P9-DHJ-296

THE HELPER'S JOURNEY

WORKING WITH PEOPLE FACING

GRIEF, LOSS, AND

LIFE-THREATENING ILLNESS

DALE G. LARSON

RESEARCH PRESS
2612 NORTH MATTIS AVENUE
CHAMPAIGN, ILLINOIS 61822
(800) 519-2707 • WWW.RESEARCHPRESS.COM

RESEARCH PRESS
PUBLISHERS

Cover design by Doug Burnett
Composition by BookMasters, Inc.
Printed by Total Printing Systems, Inc.

ISBN-: 978–0–87822–344–2
Library of Congress Catalog Number 93–84096

To Dickie

Contents

Contents

Preface

This is a personal book. I know firsthand about the challenges of caring. I have encountered the joys and sorrows of helping as a clinician, as a volunteer, and as a consultant to caring organizations. My academic research has evolved in response to these personal encounters, and *The Helper's Journey* addresses the questions that have both intrigued and troubled me on my own helping journey.

Some of these questions are as follows: Why do we help and why do we not help? Is helping a healthy and natural expression of human nature, and if it is, why do so many caregivers burn out? How can we remain caring and emotionally involved as helpers without burning out? What are the essential skills in helping, and how can we learn them? What makes caregiver teams and support groups successful? How can our work as helpers be a journey of discovery and personal growth, and of service to others? And, finally, what are the forces that nourish caring and helping, and how can we maximize those forces in ourselves, in our caring organizations, and in our society? These questions define different facets of what I call the challenge of caring.

In exploring both the theoretical and practical sides of caring and in offering specific strategies for meeting its challenge, I have drawn upon work in many areas: altruism, empathy, burnout, the helping relationship, communication training, support groups, and team development. I also present recent findings from my own work on helper secrets and self-concealment. I have chosen to use stress, self-esteem, social support, and approach and avoidance in coping as some of the major organizing ideas for the book because they reveal the patterns and relations in the phenomena explored.

At each point, my clinical and consulting experiences have acted as a filter for these ideas, testing their relevance to the real world of helping. Many of the examples and anecdotes I relate here come from the worlds of hospice, nursing, and counseling because these have been the testing grounds for me as a helper. The positive responses of caregivers to my lectures, workshops, and retreats have validated these ideas and inspired me to undertake this project.

The Helper's Journey is intended for the volunteers, nurses, physicians, social workers, clergy, counselors, and others who work at the front lines of caregiving. Because my own research and helping work are focused in the areas of hospice, oncology, and psychotherapy, most of the examples in the book are drawn from those fields. If you assist people coping with grief or life-threatening illness, there will be many vignettes and issues familiar to you. It is my hope, however, that professional and volunteer helpers and students in a broad variety of settings will find the ideas and skills presented here useful to them. Finally, if you are a friend or family member who is acting in the role of caregiver for a loved one, you might find that many of these ideas apply to you and your experience, even though I don't directly address your unique needs and issues.

This is a practical book, one that seeks to "give psychology away" and to empower the reader with new skills and working knowledge. I believe that we become more effective helpers, better team members, and more able to cope with stress primarily through the acquisition of knowledge and specific psychological skills. I don't believe that we can just pick up these ideas and skills along the way, as the popular (mis)conception would have it. To enhance your learning in these areas, *The Helper's Journey* includes many exercises and activities. I strongly encourage you to be an active reader and to practice and personalize the ideas and techniques presented here.

A central goal of this book is to provide an opportunity for you to compare your inner life as a helper with those of fellow helpers who, though they remain anonymous, can become your own valued teachers. You will read the verbatim disclosures I have gathered from other helpers describing their self-doubts, deepest fears, and frustrations, as well as their joys, rewards, and greatest moments. Some of these disclosures will shock you; some will arouse your compassion; some will inspire you. Many will no doubt offer you the relief of knowing that you are not alone in having these thoughts and feelings.

Finally, this is a book about caring in our society and in our world. The ideas presented here have, I think, far-reaching implications. Each of the caring situations discussed (e.g., a volunteer counseling a bereaved family member, a cancer patient confronting her inner fears, or health team members resolving their conflicts) can teach us something about how to create a more caring society and world.

Part One of the book focuses on the innermost personal experiences of helping, such as emotional involvement in helping and helper secrets. Part Two looks at the interpersonal dimensions of caregiving, focusing on the helping relationship and the communication skills that are the vehicles for expressing your caring. Finally, Part Three examines helping teams, support groups, and our nation as caring systems, exploring the healing potentials and the barriers to caring that exist in these systems.

A note on style and terminology: A review of the helping literature shows that the terms *helper* and *caregiver* are used interchangeably. I have used both terms to refer to the professional or volunteer who provides help. The term *caregiver,* however, is also commonly used for family members or friends/partners who care for the ill or disabled, and although many of the ideas presented here apply equally well to these other situations, my use of the term *caregiver* is not meant to include them. There is equal ambiguity concerning the best term for the person receiving help. Both *patient* and *client* are commonly used. I have used these terms interchangeably throughout the book, with a greater use of *patient* when discussing helping in medical contexts.

I hope that, as you continue your helping journey, you will find renewed strength, inspiration, and useful skills in these pages.

Acknowledgments

This book reflects my life and work over the past decade. During that time, many extraordinary individuals have shared their ideas and lives with me. To all—thank you.

Certain people have played special roles in my life and in the writing of this book, and I would like to acknowledge their contributions:

Shelly Korchin imparted his vision of psychology and his appreciation of life; he and Sylvia found a place in their hearts for me and my family.

My intellectual debt to Gerald Goodman, Allen Ivey, Carl Rogers, Richard Lazarus, and Ayala Pines can be seen throughout these pages. Ayala also read the manuscript, and her enthusiastic and illuminating feedback prevented a case of writer's burnout.

Reiner Bastine, Linda Beech, Stephen Connor, Joel Crohn, Oren Harari, Connie Holden, Annette Kaemmerer, Marcia Lattanzi-Licht, Ed Lau, Katherine Levin-Lau, Linda Norlander, and Jay VanSant gave timely encouragement and assistance.

Alberto Zucconi, through his vision and example, taught me about empathy, authenticity, and respect.

Jo Ann Vasquez challenged me to stretch myself and supported me when I did.

Ira Bates reminded me more than once that I needed to write this book.

Kalpana Asok, my research assistant, patiently and successfully negotiated my unending series of library requests.

Carol Carr read the entire manuscript, line by line, and made many excellent suggestions for improving it.

Robert Zelman, my editor/coach, gave me precise and insightful feedback on the manuscript, was always available to discuss my conceptual breakthroughs and breakdowns, and conveyed his empathy for my journey as a writer in a way that allowed me to finish the book and stay true to my ideas—and myself.

As a scholar and teacher, I have had the support of many exceptional organizations: Santa Clara University, the National Hospice Organization, the National Institute of Mental Health, the Stanford Center for Advanced Study in the Behavioral Sciences, the Fulbright Commission, the Institute for the Study of the Person in Rome, and the Psychological Institute at the University of Heidelberg. Thank you to the friends and colleagues in these institutions who have valued me and my work.

I'm very grateful to Ann Wendel, Karen Steiner, and the others at Research Press for believing in *The Helper's Journey* and for their support and many helpful suggestions.

Others have taught me about life, courage, and helping. My students at Santa Clara University have helped me test out new ideas. My clients and participants in my research have taught me about stress and life's trials, and how we respond to them. In seminars and retreats, many thousands of people have shared their experiences as helpers with me, teaching me most of what I know about the challenge of caring and how to meet it. Thanks to all of you.

My family has been my greatest source of support. My parents and my sister Leanne have always been positive and loving presences for me. My wife, Deborah Kennedy, whose intelligence and creativity inspire me daily, gave me love—the best stress buffer—and helpful feedback on difficult sections of the book. She also patiently and generously gave me the time I needed to write it, no small task because the gestation of *The Helper's Journey* coincided with the arrival of our wonderful son, Evan. My theories about caring and teamwork were tested in the crucible of becoming a family.

PART ONE

Exploring the Inner World of Helping

*This is the true joy in life, the being used for
a purpose recognized by yourself as a
mighty one; the being thoroughly worn out
before you are thrown on the scrap heap;
the being a force of Nature instead of a
feverish selfish little clod of ailments and
grievances complaining that the world will
not devote itself to making you happy.*[1]

*Life is no brief candle to me. It is a sort of
splendid torch which I have got hold of for
the moment, and I want to make it burn as
brightly as possible before handing
it on to future generations.*[2]

George Bernard Shaw

The Helper in Us All

PURPOSE IN HELPING

Most professional and volunteer helpers can identify with the feelings that inspired George Bernard Shaw to write these words. They feel a sense of purpose in their work. For them, helping expresses deep values and personal goals that allow them to make a positive difference in the world. Caring is their "splendid torch," their charge.

Think for a moment about your own motivations as a helper. What brought you into this work? What first comes to mind when you ask yourself, "Why did I initially choose to do this?" Think back to the time in your life when you made the decision that led to your current involvement as a caregiver. What were your goals, hopes, and expectations?

That moment might have been yesterday or 20 years ago. It might have been when you first picked up the phone to call a friend about volunteering. Perhaps it was when you decided to go into nursing, medicine, counseling, social work, or the clergy.

What led you to make that choice back then? What did you originally want to achieve as a helper? What mattered most to you? What was your original purpose in helping?

Perhaps you wanted to prevent unnecessary pain and suffering, or to provide quality support for seriously ill people and their families, or to help people die with dignity, or to learn about life and death. Your broader goal might have been to make a difference, to give something back, to make the world a better place, to do something significant, to develop your spiritual nature, or to connect with others in a caring way.

It is also revealing to reflect on the life events that may have shaped your helping motivations and your decision to be a caregiver. Personal encounters with grief or life-threatening illness can sensitize us to the needs of others in similar circumstances. If a sensitive

3

caregiver guides us through a personal life crisis, that can inspire us to give this kind of care to others.

Events early in our lives are often the roots of our passion for caring. For example, an oncology nurse recalled an aunt saying, "You'd be a great nurse" to her when she was 6 years old. This nurse identified that instant as the beginning of her nursing career. As a young girl, Florence Nightingale escaped from the routines of everyday life by daydreaming. In her daydreams, she envisioned a life of heroic action helping others. She spent the remainder of her life realizing that vision.[3]

Your helping motivations and the encounters that led you into this work define who you are both as a person and as a helper. My own helping motivations have their roots in my early childhood. They are rooted in my grief for my older brother Dickie. I was 5 years old and he was my 11-year-old big brother—a Little League All-Star, a paper boy, and in my eyes, a champion at just about everything.

One afternoon when Dickie was playing on a rope swing with a friend, he lost his grip on the rope and fell. Despite a serious concussion, he managed to ride his bike home. My parents had forbidden him to play on the rope swing, so at first Dickie told them he had fallen off his bicycle. But when his pain became unbearable, he told my parents what really happened. I can still see my father's hand opening the desk drawer and reaching in to get the Blue Cross card.

The next morning I was at my grandparents' home, sitting alone on the porch, listening to the adults talking in the living room. Suddenly, their conversation stopped, and they began to cry. The wave of pain going through the room hit me, and I cried, too. I knew I had lost Dickie; I knew grief. I knew I had lost my brother. The next thing I remember is reaching through the white lace of his casket to place a penny near his hand. Dickie was leaving me, and I wanted him to have candy in heaven.

The connection between this early loss and my desire to help others became clear nearly 30 years later when I happened to see the movie *Ordinary People.* This powerful film focuses on the grief of a young boy for his older brother, a victim of a boating accident. In a pivotal scene, the two boys are struggling to hang on to a raft in rough seas. The younger brother holds his brother's hand but can't keep his grip, and his brother slips into the stormy sea and drowns.

Something incredible happened to me during this scene: My brother's face suddenly appeared on the screen, replacing that of the drowning boy in the story. Waves of feeling overcame me, and pristine childhood memories related to the loss of my brother flooded my mind. For the first time, I clearly remembered conversations between my grief-stricken parents, how Dickie's room looked, and how I acted at his funeral. After the film, my wife and I went to our car. I sobbed deeply for half an hour. I said good-bye to Dickie.

Two weeks later, I urged health care workers at a seminar to "help the sibs grieve," an exhortation I had always included in my lectures. During our discussion of grief, I disclosed my experiences at the movie. Later, when I asked members of the group to describe what brought them into this work, one participant sensitively asked me if I ever thought about how my brother's death might have influenced me in my career choice, perhaps even specifically to encourage concern for the siblings of terminally ill children. I stopped, had an immediate flash of recognition, and thanked her for her insight.

Caring organizations develop mission statements to articulate the "why" of their work and then translate these statements into a vision that defines what they will need to do to actualize this mission.[4] This same translation occurs in individual caregivers. Our purposes or motivations as helpers—wanting to make a difference in the world, to ease pain and suffering, to give and receive love—make up our mission in helping. This mission is then articulated into a personal vision that defines our helping goals.

Our personal vision may express itself in the world in many different forms: leading a bereavement support group, orchestrating good pain management, holding a frightened child, giving chemotherapy, writing a successful grant proposal, or helping a terminally ill father talk to his son about his caring feelings. Any of these diverse caring acts can express your special mission as a helper.

GREAT MOMENTS IN HELPING

What I call "great moments in helping" can often reveal one's purpose in helping. In these moments, your caring expresses a core part of yourself and fulfills your personal mission as a helper. Think of the helping situations that have touched you most profoundly, the times when you thought, "This is it" or "This is why I'm doing this." These don't happen every day or even every month, but when they do occur, they remind you of your mission as a helper.

I first discovered the real power of sharing great moments in helping when I was conducting a retreat for the staff and volunteers of a large hospice in the Midwest. Rain poured down as the last remnants of a dying hurricane swept over our retreat site. Inside the meeting hall, we shared our most difficult feelings and encounters as helpers, our "helper secrets." The similarities of our disclosures surprised us. Some relief came with the knowledge that we were not alone in having these problems. Yet a sense of incompleteness was also there—something was missing.

Responding to this feeling in the group, I asked everyone to think of the most *positive* moment he or she ever had as a helper. Do this for yourself now. Even if you are just beginning to do this work, you have probably felt at times, "This is why I'm doing this." Or if you have been a helper for many years, imagine that you are writing your autobiography and are describing your most fulfilling moment in helping. Take a few minutes and write down a description of this situation, then continue reading.

At the retreat, we wrote our descriptions on note cards and then exchanged the cards to ensure anonymity. Then we slowly read the vignettes aloud, one at a time:

> After weeks of providing emotional support to an AIDS patient and his mother, helping them talk about their fears of his disease progressing and the pain of saying good-bye, they held each other and expressed their love for each other—the specialness of a beloved son to his mother and the unconditional acceptance of a loving mother. The affirmation of love was beautiful. They hugged each other and then opened their arms and hugged me.

> When a wife of a patient whose case I just opened called the office after I left their home and told my supervisor, "Thank you for sending us such a wonderful nurse." She later told me, "My husband didn't think he'd be able to share his death with anyone until he met you, and now he can."

> When a patient said to me, "I'm so glad you're my nurse today—because I wanted you to be the one to be with me on the day I die." She died at the end of my shift that day.

> My patient was deteriorating quickly, and his wife was very anxious and overwhelmed. While talking on the phone with her, I realized I needed to visit a day early. I visited and talked and listened to her. I encouraged her in caring for her husband—to keep him home and do the care herself. When the patient died, his wife was overjoyed that she had been able to keep him home and told me I was her angel of mercy.

> A young wife and mother, terminally ill and hooked up to IV pain medications, died 2 days before Christmas. Her husband was grief stricken but coping well. Before he allowed his children to come in and say good-bye to their mother, I helped him dress her in a beautiful robe, comb

out her few strands of hair, and place flowers near her bed. He looked at me and said, "Thanks for making my kids able to see their mommy as they remembered her."

I knew this woman through her husband's awful disease. He died in January. We have maintained close contact throughout her bereavement. She came in to the office to ask my permission (blessing) for her upcoming wedding. She has invited me to her wedding. It's been beautiful to share the illness, death, grief, and rebirth.

A 29-year-old man was dying of AIDS in the inpatient unit. None of the other volunteers would sit with him, so I volunteered. I sat and held his hand, talking to him and wiping his face with a damp washcloth. His mother, who lived 50 miles away, had been called, but she didn't make it to the hospice before he died. I left a few minutes later, when my shift ended. Two days later I got a telephone call from the mother, in which she tearfully thanked me for sitting with her son. After I got off the phone, I cried for 2 hours. I really felt I made a difference.

After entering the hospital room of a middle-aged man dying of kidney cancer, I spoke with him about many things. Having known him for some time, we talked about his family and his hopes for the future. Finally, I asked him what one thing I could do for him and he told me, "Help me get home to my own big bed." We made the arrangements and he left me, saying, "I love you, kid." That's where he died—in his own big bed.

A mother of a child with leukemia once said, "We come to this clinic every week and know that you care for many, many children, but when you come to see us, I feel like we are the only people you have seen that day."

A young mother with two young children was dying, and the family would not allow her to hold her children because they thought this was a terrible thing and would scare the kids. So when they weren't around I asked the kids if they wanted to get in bed with her and they said yes—so I put them in her bed and she held them.

What were these poignant encounters like for the caregivers? They said they felt "peaceful," "connectedness," a sense of "making a difference," that their purpose in the work was being fulfilled.

Now that the implicit "But why do I do this difficult work?" question was answered, the difficulties shared earlier took on a different meaning. Sharing these stories brought more tears to our eyes than discussing our worst feelings had. The intense emotion in the room made it difficult to continue reading the cards. It was as if—in these individual acts of helping—the fabric of human existence unfolded before us, and at its center we found love, compassion, caring. Helping is tough work—it is inevitably stressful, conflicted, and exhausting at times. Yet when you make a difference, when you see the real impact of your caring, any doubts about the value of your efforts disappear.

A whole lifetime of caring can be affirmed in just a few words. On his deathbed, Jim Vizzard, a Jesuit priest and dedicated helper who had fought for the welfare of migrant farmworkers for more than 25 years, described one such instance to me. Jim was thrilled when he learned that he and John Steinbeck were attending the same social gathering in New York. At the party, he approached Steinbeck and revealed that *The Grapes of Wrath* had inspired his lifetime of caring work. Steinbeck surprised Vizzard with his response: "Then it was worth writing, Jim." Steinbeck went on to say that he had followed and respected Vizzard's work for many years. The caring contributions of both men were validated in that moment.

THE CARING HELPER

Professional, paraprofessional, and volunteer helpers are commonly viewed as idealistic and altruistic in their orientations toward others. Think of the people you work with. What are they like? Do words like *dedicated, committed,* and *concerned* come to mind? I'm sure some other words come to mind as well, but the general picture probably reflects these highly positive qualities. This is because the nature of your work acts as a powerful screening device, a filter that selects for humanitarian individuals who want to work with people in these kinds of challenging situations.

Although research on volunteer helpers in the human services is somewhat sketchy, it supports our everyday observations that a powerful self-selection factor is at work here. For example, community mental health volunteers, when compared with nonvolunteers, have more internalized moral standards, more positive attitudes toward self and others, greater empathy, and more emotional stability.[5] These dimensions taken together reflect a kind of "prosocialness" or altruistic personality.

The Gallup Organization's survey of volunteers asked, "For what reasons did you first become involved in volunteer activities?" The most frequently endorsed reason was "to do something useful, to help others."[6]

In a survey of hospice volunteers, I found the following motivations most frequently cited: "Because I enjoy helping other people," "Because of my values, convictions, and beliefs," "Because I consider myself to be a loving and caring person," "To learn how to help people who are terminally ill or dying," and "To help members of my community."[7]

A variety of behaviors can reflect your altruistic orientation toward others: giving directions to strangers, volunteering, donating blood, delaying an elevator for a stranger, helping someone with a disability across a street, giving your seat on a bus to an elderly person. Are you the kind of person others can count on? Do you give to people more needy than yourself? Do you value comforting others? Do your family and friends view you as a caring, considerate, and helpful person?

The altruistic person acts in a prosocial as opposed to a self-centered way—he or she cooperates, donates to charities, shares with friends, and generally helps people when they need it.[8] These acts of kindness can reflect a deep sense of moral values. Altruistic helpers are interested in people and help out of a deep love of humanity; seeing other human beings grow and knowing that they are assisting in this growth is highly rewarding for them.[9]

In addition to their helping motives, idealism, and altruism, most helpers are likely to possess high levels of empathy.[10] Do you consider yourself an empathic person? Do you agree with the following statements psychologists use to measure empathic capacity?[11]

- When I read an interesting story or novel, I imagine how I would feel if the events in the story were happening to me.

- When I watch a good movie, I can easily put myself in the place of a leading character.

- I often have tender, concerned feelings for people less fortunate than myself.

- When I see someone being taken advantage of, I feel somewhat protective toward them.

- I sometimes try to understand my friends better by imagining how things look from their perspective

- When my friends start to talk about their problems,
  I listen to their issues and don't try to steer the
  conversation toward something else.

- It makes me sad to see a lonely stranger in a group.

You probably tend to agree with most of these statements. Most likely, you see yourself as a "people-person," and this view of yourself is a central part of your self-concept.

You bring your unique self—your purpose in helping, your empathy, and your altruistic tendencies—to every helping encounter. Research on altruism, empathy, and helping shows how these essential ingredients combine to promote and guide caregiving. Helping can be a natural outcome of these psychological forces. When we look at the altruism–empathy–helping connection in a broader context that transcends the individual caregiver, an inspiring view of our individual and collective capacities for caring and helping emerges.

THE ALTRUISM–EMPATHY–HELPING CONNECTION

Helping as a Natural Process

Our helping often has an almost automatic quality. Imagine that you are taking a nature walk and as you come to a clearing you see a young woman lying on her back, groaning and holding her leg. You see her mountain bicycle on the ground behind her, its frame bent. No one else is in sight. What do you do? Most people would certainly do something to help this person.

Put yourself in the place of the caregivers in the following situations:

A patient of mine called. She was devastated. She had
awakened and clumps of her hair were all over her pillow.
I immediately got a large selection of wigs and went to her
home. After we talked, we tried on the wigs and laughed
about being a blonde or a redhead. She felt better; so did I.

A moment came when I realized a family was not going to
have a memorial service. The husband wanted to, but the
children so disliked their mother because of an alcohol
problem they had no interest in a service. On the
anniversary, I called the husband and asked if he wanted
to get together. He said yes. I got a spray of flowers and
we went on a boat, said a prayer, and cast the flowers on
the water.

Why do we help in these situations? For most of us, the question we ask is not *why* we should help, or *whether* we will help, but *how* we can help. We listen, give pain medication, make a meal, hold a hand, grab the wigs, or call to set up an impromptu funeral service. The spontaneous nature of helping in these moments bespeaks powerful, invisible psychological forces at the heart of our caregiving.

The different elements of helping as a natural process come together in your everyday caregiving. As a helper, you are "on fire"— your helping goals are connected to a flame of caring that is burning brightly within you.

Think of your great moments in helping and all the "normal helping" you do in an average day. What is it that motivates you to help? You might be paid for what you do as a helper, it might be your job or duty, but the motivation for most of your helping comes from within. You care.

These observations concerning helping probably make sense to you. You might be thinking, "Yes, that's how it works, at least on my good days." What is not so obvious are the powerful and pervasive invisible forces that arouse, shape, and support our helping. The most fundamental, and perhaps most overlooked, of these forces is our innate altruism.

Innate Altruism: The Pilot Flame of Caring

Are love, caring, and compassion really at the core of human existence? Few of us would say there is enough caring in the world. Cruelty, not kindness, often seems to have the upper hand; conflict, not cooperation, among people and nations seems to rule the day. The media report widespread institutional greed and corruption and proclaim the arrival of the "care-less generation."

Thinking about our long-term social and health care problems— AIDS, homelessness, poverty, crime—can be deeply discouraging. Daily exposures to these failures in caring coalesce into a negative image of our fellow humans. A recent national survey of Americans showed that 43% of our population see selfishness and fakery at the core of human nature.[12] Cynicism is on the rise; it has become an inextricable part of how many people in our society view the world.

This cynical view of human nature—a kind of social Darwinism—is profoundly demoralizing. It is encouraging to work with committed and caring people and to know that you are helping people in distress, yet too often it feels like an uphill or losing battle. This is especially true when you begin to doubt your caring or are disappointed in your coworkers. As our cynicism grows, the image

of a caring world where all people—healthy and sick, rich and poor—
are treated with dignity and compassion moves further and further
from our collective consciousness and social reality.

Greed, violence, and a callousness to the suffering of others are
ghastly social problems, but their existence is not an indictment of
human nature. When we take a closer look at the world, a more encouraging perspective emerges. We begin to see that altruistic behavior is an ubiquitous and frequent human activity. This view says
that as a species we are "prewired" to be cooperative, helpful, and
altruistic, that we are programmed to be our brother's keeper. It pro-
claims that there is a hero in us all, that compassion and caring are
part of the fabric of human existence, and that human nature is essentially good and constructive. This alternative, more hopeful view
of humankind suggests that if we create the right environment, helping will naturally unfold and, further, that both the helper and the recipient of care will grow and develop through their participation in it.

What evidence is there that helping and caregiving are the
"default condition"[13] of humankind? Although a harsh and unloving
childhood can interfere with the full expression of these human tendencies, the weight of scientific evidence decidedly leans toward the
conclusion that altruism and cooperation are innate and that the tendency to help others in distress is part of our biological inheritance.[14]

The human capacity for altruism begins expressing itself early
in life:

> Many children, it appears, are able to perform a caregiver
> function well by the age of 1½–2 years. Not only do they
> comfort another person by patting, hugging, or presenting
> an object, but they also have more sophisticated and
> complex methods of attempting to help. They express
> verbal sympathy, they give suggestions about how to
> handle problems, they are sometimes judgmental in their
> helping, they appear to try to cheer others up, and they
> sometimes try alternative helping responses when a given
> technique is not effective.... The behaviors appear to be
> intended to reduce suffering in others and to reflect
> concern for the victim in distress. Many of the acts would
> undoubtedly be judged as altruistic if an older child or
> adult were performing the very same behaviors.[15]

A tendency to help distressed others is not unique to homo sa-
piens. Jean-Pierre Hallet recounts this instance of elephant altruism
in *Congo Kitabu*:

> The trunkless *tembo* [elephant] stood by idly while his
> companions tore into the trees, then he opened his mouth

and every member of the herd moved toward him with trunkfuls of twigs and leaves. Two of them jostled each other, anxious to feed him first, but the rest waited their turns patiently. In all, they brought so much food that he hardly had time to chew it; he gulped furiously until, finally, he closed his mouth tight and shook his mutilated head from side to side. Only then did the other *tembo* move away and at last start to feed themselves.[16]

Animals consistently respond to distress in their fellows. In one study experimenters taught rhesus monkeys to obtain a food morsel by pulling one chain when a red light flashed and another when a blue light flashed. The monkeys could do this with ease. Then the experimenters created a new situation. One chain administered an electric shock to a monkey in the next cage. Ten of the 15 monkeys in the experiment shifted to the nonshock chain, and two refused to pull either chain. When the shock victim was a cagemate, this altruistic behavior was much more likely to occur. Monkeys who had themselves been shocked in the past were most likely to engage in selfless behavior.[17]

Rats behave in much the same way. Again, rats sacrifice rewards to decrease the shocking of their peers, and rats familiar with shock are most likely to desist from shocking others.[18]

These experiments and other naturalistic observations of animals reveal an almost universal tendency to become aroused in the presence of a distressed member of one's own species and to act in ways to reduce this other's distress. When there is a special connection, when the other animal is a former cagemate, this tendency becomes even stronger. If this distress is familiar to the animals, if they themselves have been shocked in the past and can really "empathize" with what this distress is like, helping is even more likely.

In the human realm, helping response rates of 85 to 100% are common in analogous laboratory experiments.[19] The finding that shared difficulties lead to more intense helping efforts is also a familiar phenomenon in human helping. For example, I often notice that caregivers who have known grief in their lives are more likely to "go the extra mile" for other grieving persons. If grief is a total stranger to us, it is easier to stop short in our helping; as Shakespeare's Romeo observes, "He jests at scars that never felt a wound."

Humans also act altruistically outside the laboratory. For example, national surveys consistently find that about 50% of the population reports performing some kind of volunteer work during the past year, with 80 million American adults engaging in volunteer work in 1987.[20]

Although denial and avoidance still characterize much of society's response to the AIDS crisis, there has also been a tremendous caring response from community-based grass-roots organizations of volunteers who provide supportive care for people with AIDS.[21]

Vast amounts of natural helping also occur in self-help groups, where participants voluntarily assist one another in coping with shared problems. About 15 million Americans have at one time or another participated in self-help groups, and more than 10 million each year will participate in these groups by the turn of the century.[22] Add the informal support occurring among friends and relatives, and the estimate of voluntary helping occurring in the United States rises to a staggering figure.

Disasters often reveal something positive about human nature. Take the incident in La Verne, California in 1984, when a deranged man killed a number of innocent people in a McDonald's restaurant. A horrible event like this can sour us on humanity; we might conclude that people are "crazy" or dangerous and by doing this take a step away from our fellow humans. Yet when we examine the actual events of the incident, we see that during the melee one man tried to save a woman by pulling her into a post office. And after the event, tremendous support for the victims and their families poured in—thousands of acts of helping after a single violent act.[23]

The helper in us all sometimes appears unexpectedly. A friend of mine was once ice skating at a public rink when a large group of blind teenagers arrived. The group included only one sighted companion. My friend and the other sighted skaters at the rink immediately felt uneasy because it seemed the blind skaters would have to skate one at a time with their companion. Slowly, without discussion, a line of people formed, waiting to guide the blind skaters around the rink. The line remained for the entire evening as this group of strangers joined in their common humanity.

Theoretical explanations for these phenomena come from many vantage points. Socially oriented theorists assume that altruism is an enduring disposition acquired through social learning. They see caring as conditioned early in life (i.e., we see the reactions of others to caring acts and learn that responding with empathy and caring is rewarded and rewarding). Biologically oriented thinkers see altruism as genetically transmitted and point out that it would make sense that caring is innate in a species like ours, where our young are so entirely helpless at birth. This point will ring true for any parent. Finally, evolutionary theorists describe a model of reciprocal altruism, a kind of evolutionary Golden Rule guided by the following logic: If I help you now, you'll help me in the future and thus increase both our chances of survival.[24]

Empathy: The Bridge Between Altruism and Helping

Whatever the origins of our altruism, it is our empathy that eventually transforms it into caring action. To understand the role of empathy in helping, psychologist Harvey Hornstein argues that we must journey back in time to the savannahs of Africa, where, about 3½ million years ago, our 60-pound ancestors were struggling for survival.[25] Their survival hinged on whether they could develop the capacity for coordinated and cooperative activities. Physically, they were no match for the other predators; only their superior intelligence could save them. Fortunately, at about that time, Hornstein notes, their brains underwent a significant spurt of growth that enabled them to think and feel their way into the minds of their fellow hominids, making cooperation and other forms of prosocial and helpful behavior possible. Without this ability to empathize, to feel emotionally and sympathetically aroused in the presence of another's distress, we as a species would in all likelihood not have survived, falling prey to physically superior species. And, of course, the survival of our species has also required an intense empathic bond between mothers and their infants.

A host of studies have shown that empathy is the built-in mechanism for mediating helping behaviors—it is the bridge between innate altruism and helping. As we become aware of distress in another person, a tension develops in us and we make an effort to help that person, to reduce his or her suffering. The more aroused we are, the greater the intensity and speed of our helping acts.

For example, in one study subjects heard an experimenter in another room scream through a microphone that a stack of chairs had fallen on her. Silence followed. Those subjects with the greatest changes in heart rate were quickest to respond.[26] The almost automatic quality of helping in this and other experiments reflects the physiological basis of the altruism–empathy–helping connection.[27]

Other variables come into play, and both thoughts and feelings are involved, yet our emotional responses are most important. We can mentally take the role of the person in distress, but if we don't have the corresponding empathic feeling response, helping isn't likely.[28]

Our empathy changes as we grow and develop. The newborn baby cries reactively, but the adult can take the role of the distressed other and imagine how it would feel to be in those same circumstances.[29] Our instinctive need to help others in distress is aroused and guided by thinking and feeling our way into a state of empathy with the other person.

As children, we begin to develop our role-taking ability around the age of 2 or 3. By late childhood, we can empathize beyond our immediate circumstances and become empathically aroused by someone else's general life circumstances or prospects for the future. As psychologist Martin Hoffman observes, later in childhood our developing cognitive capabilities permit a more generalized empathic distress capability, and we begin to have empathy for the suffering of an entire group or class of people (e.g., poor, oppressed, or disabled groups of people).[30]

Bonds of We-Ness, Barriers of They-Ness

Our empathic concern develops as we extend our caring and understanding to others. Our empathy and helping usually begin with a perception of a social bond with the people needing assistance. Our hearts are open to them; we include them in our psychological worlds, and these bonds of we-ness encourage our empathy and helping.[31] This sense of we-ness is a kind of precursor to our empathy. Remember that even rats and monkeys are more likely to act altruistically toward their former cagemates, members of their "we-group."

Yet the altruism–empathy–helping connection can be blocked before it begins. We often fail to empathize with and help others with whom we don't feel this social bond. The expanded neocortex that enables us to take the role of the other and to develop bonds of we-ness also permits us to create barriers of "they-ness" that inhibit empathic concern, helping, and cooperation. Barriers of they-ness are a central psychological feature of many social ills of our society, such as the actions of hate groups, racism, the dehumanization of our enemy in warfare, and the failure to care for the distressed members of our society.

In 1968, a team of psychologists set out to study everyday altruism in the streets of New York.[32] They "lost" 40 wallets each day and then returned home to count the number of wallets returned by Good Samaritans who chanced upon them on previous days. An average of eighteen wallets were returned each day; that is 45%, a respectable rate of altruism.

The study was in full swing on the day Sirhan Sirhan assassinated Robert Kennedy. On that day, June 4, not a single lost wallet was returned. The psychologists speculated that the brutal killing of Kennedy weakened the social bonds that lead us to be concerned for another's welfare, especially that of an anonymous stranger. The boundaries of *they* had expanded, separating the person who found the wallet from the anonymous other who lost it, and empathy for this anonymous other did not develop. Maybe people thought something like "Why should I return this wallet? This person might have shot someone or done something else horrible. What's the use? People are pretty screwed up."

Other studies also show that remote events reported in our news media may influence whether we help someone in distress. Good news enhances our general concern for others and promotes cooperative and helping responses. Bad news, news that sours us on humanity—headlines of child kidnapping, greed, rape, killing—has the reverse effect, increasing apathy, competitive behavior, in-group favoritism, and even guilty verdicts in trials.[33]

Other elements can also have a negative impact on our inclination to help those in need. For example, it has been empirically demonstrated that a lack of time also hinders helping—that whether or not we help is significantly affected by how hurried we are. Professors John Darley and Daniel Batson studied how being in a hurry affects helping. They asked Princeton theology students to walk across campus to give a talk on the parable of the Good Samaritan as part of an experiment on religious education.[34]

In the original parable of the Good Samaritan, perhaps the classic helping story of all time, a man was going from Jerusalem to Jericho and was attacked by robbers, who left him half dead on the roadside. A priest and a Levite, two leading religious functionaries of the day, passed by him without stopping. Next, a Samaritan came upon the man and helped him, binding his wounds and taking him to an inn to give him further care. Because the priest and the Levite were on their way to an important religious event, they didn't want to be distracted. The Samaritan, however, saw someone in need, was moved by compassion, and helped.

In the experiment, the theology students encountered a slumped "victim" planted in an alley on their way across campus. The students had been divided into two groups: The experimenters told some of the students to hurry across campus and others to walk in a leisurely fashion. Who helped? As it turned out, 63% of the students who were not hurrying offered help, whereas only 10% of those who were hurrying did so. Darley and Batson concluded that situational variables such as how hurried we are can have a tremendous impact on whether or not we help someone in need.

The students who didn't help reported having noticed the man and acknowledged that he seemed to be in distress. The experimenter reviewed with them what happened: "You were on your way to give a talk on the parable of the Good Samaritan, you saw someone in trouble, and you didn't stop to help." The students admitted the irony of the situation but countered that they had helped—the

experimenter! They faced a conflict between helping the experimenter (by hurrying across campus) and helping the man in distress,
and the experimenter won out.

This experiment reveals something about ourselves as helpers.
When we don't have enough time, for whatever reason—too much
paperwork, unexpected crises, too many clients—natural helping
can miscarry, and we don't respond to the needs of others.

As a helper, you are in the business of opening your heart to
strangers, and this is not always easy. Many superficial elements can
influence our sense of connection with others. When we are aware of
these elements, we can make an extra effort to reach through this
veil of they-ness. The other person might be of a different faith or
ethnic group or have an alienating personality or a different life-style.
You might not feel that you have the time to help this person. Then
you might say to yourself, "I must work a bit harder to care for this
person." These efforts often lead to a deeper understanding and caring that transcends the barriers that initially separated you.

However, sometimes the barriers can seem insuperable. One
nurse described the enormous inner conflict she felt when saving the
life of a murderer:

> A patient came in for emergency surgery. This patient had
> gone for a "killing spree" from Oakland to Hayward. He
> had killed four men in 1 hour. Police had to shoot him to
> stop him, but it wasn't fatal. When he was in surgery, I had
> mixed feelings—let him die by not moving quickly, or save
> him to prove my efficiency.

Conflicted feelings of anger and guilt occur when barriers of
they-ness thwart our empathy and caring:

> I'm really angry that I now have to care for an old man
> who is sleeping with his young daughter and has a prison
> record for abuse. It's hard for me to keep the spiritual side
> of this man in focus, and hard for me to relate to him
> lovingly and nonjudgmentally.

> I hated the husband of a patient because he wanted her
> to die and did not want to care for her or be with her.
> I couldn't be totally effective because of my antipathy.
> He was selfish and I didn't help him through the crisis as
> I should have.

> It is easy to love and help those who are kind and
> considerate and want your help. But how about those who

hate you and the whole world? How do you get close to
them and give them encouragement, keep upbeat and
caring toward them when they have never cared about
anyone or anybody?

Have you ever been pinched, sworn at, spit on, or kicked by the
people you care for? Or been the recipient of a grieving family member's displaced rage? These incidents, a kind of "helper abuse," can
frighten and hurt even the most seasoned caregiver. How can you extend your caring to the anonymous stranger who is mistreating you?
It seems like a tough assignment; a saint could do this, but we mere
mortals have trouble with it.

Situations like these highlight how our sense of social connection—or lack of it—influences helping. In great discomfort, we os-
cillate between feelings of amity and enmity, between a sense of we-
ness and they-ness. One of my psychotherapy clients taught me
about this dynamic. An irate, emotionally disturbed customer had
brutally attacked him. As my client physically and emotionally recov-
ered from the stab wounds that nearly took his life, he continued to
work in his business, serving many customers of the same national-
ity as his attacker. He once said to me, "When I am a victim, I don't
want to help them, but as a human being, I want to."

The ability to establish bonds of we-ness may reflect a more
general orientation of the helper. In their study of rescuers of the
Jews in Nazi Europe, Samuel and Pearl Oliner came to the following
conclusion:

> Rescuers, like nonrescuers, worried both before and during
> the war about feeding, sheltering, and protecting themselves
> and their families. What distinguished rescuers was not their
> lack of concern with self, external approval, or achievement,
> but rather their capacity for extensive relationships—their
> stronger sense of attachments to others and their feeling
> of responsibility for the welfare of others, including those
> outside their immediate familial or communal circles.[35]

This extensive orientation of the rescuers contrasts with the constricted orientation of nonrescuers:

> Constricted people experience the external world as
> largely peripheral except insofar as it may be
> instrumentally useful. More centered on themselves and
> their own needs, they pay scant attention to others. At
> best, they reserve their sense of obligation to a small

circle from which others are excluded. Whereas extensive individuals are marked by strong attachments and a sense of inclusive obligations, constricted people are marked by detachment and exclusiveness.[36]

When self-concern is the price of concern for others, the ability to take the other's perspective and, therefore, to feel empathic concern is severely limited. The bonds of we-ness shrink to include only a small group. Spiritual teachers throughout history have, of course, championed the reverse: the importance of loving all people. Mother Teresa, for instance, doesn't make we-they distinctions when she cares for the poor. The popular song "We Are the World" conveyed this message and mobilized an enormous outpouring of support for starving Africans.

Developmental thinkers have also emphasized that as we mature we move away from attention focused exclusively on the self toward a focus on others. Psychologist Abraham Maslow described a hierarchy of needs that progresses from physiological needs to higher needs such as those for love and belongingness. The self-actualized people he studied had a commitment to something beyond themselves.[37] Lawrence Kohlberg has shown that moral development advances from self-interest to a concern with universal principles.[38] For these and other theorists, a caring extension of self toward others is the capstone of human development.

A "Feel Good–Do Good" Theory of Helping

Although our individual personalities dispose us to certain ways of responding, our general stance and openness toward the people we help is also strongly influenced by our moods. We are most likely to help and give of ourselves when we feel good. "Feel good–do good" is the rule. Sunny weather, thinking happy thoughts, feeling competent—all stimulate increased helping.

Simple everyday events—the unexpected positives in life—can have a powerful impact on kindness. Have you ever found a coin in a phone booth coin return slot? One study showed that 88% of subjects who found a coin stopped and helped someone (a confederate of the experimenter) who dropped her papers outside the phone booth, whereas only 4 percent of the people who didn't find a coin helped her.[39] In another experiment, students who had free cookies passed to them while sitting in a library were more likely to help someone outside the library.[40] In yet another study, subjects who received a free sample package of stationery were more willing to help a stranger by looking up a phone number and making a phone call.[41]

Unexpected positive events seem to ignite a "glow of goodwill" that leads to helping and a concern for the well-being of others.[42] Think of those days when you found a flower on your desk, a thank-you note from a patient or family member, or a check from the IRS. For that entire day, helping was probably easy—yesterday's hassles became that day's challenges, there were fewer "problem patients," and despite your high activity, you felt energized, not enervated, when the day was over. Here, two caregivers share uplifting events in their work:

One day my young patient with AIDS greeted me at the door with "I've been waiting anxiously for you to get here. I really need the ray of sunshine and good cheer you always impart when you come to see me. I look forward to each of your visits." And with that he gave me a big hug. It really made my day, and I felt good about everything all day long—good and bad.

One special note from a family read: "You made a difference to all of us. What could have been a terrible time for our family turned into something special. We have never been so close. Thank you."

The "warm glow of success"[43] clearly fuels the fires of altruism, yet how does it lead to increased helping? Why do you help when you feel good? The answer may lie in the expanded sense of self you feel at these times. Unexpected good fortune and positive events expand your sense of caring and we-ness. You feel "like a million dollars," and you are unusually responsive to diverse people and situations.

These extended bonds of we-ness facilitate the first and necessary step in helping: recognizing the needs and suffering of others. These bonds allow you to take the perspective of the other person; you don't overlook his or her suffering. This is the opposite of a self-preoccupation that can block awareness of the cues that lead to empathy.[44]

Another reason for these altruistic effects is that feeling good somehow alters your internal calculations of how much you can afford to give to others. Precisely because you feel good, you may seek to share your goodies and not be concerned about the returns from your giving. Your emotional largesse stems from the perception that there is an imbalance of resources in favor of yourself, and you give to help those less fortunate.[45]

Also, once your helping begins, altruism is intrinsically reinforcing, and it can make you feel better, especially when the costs of helping are low and the benefits high. Because altruism functions as a kind of self-reward, we can feel good, do good, and then feel even better.[46]

The model of helping underscores the importance of what you bring to the caregiving encounter. Your altruism and empathy connect you with the people you help and keep the flame of caring burning within you. If you are high on humanity and feel good, your caregiving is suffused with spontaneity. This doesn't mean that these positive feelings are necessary for helping to occur. As a professional or volunteer caregiver, you have to continue to help others even when you are feeling cynical and angry and dislike the people you care for. Still, when these psychological forces are present and the altruism–empathy–helping connection is activated, your caregiving will be less stressful, more creative—and probably more effective.

CARING CAN BE GOOD FOR THE CAREGIVER

When all the ingredients for natural helping are present, helping usually happens. The benefits of helping for the recipients of this care are obvious—their pain is controlled, their suffering is reduced, their coping ability is enhanced. The possible benefits to the helper are less apparent and have been overshadowed by our long-term concern with caregiver stress and burnout. We know that when the demands of helping exceed the resources available to the caregiver, negative psychological and physical consequences are likely to follow. However, a growing body of research and theory supports the idea that, in most circumstances, helping is a natural expression of the healthy human heart, and our caring connections with others in turn sustain our health.

An enormous literature already documents the health promotive aspects of social connectedness.[47] In a major study looking at the health of several thousand people over a 10-year period, James House and his colleagues found that men who reported a higher level of social relationships and activities were significantly less likely to die than were those with lower levels.[48] In other words, friends can be good medicine. Although social support has many facets, a core dimension of it involves participating in a network of caring, reciprocal relationships with others and creating a sense of belonging and a reason for living that transcends one's individual self.

We also know that *not* opening one's heart to others has significant negative health consequences. When these connections are lost, a host of medical and psychological symptoms can develop.

In *The Broken Heart,* James Lynch documents a strong positive relationship between loneliness and social isolation and cardiac disease.[49]

An expanding literature on the role of personality in health identifies cynical hostility—a suspicious, mistrustful, and resentful world view or approach to life—as a key variable.[50] A long line of research on Type A, or coronary prone, behavior suggests that the hurried, egocentric, aggressive individual who is unable to listen to and connect with others is at risk for a variety of health problems, most notably cardiovascular disease.

Lynch postulates a kind of "social membrane" to help understand how a person's internal and external worlds mesh, "simultaneously separating one from and connecting one to the rest of one's living world."[51] He has found that blood pressure lowers when people listen and rises when they are speaking. In Lynch's transactional psychophysiology therapy, hypertensive patients who talk their way into cardiovascular disease with an intense, rapid, and loud conversational style that radically elevates their blood pressure are taught to listen their way back to health.

Recommended clinical interventions for the Type A individual all point in the direction of expanded empathy, less self-focus, less hostility, more caring, and more listening. In their classic text, cardiologists Meyer Friedman and Ray Rosenman advised Type A individuals to bring more people into their lives through increased caring and communication.[52] This theme appears in *The Trusting Heart,* where Redford Williams, a leading researcher of Type A behavior, concludes:

> Characteristics describing the trusting heart emerged from
> meticulous analyses of psychological test items that
> epidemiological research had shown to predict higher
> versus lower coronary heart disease and mortality rates.
> As revealed by these analyses, the trusting heart believes
> others are basically good, is slow to anger, and treats
> others with considerate kindness. I have been struck by
> the similarity between the trusting heart and what I know
> of the "Golden Rule" so common in many of the world's
> religions.[53]

Many caregivers perceive this connection between caring for others and personal health in their own lives. Volunteer researcher Allan Luks surveyed 1,500 members of a large women's volunteer group and asked how helping feels. More than 50% of respondents reported feeling a kind of "helper's high" when helping others. Large percentages indicated feelings of strength, calmness, greater self-worth, and fewer aches and pains during and after helping.[54] I have heard these kinds of statements frequently from caregivers. One once told me, "Helping others simply feels good. A warmth comes over me when I know I've made a difference even in a small way in someone's life. I feel enriched." A woman in the Luks study described using her volunteer work at a nursing home to control her high blood pressure. Others reported enhanced self-esteem or the lifting of depression after doing something nice for someone else. In his subsequent book on this topic, *The Healing Power of Doing Good,* Luks marshals even more impressive evidence suggesting that helping others is good for our physical, psychological, and spiritual health.[55]

Although the potential health benefits of helping are only speculative at this time, volunteers' perceptions of immediate physical and psychological health benefits associated with their helping is an intriguing and significant finding. As I have mentioned earlier, research shows that when we feel good, we are more likely to do good. Now there is growing support for a "do good–feel good" hypothesis as well.

Some kinds of helping may be health promotive; others may not. Helping motivations, having control over whether one will or will not help, and other variables could play an important role in determining the relative benefits of helping for caregivers. In addition, the benefits might be due to the social ties and relationships and not to the helping act itself; the relative contributions to one's health of helping others and sheer active social relating must still be disentangled.

Ask yourself the following questions: What about helping is healthy for you? Is it the good feelings you get when you help someone? Or is it the compassionate stance, the social connectedness, or the sense of significance you have doing this work? When are these benefits missing or more negative consequences present?

The psychological benefits of helping and caring can be looked at in other ways. George Bach and Laura Torbet describe the paradoxical nature of caring:

> The Caring Paradox is that self-realization is only possible
> through caring for others. Caring for and about others
> *is* caring for ourselves. Caring for others accrues great
> benefits to us: it increases our self-esteem, attracts the
> care and concern of others, improves the environment,
> and enhances the quality of life. All caring is double-edged.
> We have impact on others by acknowledging their impact
> on us; we grow by supporting others' growth.[56]

The great humanitarian Albert Schweitzer expressed it this way: "It is only giving that stimulates. Impart as much as you can of your spiritual being to those who are on the road with you, and accept as something precious what comes back to you from them."[57] And a great deal does come back, often as intensely accelerated emotional, intellectual, and spiritual growth. Studying self-help groups, psychologist Frank Riessman formulated the helper therapy principle to describe the aid helpers receive from being in the helper role.[58]

I like to begin caregiver meetings with a brief sharing of what the group has learned or how we have benefited doing this work. Some typical disclosures include the following:

> Although there have been times when I've truly felt
> I've "made a difference," they (our patients) have, in turn,
> "made a difference" in me! I once found myself saying
> to a patient, "I feel blessed and a better person to be
> knowing you!"

> Since working for hospice, I have a profound
> appreciation—greater love and zest for my life and that
> of my loved ones. I treasure the moment more often. I'm
> more aware of the wonders of life and the bountiful gifts
> I've been given.

> When he reached out for my hand and muttered, "I don't
> know why you like to spend time with such a grumpy old
> man," my heart flew. He was so full of life to me, and his
> reaching out for me, both physically and verbally, felt so
> good. I was warm and at peace.

There are even some tentative data showing a possible link between caring connections with others and immunity to illness. In a study on the effect of motivational arousal through films, Harvard psychologist David McClelland found that merely watching a film of Mother Teresa engaged in selfless acts of caring for abandoned babies, the sick, and the dying had a positive effect on the immunological functioning of student subjects. It worked even for those students who reported a conscious dislike for Mother Teresa![59]

CONCLUSION

How can we explain these phenomena? Perhaps we are part of a social body, a social organism that reinforces acts of altruism and caring. Authors Robert Ornstein and David Sobel argue that our connections to the larger social environment are vital to our health.[60]

They point out that all societies and religions have understood this relation between social connectedness, altruism, and immunity, and thus have emphasized the importance of caring for others, generosity, and service. Although barriers of they-ness can disrupt this connectedness, our collective health may ultimately depend on our ability to see ourselves in others.

Even the "one-way giving" that so frequently characterizes helping may be healthful to the donor because it maintains this connection to the social organism. In earlier times, helping was more of a reciprocal event. You used your nursing skills to help me heal my broken leg, and I in turn helped you raise your barn. One-way giving is an unnatural kind of helping, and this is why the people you help so often want to repay you in some way by giving you something or by helping *you*. Though the earlier forms of reciprocity no longer exist in most professional helping situations, the psychological and physical benefits of helping—these brilliant evolutionary quid pro quos—continue into the present.

It makes perfect sense that, for us to survive as a species, acts of helping would be rewarded both psychologically and immunologically. What if each act of caring and helping depleted the helper, decreased his or her immunity and mood, and lessened the chances of survival? The view that caring and helping are natural and good for us is intuitively and scientifically more accurate. When we help another person, we take part in an exchange shaped and finely tuned over millions of years to ensure that when we help others we also help ourselves.

2

I don't think I can do this anymore. It hurts so bad—no one cares. I think I would make a great florist or meat cutter.

Anonymous helper

I want a 38-year-old patient dying of lymphoma to quit revealing his pain, his sadness, and his fear to me! I want him to die as soon as possible so I can be left alone! He's so draining I'm starting to hate this man who was my friend. I'm angry with him for having a relapse!

Anonymous helper

The Challenge of Caring: Emotional Involvement in Helping

THE CHALLENGE OF CARING

At this point, you might be thinking I have a one-sided view of helping, one filled with happy, saintly beings fulfilling themselves through selfless devotion in a stress-free process of helping. But my real understanding is that helping is extraordinarily demanding and that it doesn't always unfold naturally, if it happens at all. Though deeply rewarding, a commitment to caring is not without its costs—the flame of caring can flicker or extinguish. When it is shining brilliantly, it can inspire great acts of caring and lead to self-fulfillment; however, a bright flame is by virtue of its intensity more likely to burn out.

In fact, we find that the most idealistic, altruistic, and committed helpers are among the first to burn out.[1] Failures to accomplish specific helping goals (e.g., when pain is not controlled, when a grant proposal isn't funded, or when bureaucratic rigmarole interferes with the delivery of care) are most stressful to those caregivers who have a special sensitivity to the needs of their clients. The difficulties of the work tend to frustrate their idealism, undermine their sense of personal accomplishment, and exhaust their emotional reserves.[2] For these dedicated helpers, burnout is the "cost of caring."[3] Burnout researchers like to say, "What brings you in will burn you out." Psychologists Louis Heifetz and Henry Bersani make these same connections:

> One common theme in discussions of burnout is some sort
> of motivational erosion: dedication becomes apathy;

altruism becomes contempt; insomnia replaces the impossible dream; and crusaders become *kvetches.* The implicit assumption is that *burnout must be preceded by commitment.* For human service workers the focus of this commitment is fostering positive change—growth—in their clients. Any satisfactory theory of burnout must be limited to those workers whose clinical endeavors are substantially motivated by the desire to promote growth in their clients. Burnout may produce and perpetuate low levels of this motivation, but the process of burnout cannot begin unless the level of this motivation is high. Metaphorically, one must be "fired up" before one can burn out.[4]

High empathy and caregiver stress usually go together. Using the same empathy statements you responded to in chapter 1, psychologist Ezra Stotland and his colleagues found that beginning nurses who scored highest were the first to leave the rooms of dying patients; they did a U-turn at the foot of the beds of the patients they cared for.[5] The high-empathy nurses, imagining what it would be like to be in that bed, became distressed and left the room. Yet after receiving support and advice on how to relate to patients more effectively, these same nurses eventually spent the greatest amounts of time with patients and were highly successful. Empathy is a double-edged sword; it is simultaneously your greatest asset and a point of real vulnerability.

As a helper, you need to find a way to be emotionally involved in your work, to take your empathy, helping motivations, commitment, and idealism and use them without burning out. This is the challenge of caring. Whatever approach you take, it must be congruent with your unique helping style and not so draining or overwhelming that unmanageable stress results.

Meeting this challenge is a complex emotional task. The intensity of emotional involvement can vary greatly, from too involved to not involved enough. Emotional involvement also takes different forms (e.g., a caregiver can either identify with people's problems and be a constantly distressed rescuer or be a more balanced, empathic helper). The general effectiveness of your approach to stress management determines which emotional dynamics and outcomes characterize your helping. But before we discuss stress and stress management, it will be useful to take a closer look at the inner world of emotional involvement in helping.

THE VARIETIES OF EMOTIONAL INVOLVEMENT

Caregivers are constantly moving back and forth on a continuum of emotional involvement ranging from overly involved to less involved. This continuum describes the varying degrees of caregiver emotional involvement:

Continuum of Emotional Involvement

← — →

Distant, burned out   Balanced   Overinvolved
                      (detached concern)

The two poles of this continuum are vividly described by a nurse who said, "I feel either like I am encased in steel *(the distant, uninvolved position)* or like my skin has been ripped off" *(the overly involved position)*. Most veteran helpers have been at both ends of the continuum; all caregivers shift their involvement frequently, becoming more or less involved in response to various external and internal demands.

Intensity of emotional involvement can be thought about in two ways. First, there is the level of involvement you have from moment to moment as you help others. Think about some specific helping situations you have been in recently. What was your degree of involvement in each? Second, your emotional involvement in the work will vary at different points in your helping career, even at different points in the same week or day. Has your general degree of emotional involvement in the work changed since you finished your training and first began to work in this field? Where would you locate yourself on this scale when you think about your current relationships with the people you care for?

The Distant, Burned-Out Position

The more distant, uninvolved positions on this continuum can be momentary stances taken in response to a personal need for emotional distance. You might pull back for a moment or a day for some respite and to regain your sense of emotional balance. Or something in a helping situation might push an emotional button in you, and then your compassion takes leave of you as you quickly move to a less involved stance.

In these moments, it is common to have doubts about yourself and your caring. One caregiver, unsure whether her emotional involvement was as great as that of her coworkers, said:

Maybe I don't have the real capacity to love, to be truly
close to people. I deal with people every day and compare
myself to people who become so emotionally close. Is that
distance professionalism or a flaw in my ability to love?

Another described distancing herself from families:

I feel guilty. I sometimes try to avoid families of dying
patients when I feel inadequate to help them in the
situation. I try to stay detached and come across as
uncaring.

As discussed in chapter 4, these are common unspoken thoughts and
feelings of caregivers.

At this end of the continuum, we also find the more enduring and
painful experience known as burnout. Dozens of books document
burnout in caregivers.[6] The term *burnout* has become somewhat of a
buzzword, and the concept suffers from being used so loosely that
nearly all signs of stress—from depression to headaches—are seen
as signs of its presence.

Despite these definitional problems, there is a strong consensus that burnout is a real phenomenon with important implications for everyone working in the human services. There is also
agreement that burnout has three central, defining characteristics:
emotional exhaustion, diminished caring, and a profound sense of
demoralization.

All burnout theorists and most helpers I have known or inter-
viewed emphasize a deep sense of exhaustion as a central component of burnout. This is a kind of emotional exhaustion manifested in
low energy, chronic fatigue, and feelings of being emotionally
drained, frustrated, and used up. Exhaustion can occur even when
the physical demands of the job are less than usual:

I feel upset about my physical symptoms of anxiety—
muscle tension, rapid pulse, diarrhea, loss of appetite,
difficulty sleeping. Sometimes I feel trapped and just want
to get outside. And I ask myself: Who takes care of me?

Sometimes I feel I deserve more because I give more. I get
tired of trying. I'm so sick of patients draining every ounce
of energy out of me. Mostly, lately, I feel like I have no
more to give anyone. I need all my energy for me. I can't
get over being "tired" all the time. My mental acuity is
poor. Recall is almost zero.

I wear a mask. I work so hard at being "up" for others and getting others "up"—and no one really knows how tired I am. I want out.

Lowered self-esteem and depression are also part of this emotional exhaustion:

I feel so inadequate and lose my self-esteem when people reject my caring for them. Statements like "Leave me alone" or "Don't touch me" make me feel like maybe I should not be doing this work. I really take things like this personally and probably I should not. I'm too sensitive and too concerned with my own feelings.

Sometimes I judge people I serve like leeches, wanting more and more of your time—not really trying to help themselves. And when I pull away from being involved with them I feel judged, like I'm letting them down—I'm letting God down by not always wanting to give. I have feelings of anger and sadness when these situations occur—yet I put on my mask and smile.

Sometimes I feel so tired or useless I find I cannot believe in anything. Hopelessness and doubt are nightmares to cope with. Where is God?

A second component of burnout (perhaps the most painful for the caring helper) is diminished caring—for the people you help, for coworkers, and sometimes for your family and friends. You feel apathetic, have more "problem patients" (even though your patient population hasn't significantly changed) and don't want to take on any new patients and families. Barriers of they-ness can lead you to treat patients callously, as impersonal objects, even to blame them for their problems. The dynamics of exhaustion and diminished caring can be seen in these caregivers' disclosures:

For the most part, 99% of it, it's a thankless job, day to day, moment to moment. You can have a team of 12 patients, all 103 years old with multiple medical problems—their spouses died 30 years ago, their kids live 3,000 miles away, they haven't heard from them in 6 months, they don't even want to live themselves, and there you are, like "Come on, you got to eat, come on, you got to move around and get that blood pumping." At any given moment you've got 25 things you have to do. And that's

what gets to you. And there's no thanks in it. And patients
aren't saying, "Oh dearie, thank you." They don't want you.
They don't want to live. You've got to care when no one
else cares about them, and they're not even your own flesh
and blood. And we get so tired that we can't even express
our real care that we have for our own families, because
we've got to put all this out for people that are not even,
really, a part of this. But yet you feel guilty because you
should be pro-life and you shouldn't hate these people.
You shouldn't wish they would die. "You use all your
sympathy up at work." That's what I hear when I go home.

Sometimes I don't have any connection with patients'
pain. On the outside I know what to say and on the inside
I'm daydreaming or thinking about my own needs. I just
don't care.

Many times I've felt inside like Archie Bunker, complaining
and bitching that I'm stuck at someone's home during an
active dying process. Inwardly I'm hoping that the next
time I reposition the patient, he will die and then I'll be
free. I feel guilty that I can't inwardly be filled with
compassion, love, and patience. Sometimes it amazes me
that I pull it off and at least appear caring—in fact, I
overcompensate and do it up pretty well. But I'm left
feeling selfish and guilty.

The third component of burnout—demoralization—is also reflected in the statements just presented. At the heart of this attitude
is a feeling of "I can't": "I can't do well at doing good. I can't make a
difference." The sense of efficacy and the intrinsic rewards that often
accompany helping are missing. Instead, feelings of helplessness and
reduced morale dominate. New demands become burdens, not challenges. We think, "My God, what do I do next?" or "Don't ask me for
help! I don't have the answers!" There is an overwhelming sense
of futility and personal failure. A loss of idealism and enthusiasm
for our work follows. These aspects stand out in the following helper
disclosures:

I'm afraid that I am hopelessly inadequate as a
bereavement volunteer. I'm so afraid I'll say the wrong
thing. I avoid contact.

I try to act strong and capable, someone with a bag full of
answers. But I really feel helpless—weak and helpless!

I feel helpless when there is nothing positive to say or do
about a patient's condition, when they and their families
are wanting me to say or do something to improve the
situation and there seem to be no answers.

I feel like I've lost much of the compassion and enthusiasm
I had when I began this work and as a result I'm feeling
sad and ineffective.

Experiencing the pain in a patient's eyes as she searched
for some meaning to her life and death. There are
questions which have no answers and I am helpless.
I touch her and hug her and sometimes I cry.

Caring helpers confronting burnout have an exhausting struggle
with threats to their self-esteem. Their self-talk might go something
like this: "I got into this work because I'm a caring person and I
wanted to make a difference. Now I don't even want to see another
hurting person, and I don't think I'm really doing much good." Frustrated idealism, failing to move successfully toward important personal goals, guilt, and self-reproach combine to create a downward
spiral, deepening the caregiver's distress and exhaustion.

It is easy to see how burnout can undermine helping. Our empathy, our caring connections with others, and our good feelings all
disappear, weakening or severing the altruism–empathy–helping
connection. Without the remarkable forces of natural helping to sustain it, caregiving becomes arduous, empty, or even nonexistent.

Despite its pervasive effects, burnout is often a subtle, insidious
process that takes myriad forms and is often easier to recognize in
others than in oneself. Here are some questions to help you assess
your situation:

- Do you find yourself feeling apathetic? emotionally
  exhausted? tired? anxious? depressed? hopeless?
  helpless? trapped in your duties? as if you just can't
  cope anymore? resistant to change of any sort? that
  everything has turned negative?

- Do you have more "problem patients" than you used to?

- Do you frequently find yourself saying that "patients
  are complaining too much"?

- Do you have a conscious reluctance to go to work
  or to visit patients?

- Do you find you have insomnia or a lower resistance
  to illness?

- Is there an increase in your "need to relax" habits (e.g., more drinking and smoking)?

- Have you become more distant and detached with coworkers and patients?

Experiencing one or more of these doesn't mean you are burned out. Your caring flame might just be flickering. But it does suggest that you should do more to prevent things from getting worse.

You can systematically check your burnout level by taking the test in the Appendix.[7] Psychologist Ayala Pines, a leading burnout researcher and author, uses a score of 4.0 on this measure as the burnout cut-off score. In other words, a score of 4.0 or higher is in the burnout range. What's your score? By taking this test intermittently, you can monitor your current feelings.

If your burnout score is high, don't panic. It is important to realize that we can have many feelings like these and not burn out. And if we do burn out, it doesn't mean that we can't return to personally satisfying and effective helping. Many helpers, myself included, are members of the "formerly burned-out club." But it is essential that you pay attention to these warning signs—these wake-up calls—when they occur and look more closely at what is going on for you at work and at home. If signs of burnout go unattended, your problems will grow; if they are heeded, they can guide you toward a more balanced approach to helping and continued personal growth.

The Overinvolved Position

To burn out, your caring flame must have once burned brightly. So, one might even look at burnout as a badge of honor indicating that you had the courage to care. Yet, however meritorious, burnout is not fun, and it can exact a great toll on you.

It is those experiences at the other pole of the continuum— where emotional involvement is at a high pitch—that typically usher in burnout. When that involvement becomes personally distressing, helpers are more likely to take a defensive and self-protective stance, relinquishing their caring connections with the people they assist. The emotions here often include feeling out of control or "in over your head." You might think, "What happened to my life?" The distress of the overly involved helper is consuming:

When I wake up at 3 A.M., I start to panic, thinking, "How am I going to manage the next problem?" It's not always a real problem. I don't even like to think about how I feel.

Sometimes I feel that no matter what I do, I'm hitting my head against a brick wall. At times I wish I owned a Polynesian island to which I could escape for rest and quiet. Yet there always seems to be another crisis that needs my fixing, and my island retreats once again into my subconscious.

I hate coming to work because I feel once I'm here it engulfs me like fire.

I hated my patient at times because her emotions made me hurt. The negative feelings toward her made me feel guilty, and I would hate her even more, and yet I loved her. She was a central part of my life for 6 months. I thought she would never come to the stages *I* thought she should; toward the end, I thought she would never die.

The overaroused position is characterized by emotional involvement at a high pitch and strong emotions—both positive and negative. Positive feelings can include a sense of excitement, exhilaration, and getting something important accomplished. This intensity of feelings is exciting, but it is also exhausting. You think, "Nobody can do it as well as I can" or "Why aren't all the others more involved?" When the intensity becomes too great and your coping resources are strained, you may try to reduce your involvement, either by setting healthy limits or by withdrawing emotionally or physically.

Personal distress and emotional withdrawal are common at both poles of the continuum. An example from my life illustrates this. Early in my career, I was emotionally overinvolved as a helper. The intense world of my helping encounters and the empathic sorrow and anger I felt in these encounters overshadowed all else. The rest of my world—unfortunately, this included my friends, my exercise program, and other elements of a balanced life—receded into the background.

For example, compared with the intense feelings of the work I was doing, social occasions seemed vacuous. I felt guilty going to parties when my patients couldn't even get out of bed, and when I did go, one part of me was tempted to shake people, saying, "You won't be talking about your new car on your death bed. I've never heard people talk about any of this in their final moments, so go home and hug your family and thank God you can still do it!"

Then I would realize my loss of perspective and balance, and retreat to a less involved stance at work. Yet this stance was also untenable. Guilt and lowered self-esteem quickly overcame me. Helping—and not helping—became agonizing; both included feelings of personal distress and withdrawal from my friends, family, and colleagues. Burnout was not far off.

The Balanced Position: Detached Concern

The midpoint of emotional involvement has been described as one of detached concern.[8] This term describes a paradoxical quality—the state of being emotionally involved while simultaneously maintaining a certain emotional distance, of being united but also separate. In the ideal situation, the helper is in a state of balance, able to become more emotionally involved when the situation calls for it and ready to pull back if that is what is necessary. Frequently, however, the midpoint position is instead inhabited by helpers who are en route between the two poles of emotional involvement. They might have been underinvolved, felt guilty, and decided to reinvolve themselves, or perhaps they were overly involved, saw that their personal lives were beginning to suffer, and decided to take a respite and get less involved.

Shifting degrees of emotional involvement also characterize our everyday personal relationships. We all want to find a comfortable distance between ourself and others. Some people have extreme problems with intimacy; they get emotionally close to other people only to withdraw again immediately. The phrase "porcupines huddling on a cold night" captures this beautifully. But we all act this way to a certain extent. We initially test the emotional waters, then become more involved. When the emotional waters get too hot for us, we pull back. So, too, we constantly adjust the extent of our emotional involvement in the helping relationship.

THE HELPER'S PIT

Your emotional involvement as a helper varies not only in intensity but also in the quality and kinds of emotions you have. The varieties of emotional experience possible for you as a helper can be illustrated in the metaphor of the Helper's Pit. Imagine that the person you are helping is in a pit and you are on the edge of that pit. If you identify with this person's problems, what happens? You fall into the pit! If you empathize, you *feel with* the person in the pit and get inside his or her experiential world. If you sympathize, you stand on the edge of the pit and are concerned and compassionate—sympathy is *feeling for* the person in distress.

Identifying with the other person and falling into the Helper's Pit can limit your helping. You don't accurately perceive the other and you are unable to think objectively about which course of action might be best for him or her. Most important, people stuck in pits don't like to have their helpers in the pit with them; it can be terrifying for them, and it can deepen their feelings of hopelessness and helplessness. Your empathy and sympathy move you to help the person in distress, but to do so you must find a way to reach down into the pit and help the suffering person out—without falling in yourself.

Empathy, Sympathy, and Personal Distress

A conceptual map for understanding the dynamics of helping and the Helper's Pit is beginning to emerge from studies of altruism, empathy, and helping. This model views empathy, sympathy, and personal distress as three distinct responses helpers have when confronted with someone who is suffering. An additional distinction is made concerning the focus of the caregiver's attention—whether it is self-focused or focused on the distressed other.

When you first encounter someone who is suffering, the initial critical event is whether you attend to the distress of this person. Do you even look into the pit? As mentioned previously, your feeling state, sense of connection with the person, and other elements affect what happens at this point in caregiving. If you do extend yourself and open your heart to the other person, you begin to empathize and sympathize with his or her plight.

Empathy involves both cognitive role taking and an empathic emotional responsiveness. In other words, you imagine what it would be like to be in this person's shoes, inside his or her predicament, and then you have a kind of vicarious emotional response based on your sense of this person's state or condition. Sympathy is closely related yet distinct; it is more a feeling of concern for the welfare of the other. You feel moved, compassionate, tender, or warm but don't necessarily have a feeling state that matches that of the other person.

In both empathy and sympathy, your attention is markedly other-focused—you are looking outside yourself, you feel connected to the other, and you are in a balanced state. You observe someone who is suffering, and your initial empathic responses change into sympathetic feelings of concern for the other. This compassion or sympathetic distress is accompanied by a conscious desire to help.[9] Empathy and sympathy are synergistic, and both promote helping.

Personal distress is quite different from empathy and sympathy: When you are in it, you lose your balance and fall into the pit. Personal distress is a central feature of the burnout syndrome. Personally distressed caregivers can feel drained, troubled, angry, worried, or grieved—they "go to pieces," feel helpless in the middle of emotional situations, and lose control during emergencies.[10] When we are personally distressed, our attention is focused on ourselves, and our caring connection with the other person is weak or nonexistent as we focus our attention on our own pain, sorrow, sense of failure, or other emotional reactions.[11]

Both the intensity and the nature of your emotional responses contribute to determining whether you feel empathy and sympathy or personal distress as a helper. Your arousal can be so high that personal distress results. For example, if your empathic sadness becomes too great, overarousal can occur, and a more self-oriented, distressed response follows. If you believe you must continue to witness the other person's suffering and that it will not be significantly eased by your interventions, overarousal is particularly likely. You are frustrated by not achieving your helping goals, and the suffering of the person you are helping continues without relief.

Reviewing work in this area, psychologist Martin Hoffman states: "Perhaps there is an optimal range of empathic arousal—determined by people's levels of distress tolerance—within which they are most responsive to others. Beyond this range, they may be too preoccupied with their own aversive state to help anyone else."[12]

Thus, you can begin with empathy and end with personal distress. For example, we can speculate that the nurses in the Stotland study, described earlier, were overwhelmed when they walked into the rooms of the dying patients; their empathy rapidly became personal distress and overrode their feelings of sympathy and their desire to stay and help.

Interpersonal Allergies

Having our emotional buttons or vulnerable spots pushed creates another pathway to personal distress. This can instantly lead us to feel sad, angry, frustrated, detached, or a myriad of other emotions. Psychologist Norman Kagan calls these emotional buttons "interpersonal allergies"—as with physical allergic reactions, a little bit of something can evoke a strong reaction in us.[13] When these buttons get pushed, we typically withdraw from our patients, become preoccupied with our own emotional state and fall into the Helper's Pit, or both.

These interpersonal allergies are universal in human experience. They affect everyone some of the time and some people all the time and are usually related to some basic fear or vulnerability. One common example of these interpersonal allergies at work is when we find it extremely difficult to work with a certain patient or family member and are surprised when another team member is highly effective with the same individual. We can't understand how he or she can even be in the same room with this impossible person. Then we find ourselves easily dealing with a different patient, one with whom we work well but whom our coworker can't tolerate. Our differing reactions to these people and situations can be traced to the emotional history that each of us brings to these encounters.

The psychotherapy literature discusses these highly individual reactions by helpers as *countertransference phenomena*. Countertransference occurs when we see something that isn't there or don't see something that is there. It is a pathway to ineffective helping and personal distress because we are relating most strongly to our *own* thoughts and feelings, not to those of the client, and we are unable to maintain a balanced position. For example, when a client reminds you of one of your family members or friends or presents problems that remain unsolved in your personal life, you may be less effective with this person. Another example is when the grief of the person you are helping activates your own continuing grief reactions, and you quickly fall into the Helper's Pit. The test then becomes how to use this exceptional sensitivity to deepen—not diminish—your empathy for the other person.

Our allergic responses are often unconscious and can catch us unaware—suddenly we find ourselves behaving in a way we might not have anticipated in our work with a specific patient or family member. We might move rapidly to an extreme position on the continuum of emotional involvement, jump into the Helper's Pit, find ourselves withdrawing from emotional contact, or feel helpless, frustrated, or angry.

Pam, a nurse who works with people with AIDS, has her greatest difficulty working with women. Her own mother died when she was 10 years old, and she now finds herself feeling protective of the children of dying female patients and intensely interested in what it is like for the dying mothers to say good-bye to their children. By talking with the mothers about their grief and by supporting their children, Pam is able to gain some insight into what might have been happening for her own mother when she had to leave Pam. Also, she can support the children in a manner she would have wanted for herself. The double-edged nature of Pam's deep empathy with these mothers and children is clear: She no doubt is profoundly caring in her interactions with them, but she also finds herself confronting much personal pain.

Four emotional themes that frequently appear in the interpersonal allergies of caregivers are fear of our own death, fear of hurting, fear of being hurt, and fear of being engulfed.

Fear of Our Own Death

Daily confrontations with life-threatening illness can push perhaps our most powerful emotional button, the fear of our own mortality. We can work for long stretches of time without consciously feeling this fear. Then, suddenly, we have a patient with our birthday, or who looks like our child or our sister, or has our mother's name, and instantly we have an "ego chill" experience in which we lose our sense of "this is not me" who is dying. For that moment, we jump into the Helper's Pit.

How we handle our reaction determines whether we can continue to provide help in an effective manner. This is a good example of a moment in helping when we need to maintain our balance and neither let our empathy switch to personal distress nor allow ourselves to unconsciously distance ourselves emotionally to reduce this distress.

No matter how often I ponder my own mortality or however many dying patients I work with, I still have a hard time thinking about my death. I'm not death phobic, but I have a "death button" that can get pushed. This often happens when I am working with someone my age who is a lot like me.

As Freud noted, the ego cannot imagine its own dissolution. In one of his lighter moments, he is said to have told his wife, "If one of us dies before the other, I think I'll move to Paris." The fear of our own mortality is something we continually face. And our work forces us to look at it or to work at avoiding it.

Regardless of how we cope with this fear, the pressure is still there. When this button is activated, you might find yourself leaving the helping field altogether, making a referral, or maybe becoming emotionally distant while you are still physically present. In one study, hospice volunteers with lower scores on a measure of death anxiety continued working in the program for longer periods of time than did volunteers with higher scores, suggesting that the group with high death anxiety had greater difficulty keeping their emotional balance.[14]

You are less likely to react in these ways if you have been working with the dying on a continuing basis. For example, one study showed that palliative care nurses working with the terminally ill had more positive attitudes toward death and less death anxiety than nurses who did not work regularly with the dying.[15]

Fear of Hurting

Another interpersonal allergy is the fear of hurting the person you are helping.[16] This is not always an irrational concern. Indeed, administering chemotherapy, doing a spinal tap on a 5-year-old child, delivering bad news, or making many other routine interventions is quite painful. Your helping often hurts. And that makes helping more stressful for you.

The fear of hurting others is compounded by the pressure to be perfect and by the fact that you must often make decisions based on ambiguous or incomplete information. Technological developments occur so rapidly that it is almost impossible to stay current with medical facts. Mistakes can be costly, sometimes even life-threatening. Consequently, many of us work with a "terror of error" that can grind us down and make it harder to be emotionally involved with the people we care for:

> I'm afraid of being caught in a crisis (life/death) situation
> of mother and/or baby when no doctor is around and other
> staff are too busy to help me—I'll do something wrong or
> fail to do the right thing.

> Before a sick baby is born, I feel I will not do the right
> things to save that baby from dying!

> I'm afraid that someday I'll accidentally say the wrong
> thing and take away someone's last hope.

Errors inevitably do occur, and the emotional consequences for the caregiver can be powerful and persistent, as these caregivers' disclosures reveal:

> Sometimes I feel that I've been careless, giving the wrong
> IV and rate to a patient. Instead of helping him, I'm making
> things worse. God! I feel so guilty, and I have sleepless
> nights worrying what the consequences can be.

> I made an error once and never told anyone and have
> always worried about it.

> In my first nursing job, I was in a treatment room dealing
> with trachs and dressing changes. A patient was brought in
> who had trouble breathing. I went to help him, suctioned
> and removed the dressing in the pharyngeal area. As I
> turned to do something, it seemed as if a small part of the
> dressing fell in the larynx, but I was never sure. The
> patient got worse after this and died later that night.

Early in my nursing career, another nurse and myself were
caring for the patients on a pediatric unit. An infant was
receiving blood and I could not monitor 1:1 because we
got an admission with croup and the second nurse sent
me to assist. The baby received too much normal saline
after the transfusion and went into congestive heart
failure, and his existing heart condition was compromised
and he died. If I would have been more knowledgeable and
insistent about having a doctor come in for a late
deceleration, that baby would be about 4 years old today.

Fear of Being Hurt

The fear of being hurt is also a frequent concern for helpers. The
kind of hurt we fear—and often have—can take many forms. First,
there can be direct physical and psychological aggression. An amazingly high percentage of caregivers have been kicked, spat on, sworn
at, pinched, or mistreated in other ways I lump together as helper
abuse. If we lose control and respond in kind, our self-esteem can be
seriously eroded:

I had a difficult patient who became angry at my attempts
to help her. She spit in my face. Without thinking, I spit
back in her face. I could have died with shame. I was there
to make this more comfortable for her, and I failed
miserably. I don't think anyone else would have reacted
so impulsively.

Second, displaced rage from patients and family members can be
extremely difficult to cope with. For example, an oncology nurse related how she had struggled to provide excellent care for a patient
with open wounds. The nurse was covered with blood and was standing near the husband, expecting him to thank her for her tremendous
caring efforts. Instead, he slapped her face and said, "Even *you*
couldn't save her!" This nurse could eventually see this outburst as
displaced rage, yet, in the moment, the pain and hurt for her were all
too real. The struggle to keep one's heart open—and one's commitment to helping intact—in difficult moments like these can be very
stressful.

Third, we can feel hurt and grief when our patients die. We grieve
for them and for their families and even for what we did or wished we
could have done. An important issue for teams and individuals in
health care is helper grief. If we work with dying patients, grief is a
constant part of what we do, and it builds up if it is not confronted

and worked through. In addition, grief from your personal life can be activated in helping encounters:

> The majority of people who are dying that I must care for have terminal cancer. I often feel anger, frustration, and fear when dealing with these patients and their families. I of course try to hide these negative thoughts. My problem is I watched my father die a miserable death from lung cancer over a 10-month period. My new patients and their problems bring up old feelings I felt when my dad died.

Fear of Being Engulfed

This concern is best captured by the thought that if I let myself become involved, I'll be sucked into the bottomless pit of the patient's emotional neediness. When activated, this emotional button can push us from feeling empathy and sympathy into an experience of distress. These helper disclosures vividly convey what this experience can be like:

> When I was there Monday she was very, very frightened. It was like she was clinging, and there was so much power in that I had to just stand back from that. It became almost manipulative. I felt like I was going to get sucked in.

> I have a fear of becoming so attached to my clients that I won't be able to detach myself when I go home to my family. I'm afraid of cheating my family out of having fun because I feel depressed over the client's situation. I can't turn my emotional state on or off easily, and I worry about my attitude toward my family and friends.

By blaming ourselves or getting stuck in helplessness when things go wrong, we often make a difficult situation worse. Coping with our fears, vulnerabilities, and other emotional responses also adds to our stress level. These internal stressors take their toll. But the toll often goes unnoticed. Maybe we start avoiding certain topics with patients or family members. Perhaps we become emotional for no reason. We might get sloppy in our communication—interrupting more; questioning more; telling people how to act, think, or feel; or not paying attention to our real impact on others.

When the toll is too great, when we have ignored our own needs for too long, the result is that we cut ourselves off emotionally from those we help—we tune out, stop listening, and disconnect. The antidote is to recognize and understand our fears and to retain our inner balance when our emotional buttons are triggered.

STAYING INVOLVED AND BALANCED

Finding a way to be empathic and emotionally involved without falling into the Helper's Pit is perhaps *the* central challenge for the caring helper:

> Helpers must be able to find joy in bringing people through these dark places rather than take on their clients' problems as their own and suffer with them. Helpers must learn to grow and increase their strength through wrestling with the pain of others rather than let that pain drag them down too.[17]

The alternative—to remain emotionally uninvolved—has powerful negative effects on us as helpers, as Eugene Kennedy and Sara Charles vividly describe:

> If we remain uninvolved, nothing much will happen, and the potential stress of emotional engagement will be transformed into a different kind of difficulty commonly known by the reluctant counselor. Such helpers experience the problems of others as burdens or downright impositions; they struggle through relationships like a downed airman crossing a swamp with a parachute dragging behind him. There is nothing sadder than helpers who steel themselves against their tasks, who speak of "having to see all these mixed-up people," and who seem more grimly dutiful than interested in their work. The stress associated with noninvolvement is not very dramatic, of course; the heart does not leap with enthusiasm in these situations. It is like being caught between two grindstones which crush us slowly into a fine, dry powder. Few things are worse than working with people and not enjoying it.[18]

Because emotional involvement is essential, how can we tell when we are overinvolved? I believe that we can have extremely strong emotional responses without falling into the Helper's Pit. Strong emotions are a natural part of helping people cope with grief, loss, and life-threatening illness. You can be balanced even as tears roll down your cheeks as long as you are still focused on the other person and your own feelings don't shift from caring to distress.

In one of my own helping encounters, I was talking with a bereaved, usually unemotional husband about his final conversation with his terminally ill wife. She had told him, "Share your tears with our sons." He cried as he described this. Tears also ran down my face, and he saw them. We continued talking. Was I in the Helper's Pit? I don't think so, and this is because I still could think about his situation as other than my own, though I was resonating to the depths of my soul with it.

Being close and helpful without being distressed requires that we know ourselves and respect our own feelings. When we misinterpret, don't know, or cover up our genuine feelings and reactions, we risk the hazards of overinvolvement. Strong and sometimes irrational feelings are part of helping; they become troublesome only when we don't give ourselves time or permission to explore their roots, to reflect on why we are having these particular feelings at this particular time. When you find yourself overreacting, clinging, rejecting, feeling possessive of a patient, or saying this is the best or worst person you have ever worked with, it is time to look inside and try to make sense of what this relationship really means to you.

We must also remain separate as we draw closer to the other person, a suggestion that may on its face sound paradoxical. But it is only as a separate person that we can care for someone without the fear that our concern for him or her will drag us into the Helper's Pit. Carl Rogers once made a distinction in his definition of empathy that is useful here. He wrote that "to sense the client's private world as if it were your own, but without ever losing the as if quality—this is empathy."[19] This balanced way of relating to our inner and outer life is analogous to the way family therapists describe healthy patterns of interrelating in families. For them, the optimal style of relating is somewhere between the extremes of being overly involved or "enmeshed" and distantly disengaged.

We must have a real relationship with the people we care for. The greatest gift we can give is that of human presence—the feeling that they are not alone in their struggles. We can give this gift only if we are willing to take the risk of becoming involved with this stranger who seeks our help. Yet we must somehow find a way to do this without becoming enmeshed with the other.

In both the intrapersonal and interpersonal realms, we want to be close enough to have contact but not so close that we lose our balance and identify our whole selves with what we encounter. Whether it is your patient's pain or the sadness you feel when a patient is suffering, you must befriend and acknowledge these feelings while also remaining able to step back and see the larger picture. Without this skill, your potential for caring and compassionate helping is severely limited.

Within the Helper's Pit metaphor, we might think of empathic caregivers as holding onto tree limbs to maintain balanced emotional involvement. These tree limbs are the various coping resources (personal strengths, social support, and stress management skills) and the helping skills that support them in their caregiving. These resources and skills will be explored in greater detail in chapter 3 and chapter 6.

Assessing how we are doing in our pursuit of greater emotional balance as helpers is a complex task. When we have a big emotional button pushed or when we are clearly in over our heads, it is easy to recognize that we are having a problem. However, our helping is often activated by personal distress, low self-esteem, guilt, and other more subtle psychological forces. Let's take a look at some of these other varieties of caregivers' emotional experiences and see what they can teach us about keeping our balance as caregivers.

EMPATHY-DRIVEN VERSUS DISTRESS-DRIVEN HELPING

Empathy and personal distress are related to different patterns of helping behavior. As we saw earlier, empathy-driven helping is caregiving powered and guided by our empathic responses to the people we care for. Our focus is on the other person, and a promotive tension within us moves us to help. Distress-driven helping, in contrast, is helping powered by personal distress. Here the caregiver is more self-focused, and the task of reducing his or her personal distress begins to compete with that of reducing the other person's distress. Unhelpful responses like blaming the victim, distancing oneself emotionally, self-preoccupation, and other burnout-related phenomena become more common. Another way to say this is that when the caregiver falls into the Helper's Pit, empathic distress, a "prosocial" motive, is transformed into personal distress, an egoistic motive.[20]

Let's look at this phenomenon more closely. What does *egoistic* mean here? If our helping is driven by personal distress, we are more likely not to help if escape (e.g., physical or emotional withdrawal) is easy; that is, our helping is egoistic or "selfish" in the sense that our ultimate goal is the relief of our own, not the other person's, distress.[21] If escape is too costly (e.g., negative responses from a supervisor, coworkers, or oneself), we can still escape by distancing ourselves physically or emotionally—for example, by leaving the scene or not answering phone calls. If we choose escape, we may try to discharge our guilt by blaming the victim, saying things like "He's totally impossible" or "She just won't help herself."

During the course of caregiving, there are often many opportunities to stop or diminish your helping. You can decide to spend less time with this person, or you can refer the person to another agency or caregiver. If these forms of physical escape are not possible, you can pull back emotionally and do only what is necessary. But what is most revealing here is that we usually do not avail ourselves of these escapes from helping: Our empathy for the distress of others usually keeps us moving steadily toward a positive helping outcome.

However, the picture changes dramatically in distress-driven helping. Here the balance shifts to relieving our own emotional pain. True, unless you escape the field, you are still helping the other person, but the entire complexion of helping is different and the features of burnout begin to overshadow the positive qualities of helping.

The distinction between empathy-driven and distress-driven helping raises a more general issue concerning our motivations for helping. Is altruism ever really the motivation for our helping, or is our caregiving always primarily self-centered? Think back to the scene with the young woman who had fallen from her mountain bike. Let's assume that you were "empathically aroused" when you encountered her and that you helped. Did you help her to relieve her distress or to relieve yours? The more general question is, Are "altruistic" acts actually egoistic? In other words, do we just help others to reduce our own negative feelings, helping being the most efficient way to do this?

This question receives much attention by research psychologists, who reason as follows: If we are helping for egoistic reasons (to reduce our own emotional pain), we won't continue to help if we can easily escape from the helping situation (assuming there are low costs for escaping). If these options are readily available, we will escape by avoiding being assigned this person, not answering the phone, or getting another volunteer or staff person involved. We might also withdraw emotionally. If, on the other hand, our motivation to help is truly altruistic, the ease or difficulty (costs) of escaping the helping situation will have no impact on whether or not we help because this is irrelevant to our goal—namely, relieving the other person's distress.

Most researchers now agree that empathic emotion produces a truly altruistic desire to reduce the distress of others.[22] We act first and foremost for the other person; the relief of our empathic distress (as opposed to personal distress) is a positive outcome, but it is not the motivation for our actions. This finding explains why we persist in helping in situations where giving up or leaving the scene could be a tempting alternative. It also supports the view that altruism and helping are a fundamental aspect of human nature.

"I CARE, THEREFORE I HELP"

Another intriguing finding is that for the empathy-helping connection to occur, we must personally interpret our arousal as empathic concern and not as private distress or some other aroused state. Consider the following study done by psychologist Jay Coke and his colleagues.[23] Undergraduate subjects listened to a fake newscast about "Katie Banks," a senior at their university whose parents had recently been killed in an automobile crash. Katie needed money, and she also needed help with grocery shopping, chores, and baby-sitting for her two younger siblings. Subjects were told that because Katie was nice enough to let them use the newscast in the study, the professor in charge of the research wanted to do something for her and had a list from Katie of things subjects could do. The measure of helping was the amount of time volunteered to help Katie.

Some subjects were instructed to imagine Katie's condition during the newscasts; another group was instructed to identify specific broadcasting techniques. Both groups had some subjects who were given a placebo pill they were told would either relax or arouse them. The subjects who were instructed to empathize but were also told that they had been given an arousing placebo did not help. It was the subjects who were told they had been given the relaxation pill and to empathize who helped the most. They knew that their arousal was due to empathic concern, and they proceeded to offer the most help, often many hours of volunteer assistance. When we are empathically aroused in response to distress in others *and* we perceive our arousal as empathic concern, we help.[24]

It is important to note at this point that, just as not all empathy leads to helping, not all helping is a result of empathy. Helping, spontaneous or otherwise, doesn't always require personal in-the-moment empathy. Many, perhaps most, of our interventions flow from a more cognitive understanding of our clients' needs and can be based on diverse sources of information, from test results to predictions based on previous clinical encounters. For example, consider a routine phone call to a family on the first night of home care. This intervention makes good clinical sense and might seem extremely empathic to the family, but it does not necessarily stem from emotional empathy, though a deeper empathic involvement might develop during the phone conversation.

Indeed, most of our helping moments are imbued with a more general sense of empathy for the people we care for. We develop a picture of their suffering in the present and in the future, and this larger sense of concern and empathy guides our actions. When we sit face to face with them and discuss emotional issues, more specific empathic reactions develop and add further impetus and focus to our helping.

In this way, some of our helping can be almost purely cognitively driven. The cognitively driven helper thinks, "I know what they need at this time, and I will do it." Although often on target, this kind of helping can be somewhat pro forma and out of touch with the unique needs of the people we care for. For example, after many years of working with patients and families, we often know what to expect; even the most poignant disclosures—things said for the first time, words finding form from raw experience—can be similar in structure to what we have heard hundreds of times before. This can lead to a tendency to anticipate and not listen, to act before hearing the full story, to slip into advice giving, and generally to do what we know will usually be helpful to people facing this kind of circumstance.

Still, cognitively driven helping has some unique advantages. This kind of helping can get you through many difficult helping situations. You might not have empathy for or even like the people you are caring for. However, you know what they need, you are committed to serving them, and you go on to make effective interventions based on your understanding of their situation and the personal values, ethical beliefs, and goals you bring to your work.

DOWNWARD AND UPWARD COMPARISONS WITH OTHERS

When people are distressed, they often find some relief in comparing themselves with other less fortunate people. Psychologists know this as *downward social comparison*.[25] For example, the people we care for, even in the worst of circumstances, often comment that others are worse off. A mother agonizes over the loss of her child but knows another woman who lost her entire family. Knowing that things could be worse is comforting.

We also experience downward social comparison as helpers. The suffering of patients and family members, although a source of deep concern and a constant reminder of the fragility of life, also deepens our appreciation for the health of our own families. Difficulties in our personal lives pale in comparison, and this comparison can fuel our helping. We think, "If they have the courage to deal with this, I must have the strength to help them in this time of need."

When comparisons go in the reverse direction, however, the empathy-helping connection can be derailed. For example, in one study subjects asked to empathize with the positive feelings of others were less likely to offer help to these perhaps more fortunate others. Empathic sadness promotes helping, but empathic joy lessens it.[26] How can we explain this? It seems that we unconsciously assess whether our needs are being sufficiently met to allow us to empathize with the suffering of others. If we perceive our own sadness as out-weighing another's, our attention shifts to ourselves, and our empa-thy transforms into personal distress. You find yourself feeling angry or thinking, "I need comfort and help" and then feel inadequate or guilty for having these thoughts:

> Last month I felt no sympathy for and was even angry at a man who had lost his wife after 50 years of marriage. He was distressed that he had no reason to go on. All I could think was that he had 50 good years with her and that I may never marry—and then I felt guilty.

> I get so angry when mothers of healthy term newborns use me as a baby-sitter or refuse to care for their own baby when I have been trying desperately to conceive a child of my own.

Even when you just have a bad day, one peppered with daily has-sles or small misfortunes, you must work harder to help people who are having an easier time. When you need help, when you are in your own pit, helping others is more difficult, and your vulnerability to burnout is heightened.

GUILT, LOW SELF-ESTEEM, AND HELPING

Everyday helping, though fueled primarily by the altruism–empathy–helping connection, is frequently sparked—and healthily so—by many egoistic motivations. Altruism and egoism are often closely and positively related in helping. You can grow and develop during helping, your self-esteem can be enhanced, you can feel good be-cause of the good works you do, and you might even accrue certain health benefits. Still, many caregivers are a bit hesitant to acknowl-edge these rewards, feeling that these "selfish" elements somehow diminish their helping motivations. I believe that these benefits should be celebrated as affirmations of the notion that helping is nat-ural and healthy. Helping is often difficult and stressful, but it is also the most rewarding endeavor in which we can engage.

There is, however, a kind of egoistic involvement in helping that is problematic. As already discussed, helping often gets derailed, and empathy-driven helping can be replaced by helping that is motivated by personal distress. Guilt and low self-esteem are two emotional states that can play particularly important roles in distress-driven helping.

Guilt can induce us to help others. In laboratory experiments, if someone does harm of any kind (e.g., he or she hurts someone's feelings, breaks something, or administers an electric shock to someone), that person is very likely to engage in helping behavior. Think about the times you have made a mistake as a caregiver and have immediately gone out and made up for it. Speaking personally, I know that each time I've said the wrong thing in a helping situation, I have subsequently redoubled my efforts to do something positive. We also know that the *absence* of guilt reduces prosocial behavior. Churchgoers, for example, are less likely to contribute to charity following confession than before it.[27]

A kind of existential guilt can also motivate our helping. This is guilt resulting from seeing yourself in an extremely advantaged position in relation to the people you help. They are in so much pain and in such awful predicaments, whereas we who are relatively happy and healthy go home at night to our friends and families. This guilt persists, even though we consciously recognize that our advantaged position is a fragile one.

Low self-esteem is another negative feeling that can motivate helping behavior. When our own self-esteem is at a low point, the internal and external rewards of helping can serve to improve our reputations with ourselves.[28] Then the enhancement of self-esteem is no longer a fortuitous byproduct of helping; it is the goal. In their study of the motivations of volunteers, psychologists Gil Clary and Mark Snyder found that volunteering can serve an *"ego-defensive function, helping people to cope with inner conflicts, anxieties, and uncertainties concerning personal worth and competence."*[29]

THE CODEPENDENT CAREGIVER: A DANGEROUS MYTH

This discussion raises the specter of the "codependent caregiver," the helper who allegedly satisfies personal needs through the people he or she cares for.[30] This term increasingly is invoked to explain the difficulties of caregivers.

In a recent critique of codependency theory, Edith Gomberg chronicles the expansion of the term *codependent* beyond its use denoting family members of the alcoholic or drug abusing person.[31] The first people labeled as codependent were wives of alcoholics in the 1950s and 1960s. These women, seen as dependent and frustrated, and as marrying their husbands to meet their own neurotic needs, were referred to as "Suffering Susans," "Controlling Catherines," or "Punitive Pollys." The "codependency epidemic" then spread to coworkers and friends of the addicted person and now affects the relationships of virtually everyone to everything, explaining our dependence on food, religion, and even on the people we work with as helpers. This although no scientific research supports any of these applications.

The continuing proliferation of codependency is fostered by the unclear criteria for and vague conceptual boundaries of the concept. When we look at any of the myriad statements on codependency, we always find lists of characteristics that are easy to agree with, such as the following:[32]

- Do you have a "need to be needed"?
- Are you a controlling caregiver?
- Do you ever have low self-esteem and problems with boundaries?
- Are you afraid to express your needs and opinions?
- Did you grow up in an emotionally repressive family?

Like the rest of the helper population of the United States, you probably answered yes to one or more of these questions, suggesting that you have a mild or perhaps even a full-blown case of codependency, the "social disease of the 1990s." Or do you? In fact, because there are no valid and reliable testing instruments for measuring codependency, we cannot really differentiate the codependent person from anyone else in the population. In psychology, we call this a lack of discriminant validity; in everyday life, it means that you can never exclude yourself from codependent status.

As a long-time advocate of mutual support groups and someone who believes that Codependents Anonymous (CODA) groups have helped many people stand up for themselves and leave abusive relationships, I have been surprised by my growing discomfort with the notion of "codependent caregiving." What could be wrong with this kind of attempt to pay more attention to our difficulties as helpers?

The reasons relate to some unintended and negative consequences of looking at ourselves and our caregiving this way. Viewing our difficulties in helping as symptoms of a disease is an unhealthy, self-defeating approach to these problems. Richard Lazarus, a leading stress theorist, cautions against explaining our distress this way, arguing that we

should be wary of the pathology mystique in which
emotional distress and dysfunction are automatically
relegated to the idea of sickness rather than being seen as
active adaptational struggles of a person under stress who
is trying to cope as best as he or she can.[33]

Research on the effects of different attributional styles demon-
strates that interpreting our difficulties this way engenders feelings of
helplessness and depression.[34] We come to believe that the source of
our problems is internal ("It's me"), stable ("It won't change"), and
global ("And it will affect all other areas of my life"). In our culture,
the line between self-responsibility and self-blame is already thin.
When we add the stigma of a disease diagnosis, our tendency to
blame ourselves is intensified.

The key lesson of recent work on caregiver burnout is that the
major source of problems is usually in the situation or context, not in
the caregiver: Burnout results not from "bad apples" but from the
"bad kegs" the apples are in.[35] The recommendation of burnout experts is, accordingly, that we need to shift from asking "What's wrong
with me?" to asking "What can I do about the situation?"[36] However,
as psychologists Christina Maslach and Susan Jackson point out,
when the quality of care begins to decline, people and not the work
environment are usually first to be blamed (either "bad patients" or
"lazy staff"):

> Although personality variables are certainly an important
> factor in burnout, research has led us to the conclusion
> that the problem is best understood (and modified) in
> terms of the social and situational sources of job-related
> stress. The prevalence of the phenomenon and the range
> of seemingly disparate professionals who are affected by it
> suggest that the search for causes is better directed away
> from the unending cycle of identifying the "bad people"
> and toward uncovering the operational and structural
> characteristics of the "bad situations" where many good
> people function.[37]

The tendency to explain negative events as reflecting something
about the people experiencing them rather than the situation itself is
a pervasive human phenomenon and follows from a more general
bias known in psychology as the *fundamental attribution error.*[38]
Viewing ourselves as codependent caregivers is a doubly dangerous
error because, besides heightening self-blame, it shifts our attention
away from the situational determinants of our stress and undermines
our efforts to change them.

Perhaps the most destructive consequence of the codependent caregiver concept and others like it is that the web of blame and cynicism it fosters can undermine your external support for doing this work. With the arrival of codependency in the popular press, your disclosures of any kind of distress associated with your work are more likely to be greeted with "Maybe you shouldn't be doing this kind of work. By the way, have you read anything about codependency?" The message is clear: Caring for others must always stop short of personal inconvenience or distress.

Support from administrators, coworkers, and supervisors can also be undermined by the codependency model. We already witness discussions about "codependent" employees and coworkers. Listen carefully the next time someone in your work setting uses the term to describe someone. Is it used with compassion? Is the message "This person is hurting and we need to do everything we can do to help her" (e.g., add staffing)? Or is it tinged with blame, more like "She's got a real problem"? Because of this negative aspect, helpers become even more likely to conceal their pain.

Finally, the codependency model makes us doubt ourselves. If we label our caring motivations as codependent needs, our altruistically inspired helping becomes a product of emotional instability. When we go out of the way for others—something that is part of everyday caregiving—we wonder why we are doing so. We ask ourselves, Is this just a need to please? As writer Alison Humes puts it, codependency theory "makes loving people an addiction."[39]

Codependency theorists fail to see that the wellsprings of human caring run much deeper than dysfunction and addiction. What is most noble in the human spirit—and in caregiving—becomes suspect. These doubts about our helping motivations can erode the best buffer against stress in caregiving—your sense of purpose in the work. You jeopardize your most precious resource—your love— if you view yourself and your caring as something less than what they are.

Each of us has a unique blend of motivations driving our helping efforts. Guilt, low self-esteem, personal distress, and "selfish" motivations are probably a small part of every helper's motivations. All caregivers must find a balance between responsibility to self and responsibility to others, between balanced helping and rescue operations. We need to closely examine all the ways that we might land in the Helper's Pit and look at whether we are being overly controlling, communicating ineffectively, not setting boundaries, or vicariously living through the lives of the people we care for. And when we identify these bad habits, we need to change them, but we don't need to have a disease to do this.

CONCLUSION

Helping relationships are *personal* relationships. To be successful as caregivers, we must enter into meaningful emotional relationships with the people we assist; we must make room for them in our emotional worlds. Why is this emotional involvement so necessary? Research on helping confirms the old adage that "people don't care what you know until they know that you care." We know that prizing and valuing the other, a real interest and concern, and a kind of non-possessive warmth are essential elements of effective caregiving. In the highly personal and intimate helping relationship, something akin to love may be the most effective agent for healing and growth, as psychologist C. H. Patterson observes:

> A loving relationship is the therapy for all disorders of the
> human spirit and of disturbed interpersonal relationships.
> It is not necessary to wait for a "breakthrough" or a
> discovery of new methods or techniques of psychotherapy
> or human relations. We already have, in essence, the
> answer—the answer that has been reached through
> thousands of years of human experience and recognized by
> the great philosophers of various times and cultures.[40]

Your effectiveness as a helper and the personal and professional growth you have in that role can be threatened if personal distress and emotional overload keep you in the Helper's Pit. Your relationships with the people you care for are only one source of this distress. Your relationships with coworkers, problems in your organization, and events in your personal life also contribute significantly to your distress quotient. To meet the challenge of caring, you must find balance on your helping journey, balance between the demands you face and the resources you have to meet them, between giving to others and giving to yourself.

3

There are times when I feel like screaming or kicking or hitting something—like I'm about to lose control—but I usually just make tight fists, breathe, and then return to the situation looking (and hopefully acting) calm, in control, and like a nurse. It's very hard, often painful.

Anonymous helper

The very worst times are the ones when I have felt so much and hurt so long for a family that finally I can't feel anything at all.

Anonymous helper

Sometimes I wish I could let go of some memories of one child whom I could not help. To this day I picture her and try to reach out and help, but even I could not help this terminal patient. I feel sad and the memory lingers.

Anonymous helper

Once when caring for an elderly Jewish woman who had been in the concentration camps, I had to get her up in a chair per M. D.'s order. She had severe pain and sarcoma diagnosis. She glared at me and said, "You're worse than Hitler!" Being Jewish myself, this hurt worse than anything she could have said. It still makes me reflect on how poorly I handled the situation.

Anonymous helper

Finding the Balance: Managing the Stress of Caregiving

STRESS

We all know stress when we see it or feel it. We see it in the eyes of the people we care for. We feel it within ourselves when a child in our care dies, when we are emotionally drained, when we have conflicts with our coworkers, or when personal problems grind us down.

Think of your current work as a helper and rate yourself on a 10-point scale, where 1 is "almost no stress" and 10 is "extremely stressed." The actual rating you give yourself is less important than the events and situations that flash through your mind while you are making the rating. Jot down these events and situations on a sheet of paper.

Also take a few moments and write out your purpose and goals in helping (see chapter 1 for a discussion of these issues). These can include your broader purpose or mission, such as the desire to give something back or to ease the suffering of others, and the specific helping goals that make up your personal vision as a caregiver. They are the things in your work that give you a sense of personal significance.[1]

Before you take a closer look at what you have written, let's explore two important ideas that will provide us with a framework for viewing the lists. The first idea focuses on the fact that your motivations as a helper have a double-edged quality: They inspire and fuel your helping, but at the same time they make you more vulnerable to stress. This idea was presented at the beginning of the previous chapter, where the relation between commitment levels and burnout was discussed and the adage presented that what brings you into the work is also what can burn you out.

59

Some examples will illustrate these connections. If pain control really matters to you, uncontrolled pain in someone you are caring for would be highly stressful for you. If you value treating the entire family as a unit, late referrals that preclude effective family interventions would be especially painful for you. If you like to facilitate open communication in families, a family locked in avoidance would probably be high on your list of stressors. If you are an administrator whose personal vision includes fostering high levels of trust and openness in your organization, unresolved interpersonal conflicts among team members will tend to grind you down. In each case, your personal vision of what helping is all about is being frustrated and blocked from its full expression.

The second idea concerns the role of self-esteem in stress. Essentially, self-esteem is how much we like or dislike ourselves; or, as Nathaniel Branden puts it, it is the reputation we acquire with ourselves.[2] Human beings are constantly engaged in preserving, enhancing, or restoring their self-esteem. Self-esteem, and its fluctuations, plays a central role in all interpersonal relations and is a powerful predictor of how we behave at work and at home. When our self-esteem is threatened or injured, conflict, avoidance, resistance, and other defensive responses to stress often result. Think about your own relationships and interactions. When someone's actions threaten or lower your self-esteem, even just a little, do you want to spend time with that person again? Probably not.

Thus, besides wanting to make a difference and realize our personal visions as helpers, we seek to maintain and enhance our sense of self-esteem. When our self-esteem is threatened at work, stress will predictably follow.

Now look at your lists of stressors and your purposes and goals. (I use the words *stressor* for the stimuli that affect us and *stress* for our responses to the stimuli.) Can you see any relation between the events that frustrate you most and the blocking of the purposes and goals that matter most to you? Do any of your personal stressors include events that somehow involve either a major or a minor blow to your self-esteem?

This exercise reveals how our goals, values, and self-esteem interact with external events to affect our stress levels. Often we move so quickly that we don't stop and reflect on exactly why a given event bothers us so much. When we do, we can start to realize that the event somehow connects us with the deeper parts of ourselves, to the basic motivations that move us along our paths as helpers.

Our struggles with time pressure illustrate these connections. A common stressor for caregivers is work overload. Too much paperwork, understaffing, and unexpected problems create a situation where there is no slack in the system and everyone is always rushed. When you are that busy, taking the time to talk with your patients and give them special care can feel like a luxury and might even be forgotten. (Remember the discussion in chapter 1 of the hurrying Princeton theology students who didn't help the person in distress while on their way to give a talk on the parable of the Good Samaritan.) Eventually, you realize that you can't give quality help to those in need:

It's frustrating when you finally get a day when the census is low enough that the staff can do what they can do, and then they call and make you stay home, so the staff that's left is working just as hard as when it was crowded.

Sometimes I feel all I'm expected to do are the mechanics of nursing—there is no time to deal with the family or baby as an individual. I'm not given the time to care.

When hurried circumstances deny you the opportunity to do what you can do and the time to care, feelings of resentment, guilt, and lowered self-esteem tend to replace your empathy and ability to care.

In addition to fulfilling one's purpose in helping and maintaining one's self-esteem, most caregivers share many other values and goals that can be jeopardized during helping. For example, caregivers value quality patient care, good relations with colleagues, and being treated with respect and fairness, and they usually feel stressed when these goals and values are threatened.

Stress Is Interpersonal

As you review the events associated with stress for you as a caregiver, do you find that most of these stressors involve difficult interactions with other people—whether they are patients and families, coworkers, or administrators? During the past few years, I have asked people I have come into contact with in everyday situations, from the supermarket to the photocopying store, the same question: "What's the biggest source of stress for you in your job?" The answer has invariably been other people.

People are also a major source of stress for caregivers. Coworkers, not patients and their families, may be the main source of helper stress. For example, in their study of 1,800 intensive care nurses, Karen Claus and June Bailey found that interpersonal conflict—with physicians, supervisors, or other staff nurses—was the most commonly reported source of stress.[3]

In a major study of caregivers working with critically ill, dying, and bereaved populations, psychologist Mary Vachon found that the most frequently cited stressor had to do with team communication problems—not direct patient care.[4] Interacting with patients and family members who had personality or coping problems was the second major stressor reported by her subjects. After noting the somewhat surprising and counterintuitive nature of this finding, Vachon concluded: "This finding is similar to other studies of occupational stress which often show that work stress does not primarily involve the job one chooses to do but rather derives from the hassles which accompany attempting to perform these functions."[5]

In the Claus and Bailey study, patient care was rated as the major source of satisfaction, as well as the third greatest source of stress, behind interpersonal conflicts with other staff and management of the unit.[6] It is interesting that, at the same time, interpersonal relationships at work were cited as the second greatest source of satisfaction. The researchers concluded that these nurses liked doing direct patient care, that the stress of caregiving was much less significant than the stress associated with interpersonal conflicts at work, and that efforts should be made to support nurses in their bedside caregiving.

A paradox emerges from these findings: People burn you out, but at the same time people are what keep your caring flame burning. Interpersonal relationships are the crucible in which caring is either nourished or transformed into personal pain and burnout.

Unrealistic Expectations of Self and Self-Blame

Stress may be profoundly interpersonal in nature, but its origins are also firmly rooted in our relationship with ourselves. Although more difficult to see and measure than some external stressors already discussed, unrealistic expectations of ourselves can be a major source of stress. Do you ever think that you must be successful with everyone you work with? Or that if other people were aware of how much you don't know, they wouldn't want you as their caregiver? Do you occasionally think to yourself, "Nothing I do will even begin to make a difference in these awful situations" or find yourself wanting everyone you work with to appreciate and like you? Or are you always waiting for things to settle down and disappointed when they don't?

It is easy to see how irrational and self-defeating beliefs like these can affect our stress levels.[7] If you believe you must be successful with every patient you work with, any helping intervention you perceive as an actual or potential failure will be highly threatening to you and will jeopardize your self-esteem. If you need to be liked by everyone you help, a small rebuff or an angry response might be particularly difficult for you.

This kind of self-dialogue also ensures that the on switch will be activated when you evaluate your ability to cope with these threats—how can you ever have enough resources to balance the demands for perfection that you are placing on yourself? In this manner, these uncompromising thoughts and beliefs engender unattainable goals and lead to negative self-talk that erodes self-esteem. As Milton's famous couplet reminds us, "The mind is its own place, and in itself/Can make a heav'n of hell, a hell of heav'n." Imagined failure accounts for a much greater share of our stress than does real failure.

Another intrapersonal source of stress is the tendency toward self-blame. When caregivers approach burnout, they often tend to misperceive its cause. We tend to think that our exhaustion or inner conflicts reflect a lack of competence on our part. Though we know our work is stressful and recognize the many sources of stress in the environments we work in, when we are tired or feeling low, we tend to blame ourselves for our problems. We say to ourselves, "I guess I'm not as strong and competent as the others" or "Why am I being so hostile? I thought I got into this work because I'm a caring person."

This kind of mea culpa reaction is fostered in several ways. First, burnout usually results from exposure to chronic stress over a long period. When burnout is reached, there are often no distinctive external events (e.g., an extremely difficult caregiving situation, major changes in staffing, or a crisis in our personal lives) that can adequately explain our feelings of burnout.[8]

A second reason we attribute our difficulties to something inside us is that we don't know others are having the same experiences. If we did, we might see that our stress has more to do with the situation we are in than with some defect in ourselves. But this usually doesn't happen because often neither we nor our coworkers disclose the details of our stress experiences. So, rather than seeing them as part of a *shared* stressful situation, we attribute our problems to a character flaw or personal inadequacy. We may think, "I'm lazy . . . selfish . . . needy . . . stupid . . . too angry . . . impatient . . . insensitive . . . codependent." Then, clearly unable to share this negative view of ourselves, we try to look cool, be cheerful and efficient, and work even harder. When that doesn't help, we become confused and further avoid looking at what we feel inside. All this self-blame only speeds us along the path to burnout.

A simple yet telling example of this predilection for self-blame can be seen in caregivers' feelings of self-doubt and self-criticism when they forget the names of people they care for. They might not have seen the patient or family member for a year or more but still feel bad when the person's name escapes them. They think, "I was with this person in the most difficult of times. We shared such intimate and important experiences! Now I don't even remember her name! Am I uncaring? Have I become too detached?"

Fear of embarrassment in these situations can sometimes lead the caregiver to avoid the patient or family member. Ironically, this response, meant to avoid presenting the image of someone who is uncaring, can have exactly that effect on the person being avoided when he or she sees you walking away or notices the urge to escape in your manner.

When we step back and look at this situation more objectively, it is apparent that whereas clients and families have only a few helpers' names to remember, helpers have a roster of hundreds of client and family names. It becomes clear that forgetting simply comes with the territory and that this does not in any way reflect on our level of involvement, compassion, or commitment to the work.

Self-blame is usually accompanied by feelings of guilt and lowered self-esteem. The telltale signs are thoughts that start with "If only I were":

- If only I were more skilled, this person would get well.

- If only I were a better helper, I could get this family together.

- If only I were a better listener, I would have known what she really meant, and I could have helped her talk to her daughter before she died.

I call the "if only I were" phrase a "burnout mantra." Repeat it to yourself often enough, and you will achieve a state of not-so-blissful burnout.

At its extreme, this way of thinking goes beyond what we can realistically expect of ourselves. It leads to illusions of omnipotence, reflected in statements such as "Maybe I could've prevented Mr. Smith's death." Or the flip side: "I'm responsible for how he died." This kind of self-incrimination is reflected in these caregivers' disclosures:

I can't accept that there is no humanly possible way to constantly meet EVERY need of every patient/family, my spiritual needs, family, health needs, etc. After all, with God guiding my life, I *should* feel good about what I am able to do. But it's never enough.

I am never loyal. My lack of [support for] another human being . . . no matter what they do to themselves or to me is a serious flaw. When it gets really bad, I leave or threaten them I will leave if they don't change. I can't be counted on because I am self-centered and selfish.

I'm selfish with my time. I only want to give them as much of my time as *I* want to give. I feel angry and put out when I find they need or ask me to stay longer than I'd planned. I don't like being "put-out," inconvenienced. I feel I should be totally giving.

Questioning ourselves and the work we do is inevitable; self-examination is an important skill. But blame and guilt can corrupt this inner questioning and lead to troubling thoughts and feelings that can undermine your well-being and your ability to care. These "helper secrets" are discussed in chapter 4.

A Transactional Model of Stress

A good model of stress can explain the connections between what we value and what causes us stress. It can also help us understand why certain events trigger the stress response in us whereas others don't. One such model has been proposed by psychologist Richard Lazarus and his colleagues, who define stress as follows: "a particular relationship between the person and the environment that is appraised by the person as taxing or exceeding his or her resources and endangering his or her well-being."[9] Let's look at the different elements of this definition and relate them to our everyday encounters with stress.

One key element of this definition is the idea that stress is not an objective *thing*, but the product of an ongoing relationship or transactions between a person and his or her environment (*environment* meaning other people and the situations we find ourselves in). Depending on the way we evaluate the demands confronting us, what is stressful at one moment might not be stressful the next. Also, what is stressful for one person might not be stressful for someone else. This model also implies that how we view events has a major impact on whether and to what extent they are stressful to us (i.e., it shows us that stress begins with our appraisals of ourselves and what is happening in our lives at the moment).

Am I OK?

Appraisals are our ongoing evaluations and judgments about the demands of the current situation and our resources for handling those demands. Our appraisals are of central importance because they act as critical on-off switches in the stress response.

The first or primary appraisal we make concerns the significance of the stressor. In essence, we ask, "Am I (i.e., my physical and emotional well-being) OK, or am I in danger?" In other words, is this really worth getting upset about?

This question is the starting point for the stress response, and several different appraisals are possible. First, our judgment might be that the event has no bearing on our well-being. Most of what we experience is probably seen in this way, and the stress response is never initiated. Second, we might view the event as beneficial to our well-being and feel good about it. A pay raise or a compliment from a supervisor or colleague would most likely be viewed this way. Third, we might see the event as possibly involving loss or harm, a threat, or a challenge. Judgments of loss or harm might be initiated by an illness, a death, or getting fired. Judgments of threat concern anticipated losses or harms, either to our physical or psychological selves. For example, if you have a new supervisor you don't get along with or you realize that funding for your agency is being cut, you will probably feel threatened because you are anticipating future losses or harm and have to start coping with them.

When we appraise a situation as a challenge, we view it as not just having a possibility of loss or harm but also as holding some potential benefit if we are able to meet its demands successfully. Some people seem more likely to see things in this light. We know, for example, that when presented with the same external situation, some caregivers will make threat appraisals whereas others will see the demands of the situation as challenging.[10] Consider the example of the seasoned and accomplished helper who is asked to intervene in an extremely complicated and difficult family situation. A less experienced caregiver might balk at the request, but our veteran helper welcomes the challenge of tackling this difficult assignment.

Thus, our interpretation of an event plays a central role in our stress. Many philosophers and poets have noted this. The Roman philosopher Epictetus stated that men are not worried by things, but by their ideas about things. In other words, objective events in our personal and work lives are stressful only when we subjectively appraise them as harmful or threatening.

This model of appraisals also clarifies why cancer and other life-threatening illnesses are so tremendously stressful. In essence, the appraisal process, which prompts us to figure out quickly how we should react to each twist and turn of our lives, goes haywire when we are forced to negotiate the uncertainties surrounding diagnosis, treatment, and prognosis. The appraisal of "Am I OK?"

taps into a wide range of vulnerabilities associated with physical survival and quality of life, and the answers in each domain are rarely clear-cut. Evaluating whether you can cope with these complex and profoundly demanding events is equally difficult, generating tremendous anxiety.

I tell my clients that anxiety is what happens when you are driving on a freeway, a car unpredictably slows down in front of you, and for a moment you think, "Did I get my brakes checked recently?" Fear is the feeling that occurs when you are in the same situation, push on your brake pedal, and discover that you have no brakes.[11] A diagnosis of cancer evokes both anxiety and fear, but the emotional reality is a painful blurring of the distinction between them. In addition, cancer is usually perceived as undesirable, uncontrollable, and unexpected—the same three features that researchers agree affect people most negatively.[12]

Feelings of being threatened, harmed, and challenged are probably familiar to you, both in your personal life and in your role as a helper. Lazarus argues that if we make clearer distinctions among these different feelings, we will begin to get a more complete understanding of what is going right or wrong for us than if we use the unidimensional concept of stress.[13]

Like other emotions, Lazarus argues, each of these feelings is both an indicator, telling us something about our relationship to the circumstances we are in, and a motivator, prompting us to act in particular ways. The sadness that accompanies certain events tells us that we have experienced something harmful and pushes us to seek help and support. A feeling of being threatened stems from an ambiguous answer to the question "Am I OK?" and motivates us to escape that harm. Feeling challenged, which goes with an active and optimistic relation to our external world, is a sustaining emotion that pushes us toward mastery. This perspective underscores the adaptive nature of our emotions: They are a rich source of information about our connection to the world and guide us toward specific kinds of actions.

Smith and Lazarus note that our emotions evolved as an adaptational system from the simpler and more rigid reflexes and physiological drives that once dominated our behavior. In this evolutionary progression, our judgments of threat and harm became more reliant on how we appraised the meaning of events, thereby permitting a greater flexibility of response to them.[14] Unfortunately, there hasn't been a corresponding evolutionary updating of our stress response system to go along with this more sophisticated way of evaluating our environments, and this creates problems for us. In prehistoric times the potential harm of stressors was clear—

predators and a harsh environment often jeopardized our survival. The stress response system that dealt with those situations worked extremely well for much of our history, but it gets us into trouble today. The main problem is that this system doesn't differentiate between an insult to our self-esteem and a saber-toothed tiger's chasing after us; in either case, we experience the "fight or flight" reaction. In the civilized world, it is unlikely that we will choose either of those two options. Then, because they aren't being expended through physical activity, the stress hormones that are generated tend to make us sick and exhausted instead.

Can I Cope With This?

After we appraise an event as harmful or threatening, we make a secondary appraisal in which we ask ourselves, "Can I cope with this?"[15] Here we assess our ability to deal with the loss or harm, or to reduce the threat (i.e., we examine the balance between the demands of the situation and the resources—time, energy, skills—we have available to us). If we perceive a balance between these two elements, a stress response doesn't occur.

If we generally perceive ourselves as competent and skilled in a particular area, we are more likely to see our resources as meeting the demands facing us. Psychologist Albert Bandura has shown that some people are more likely than others to respond this way and to perceive themselves as being able to perform successfully in a given situation—a trait he calls *self-efficacy*.[16] If, however, our evaluation is that we cannot meet these demands and that we cannot reduce the continued threats to our well-being, distress ensues, along with continued coping efforts and heightened physiological arousal.

Let's look at an example of this in the nurse with a strong commitment to quality pain management. When confronted with a patient whose pain is not being managed successfully for whatever reason (e.g., difficult symptoms, a new and inexperienced coworker, an uncooperative primary caregiver), this nurse will feel threatened because an outcome that matters a great deal to her is jeopardized. If she doesn't find a solution to this problem, her secondary appraisal might be that she cannot cope with the demands of the situation.

At this point, the stress response occurs, and her body tries to preserve its homeostasis, or balance, through a variety of adjustments: increased perspiration and respiratory and heart rates, higher blood pressure, the release of cortisol and other stress hormones, and suppression of the immune system. This "fight or flight" physiology, particularly when it is chronic or of high intensity, can eventually lead to the development of stress-related symptoms and illnesses.[17]

The idea of a balance between the demands being placed on us and our resources (perceived or real) is crucial. Usually, the demands in our lives and the resources we have available to meet them are fairly well balanced. Changes in the demands placed upon us can disturb this homeostatic equilibrium. However, change as such is not bad for us. In fact, arousal in moderate amounts can be pleasurable. When we see ourselves as having the skills necessary to cope with the demands facing us, our actions can be almost effortless; feelings of exhilaration and fulfillment can overtake us, to the point where we find ourselves in what psychologist Mihaly Csikszentmihalyi calls a *flow* experience.[18]

Life is full of changes; it is the personal significance of those changes that determines whether they are stressful and have negative consequences.[19] A promotion may be a positive event for one person but highly stressful for another who finds the added responsibilities and increased administrative work that come with that career change extremely unpleasant.

When demands exceed the resources available, there is a period of stress and readjustment in which we struggle to reestablish a state of balance and equilibrium.[20] Stress ends when we reevaluate the situation and find that we no longer perceive the threat or when we feel that we are now able to meet the demands it poses.

Loss, Stress, and the Self-Concept

We have seen the important role that the perception of actual or potential loss plays in the stress response. We assess events as threatening when the things that we care most about are jeopardized. When nothing we care about is at stake, we don't have stress. The intimate relation between stress and loss is reflected in the theory of stress just presented and in our instruments for assessing stress. Most of the items in life events questionnaires assessing stress are in fact loss events—death of a spouse, divorce, marital separation, retirement, being fired at work, and so forth.[21] There is an aphorism that says we are shaped and fashioned by what we love; we are also vulnerable to stress when we love because fate—an accident, an illness, or any negative life event—can take what we love away from us.

The relation between stress and loss is also apparent in our daily work as caregivers. We have all seen how a string of losses can create enormous stress in patients and families—loss of health, work, insurance, financial security, status, and even life. Without loss, according to psychologist Stevan Hobfoll, "change, transitions, and challenge are not of themselves stressful."[22]

In the case of burnout, our self-concept is repeatedly threatened and spirals downward, propelled by feelings of inadequacy, guilt, and failure. Acknowledging the stress we feel as helpers is sometimes difficult because this admission entails a further loss of self-esteem. One helper explained:

> It is difficult for me to admit or acknowledge my own
> (personal) stress as it affects my caring for others. They
> should be first, and I should be strong enough to
> overcome my problems in order to care for others.
> I am afraid of being inadequate.

This caregiver fears that others will think less of her if she discloses her feelings to them. By being afraid to discuss her problems, she won't discover that others are having similar difficulties, and she won't be offered any help in dealing with them. She also might begin to deny her painful feelings to herself, or she may not be able to stop ruminating about them.

Avoidance and Approach: Two Basic Responses to Stress

When confronted with a threat, we can either move toward it or away from it.[23] The avoidance or denial of anything that triggers unpleasant emotions is a pervasive feature of human behavior. It is this tendency that underlies such diverse phenomena as the denial of death or illness, the avoidance of threatening thoughts or memories through repression, and the reluctance to express negative feelings to our spouses or coworkers.

Avoidance of conflict and other kinds of threatening experiences in turn leads to lowered self-esteem. We know we are avoiding something that makes us feel uncomfortable or anxious—and the momentary relief gained through avoidance is eventually replaced by a more long-term disillusionment with ourselves. As psychologist Richard Bednar and his colleagues note:

> The moment we choose avoidance . . . we openly and
> undeniably announce to ourselves (and any others who
> care to observe) that we have detected impulses that are
> so unacceptable that they cannot be faced realistically. It is

as though we try to say to ourselves that this is too
unpleasant to be true and then proceed to act as though it
were not. . . . Obviously the prospects for personal growth
are virtually nonexistent when the individual's response to
threat is *to deny that which it has already glimpsed to be
true.*[24]

Think of a chronic problem in your work that you have avoided
facing. Visualize this situation—the people, the events, the feelings—and your behavior in it. Take a minute to do this. Now ask
yourself, "How do I feel about myself in this difficult situation?" Next
visualize the problem situation again and imagine yourself acting as
if you were the kind of person you would like to be in this situation.
What words come to mind when you describe yourself in this second
scenario? Then ask yourself about how you feel about yourself in this
second scenario. What words come to mind?

Like Bednar and his colleagues, who created this exercise, I have
found that most people describe their avoiding selves with words like
weak, cowardly, shameful, and *frightened.*[25] In the second condition,
these self-critical feelings disappear, and the self-descriptions instead portray a competent, courageous, and often caring person. In
other words, avoidance usually lowers our self-esteem.

The negative consequences of avoidance extend far beyond lowered self-esteem in the avoiding individual. When avoidance becomes a dominant theme for caregiving teams and organizations, it
can severely impair the kind of openness, trust, feedback, and creative problem solving essential for productive group efforts. People
stop telling the truth to one another, manipulation increases, trust
levels drop, and the group fails to do and learn what is necessary to
ensure its future success.[26]

Given its strongly negative consequences, how can we explain
the persistence of avoidance as a coping strategy? One classic animal
study illustrates the powerful nature of avoidance as a learned response. In this study, dogs were placed in a compartment equipped
with a light and a metal floor attached to a device designed to ad-
minister electric shock. A small, low barrier separated them from a
second, shock-free compartment. The experimenters turned the light
on and gave the dogs a strong electric shock, causing them to jump
immediately into the other compartment. After repeating this sequence several times, the experimenters turned the light on but dis-
connected the shock device. What happened? In this new shock-free
condition, the dogs continued to jump after the light came on until
the researchers stopped the experiment more than 50 trials later.[27]

The experimenters then simulated "reality testing" by putting a glass barrier between the dogs and the second compartment, thus forcing the dogs to stay in the first compartment after the light came on and see that no shock was forthcoming. But even after many trials with this condition, the dogs continued to jump when the glass barrier was removed.

The key to the persistence of the dogs' avoidance was that when they jumped—even when there was no real threat—their anxiety was reduced, and thus avoidance was rewarded. Like the dogs in this experiment, we often "jump" when there is no objective threat. Although this strategy reduces our fears, we don't learn from our experience and thus continue in our self-defeating behaviors.

Here is a good example of this kind of learned avoidance pattern: Imagine that a young woman is about to get married and, at the last moment, after the announcements have been sent, her fiance says he doesn't really love her and leaves the relationship. In her next relationship, this once-spurned lover might find herself getting panicky when the topic of marriage first arises and may even bolt from the new relationship. After going through this same cycle with two or three other relationships, the long-term pain starts to take its toll, and the woman goes to see a counselor. She has begun to realize that she must do something to change this destructive pattern in her life.

Most neurotic behavior has this same puzzling quality: We can continue to engage in self-defeating behaviors even while recognizing the counterproductive nature of what we are doing—what is known as the *neurotic paradox*.[28] The general principle that helps explain such behavior is that the short-term gain (anxiety reduction) of avoidance is more immediate and thus seems to outweigh the long-term pain that exists only in the future.

Avoidance of anxiety has been a central concept of psychodynamic theorists from Freud on. All defense mechanisms share a common function: anxiety reduction, primarily through the avoidance of threatening thoughts and feelings. Most of the interventions of cognitive-behavioral therapists include offering the client some form of safe exposure to threatening stimuli. In fact, nearly all psychotherapeutic approaches agree that facing unpleasant thoughts and feelings and processing threatening information are prerequisites for emotional healing and growth.

In our stress model, avoidance is a product of our appraisals that we are in danger and can't cope with a situation and thus must escape it. When a thought, feeling, object, or person becomes associated with a powerful fear, avoidance becomes almost automatic. In *Vital Lies, Simple Truths,* psychologist Dan Goleman describes the many ways our psychological lives feature a trade-off between attention and anxiety.[29] Rather than confront fears and anxieties, we protect ourselves by diminishing our awareness through self-deception and blind spots in our perceptions.

Existential theorists see our evasive behavior as ultimately driven by our fear of death. In *The Denial Of Death*, Ernest Becker contends that our avoidance of death-related anxiety is an element common to all psychological disturbances.[30] He argues that our self is shaped in a way that diminishes and deflects anxiety. We find anxiety-free domains to move about in, however limited these might be, and we remain there even when the limitations become painfully confining.

Psychiatrist Irvin Yalom also asserts that death-related anxiety is at the core of neurotic conflicts.[31] In his view, our defenses against death awareness lead to a neurotic adaptation in which we engage in rigid patterns of behavior—a kind of partial death. Yalom interprets Otto Rank's statement that the neurotic refuses the loan of life to escape the debt of death as meaning that we buy ourselves "free from the fear of death by daily partial self-destruction."[32] Approaching these fears, says Yalom, "can transport one from a mode of living characterized by diversions, tranquilization, and petty anxieties to a more authentic mode."[33]

The "terror management" theory of self-esteem proposed by Sheldon Solomon and his colleagues integrates much of what has been discussed so far in this chapter.[34] They argue that self-esteem "consists of the perception that one is a valuable part of a meaningful universe"[35] and serves the defensive function of protecting us from anxiety, which is (as Becker, Yalom, Rank, and other theorists concur) ultimately and intimately connected to the fear of death. By meeting the standards of our parents, significant others, and culture, we acquire a sense of safety and protection from the unsettling truth of our own mortality. We struggle to preserve this sense of security, which I think is most profoundly grounded in the attachment experiences of our early childhood. Direct threats to our self-esteem and frustration of our helping goals create stress because they threaten our feeling of having a uniquely valuable role in a meaningful universe.

Thus, there is a consensus that avoiding anxiety, conflicts, and psychological threats plays a major role in many of our psychological problems. The alternative to avoidance and its many unhealthy consequences is the willingness to approach what we fear most. When we face difficult and threatening experiences, new dimensions of personal growth and effectiveness become available to us.

I have asked many groups of helpers the following question: "Have any of you ever experienced significant and lasting personal growth without feeling any pain or suffering as an essential part of that growth?" Over many years, and thousands of individuals, not one person has answered yes to this question.

The changes in identity that are part of growth, and part of grief, include a loss of what was and the birth of something new. If we are faced with an inner experience that is uncomfortable or that doesn't fit our vision of who we are or want to be and we move toward the threatening content, our self-concept gradually expands to include all we truly are. Self-actualization does not mean becoming someone or something you aren't; instead, it is simply becoming who you *are,* including those difficult aspects you have resisted—in the words of Kierkegaard, becoming "that self which one truly is."[36]

The benefits of approaching difficult and traumatic thoughts and feelings may also extend to our physical health. In one study, a group of undergraduate subjects were asked to write for 20 minutes a day for 4 days about their deepest thoughts and feelings concerning a trauma. Another group of students were asked to write about a superficial topic. The students who wrote about their traumas showed heightened immune function following the experience when compared with the students who wrote about more superficial topics. The trauma-confronting students also made fewer visits to the student health center in the period following the study.[37]

Based on this and other studies, psychologist James Pennebaker concludes that the failure to confront traumas forces us to live with them in an unresolved way and that the act of avoiding—accomplished by inhibiting and controlling our thoughts and feelings—increases our stress and our chances of becoming ill.[38]

The consequences of avoidance are equally dramatic in our work as helpers. Because we have the option to turn away from the suffering of others and from our own, the tendency to avoid has profound implications for helping. We might choose to avoid something when our emotional buttons are pushed or when we have conscientiously stayed with the client to a certain point but know that what lies ahead is frightening or painful. Isolated instances of avoidance like these are fairly common in helping, but when our responses as helpers reflect a general pattern of avoidance, we can be of little real assistance to others.

Emotional and physical avoidance and distancing—often a feature in the burnout syndrome—are familiar experiences for many caregivers:

> I sometimes have patients who become very close, yet
> when they are getting close to "the end," I avoid them. Yes,
> I WANT to go and talk with them and tell them how special

they are to me and hold their hands, but I just can't. I had one very dear lady that I distanced myself from. After she died, I went back to the hospital room where she died, many times, over almost a year. I talked with her and told her how much I missed her. Why couldn't I do that while she was still alive?

Patients who are very dependent are very difficult for me. I don't want to visit them, to be near them, because they cling. I just want to distance myself as far away as possible.

Sometimes when caring for a critical baby I shut myself off from the parents and avoid them at all costs—sometimes I also avoid that baby if possible. I feel like I'm abandoning the parents and I'm "dumping" the baby on someone else, especially if it's a baby I took care of continuously when he or she was well.

Sometimes, however, we find the courage to approach the most distressing of experiences:

Joan, my patient with ovarian cancer, had a fistula. It was so *upsetting* to her to have constant drainage of stool from her vagina. She was spending most of her time in the bathroom. She was filled with anxiety and tears. I went into the bathroom with her and sat on the floor in front of her and we cried together. "How could this happen to me?" she asked. I responded—"I don't know, but I'm with you and *I* care." And she knew it. It was beautiful.

Although confronting suffering in the people we care for doesn't always lead to the kind of healing moment that these two women shared, if we can find a way to remain open and compassionate toward frightening and foreign experiences—in ourselves and in others—we can realize our fullest potentials as helpers.

COPING

Coping, like stress, is a process. It involves our ongoing efforts to manage stressful internal or external demands (i.e., demands that we appraise as taxing or exceeding the resources we have available).[39] In their extensive studies of how people cope with stress, Lazarus and his colleagues have identified eight key coping strategies:

1. Confrontive coping ("I stood my ground and fought for what I wanted.")

2. Distancing ("I went on as if nothing had happened.")

3. Self-control ("I tried to keep my feelings to myself.")

4. Seeking social support ("I talked to someone who could do something concrete about the problem.")

5. Accepting responsibility ("I criticized or lectured myself.")

6. Escape-avoidance ("I wished the situation would go away or somehow be over with.")

7. Planful problem solving ("I knew what had to be done, so I doubled my efforts to make things work.")

8. Positive reappraisal ("I found new faith.")[40]

Lazarus and Folkman also make a distinction between problem-focused and emotion-focused coping.[41] Problem-focused coping refers to efforts to change our relationship to our environment by either changing our behavior or by changing the environment itself. Emotion-focused coping efforts, in contrast, have as their goal altering our emotional reactions to the situation, even though the situation has not changed.

Different people cope differently at various points in any stressful situation, and our responses to most stressful situations include both problem- and emotion-focused coping. For example, imagine that you are working with an extremely difficult family with one actively suicidal member. Problem-focused coping might include reading up on the management of suicidal people and carefully planning any interventions you will make with the family. Emotion-focused coping responses might involve exercising more frequently, seeking the comforting support of a friend, avoiding thinking about the problem, reappraising the meaning of the situation, or meditating. We usually have problem-focused responses when our secondary appraisal is that there is something we can do about the stressful event. Emotion-focused coping is more likely when we perceive that there is little we can do in terms of changing the situation itself.

The range of possible coping responses in any stressful situation is enormous. Psychiatrist Avery Weissman outlines some possible coping responses of people with cancer. Specifically, a person with cancer can seek information, share concerns with others, laugh it off, hope a miracle will happen, put it out of his or her mind, stay busy, confront the issue, redefine the situation and take a more sanguine view, become resigned, review the alternatives, escape, do what is expected or advised, blame or shame someone, ventilate his or her feelings, or deny the reality of the situation.[42]

Helpers can respond to and manage their stressors in many of these same ways. We can seek out more information, share our concerns with peers or team members, try to forget the whole thing, focus on something good that can come out of the situation or on what we might learn about life, accept our limitations, blame ourselves, or ventilate our feelings or keep them to ourselves.

Look at the list of stressors you made earlier in this chapter and pick the two most stressful events. How do you typically cope with these types of stressors? What do you do in response to them? Has your response changed over time? Do you take any actions to prevent stress, or are most of your actions geared toward stress that has already occurred in your life? How effective are you currently in coping with these two stressors? Do you have any ideas about what is keeping you from being more effective in coping with or preventing similar stressful events from happening again?

There is now some general agreement about the differences between successful and unsuccessful copers. Unsuccessful copers tend to blame themselves for their problems and engage in more denial and avoidance—they feel helpless and out of control. They tend not to enlist the support of others and react without much planning and flexibility. Successful copers tend to take responsibility—without blaming themselves—for finding a solution to the problem they are confronting. They tend to be flexible in their use of different coping strategies, enlist the support of others, and feel optimistic concerning the outcomes of their efforts. They also usually view their difficulties as opportunities for personal growth, even though they would have preferred that life had been otherwise.[43]

Although stressful events are difficult for all people, they don't affect everyone the same way or to the same extent. Some individuals are more likely to cope successfully and less likely to develop stress-related illnesses. These stress-resistant individuals typically have a strong sense of self-efficacy or control, high self-esteem, and a good social support system. In addition, they are also fairly optimistic.

These and other variables that predict who will—or will not—stay healthy when exposed to high levels of stress are called *stress buffers* because they temper the stress-distress connection. In other words, if we feel good about ourselves, are confident in our ability to manage or adapt to stressful circumstances, are able to access and receive support from others, and have a positive set of expectations for the future, we are more able to cope with the inevitable stressors our work and personal lives bring us. We are also less likely to become sick in response to them.

Consider in particular how your sense of control and efficacy as a helper buffers you against stress. Our confidence as helpers usually increases with experience and training. If we have been helpful in similar situations in the past, or if we have learned specific skills for this kind of situation, we will probably expect to be successful this time as well. The veteran caregiver thinks, "I've been here before and I've always been able to make something good happen, so chances are I can do it again." If you are a novice helper, you may not have had enough successes or training to have this feeling of confidence.

Successful performances lead to a feeling of emotional well-being; perceived failures and ongoing self-doubt lead to stress. In other words, a person who has high self-efficacy as a helper will typically experience less stress than a low-efficacy helper.

STRESS ANTIDOTES: STAYING OUT OF THE HELPER'S PIT

What recommendations for reducing stress and preventing burnout emerge from this profile of the successful coper and from this model of stress? This section includes some general suggestions for managing your stress as a caregiver. But first it is crucial to underscore that stress is an extremely individual and personal experience. What stresses one person may not even bother someone else.[44] Thus, it is important that you take the time to identify what the most taxing and demanding events are for *you*. These can be either internal or external events (e.g., self-blame or work overload).

The recommendations for managing stress and preventing burnout that follow can be distilled into a single word: *balance*. The main goal of stress management is learning how to maintain a balance between the internal and external demands you confront and the resources you have available to meet them. Each of the following techniques for stress management and burnout prevention can be viewed as a way to strengthen your resources and coping capacities—the tree limbs that can keep you from falling into the Helper's Pit (see chapter 2).

Of course, for these techniques to be effective, we must put them to use. Unfortunately, when we are most stressed, we are often least likely to use stress reduction techniques. "I don't have time" or "As soon as I get through this one I'll take care of myself" are familiar refrains. This is why it is extremely important to have a good personal stress management program firmly in place—so that you have a routine that is less likely to be dislodged by unexpected stress.

It is helpful to think about the different techniques presented here in terms of when they occur in the stress process. The typical sequence of events in the stress response is as follows:

- Stage 1—a potentially stressful event
- Stage 2—an appraisal of this event as involving harm or loss
- Stage 3—the stress response (physiological and psychological arousal)
- Stage 4—stress-related symptoms or illness

If we try to change the stressor itself, we are intervening at Stage 1. For example, we might decide to take a vacation or to work with different client populations. Interventions at Stage 2 might include changing the way we appraise the demands placed on us and how we think about our ability to cope with them. No matter how effective interventions are during Stages 1 and 2, every caregiver will experience some stress as part of his or her work. This is when interventions at Stage 3, such as seeking support, exercise, and relaxation, are most appropriate and beneficial. If a stress-related illness does develop (Stage 4), it needs to be diagnosed and treated. It is also important to focus again on the first three stages of the stress response to prevent a worsening of the condition.

The following suggestions are presented in a sequence beginning with interventions that target the early stages in the stress response and ending with interventions that are aimed at mitigating the effects of stress once it has occurred.

Be Proactive: Stress Management Begins Upstream

There is a contemporary fable of a man who is walking beside a river and notices that someone is drowning. He jumps in, pulls the person to shore, and revives him. Then another drowning person calls for help, and again the man successfully rescues him. As the man is about to walk away, a passerby shouts, "Hey, there's another person drowning out there! Where are you going?" The man replies, "I'm going upstream to see who's throwing all these people in!"

Much of our helping is downstream, rather than upstream, work. Patients and their families have already suffered a great deal before coming to us; their relationships are strained, their bodies are ravaged, and their pain is deep. It is too late for prevention. You can't jump into a time machine, go back 30 years, and convince a patient to stop smoking. We have to work downstream, at the end of the line, even though it is often frustrating and exhausting to do so.

Working downstream can threaten many of our goals. The classic example of this in hospice work is the last-minute referral of a dying patient. In a day, or perhaps an hour, the hospice team must attempt to do all they can to relieve that person's and the family's suffering. The problem is that this is a nearly impossible task because there is almost no contact with the family, there is no time to monitor and control pain, and so forth. Thus, a late referral can be a powerful external stressor for hospice staff. The upstream answer lies somewhere in an educational intervention geared to physicians and others making these later referrals, but the downstream reality is a patient who is admitted to hospice with many complex needs and insufficient time in which to address them all.

The mental health and health care fields are moving, albeit slowly, toward a greater emphasis on prevention, or toward a more upstream approach. This makes sense because no disease has ever been conquered through downstream, curative interventions. Upstream approaches such as immunizations, pollution control, changes in health behaviors, and the acquisition of conflict resolution skills hold the ultimate answer to eliminating the physical and social diseases that now plague us.

As caregivers, it is helpful—both to us and to the people we assist—to look for any upstream interventions we can make. It is also less stressful to work upstream, where problems begin and changes still can be made. For example, you might do some community education work or try to make an early evening phone call to a family telling them what to expect during the night. These kinds of interventions can prevent some of the difficulties we repeatedly encounter downstream in helping.

Take Charge

Whether your intervention is proactive or reactive, what is most important is that you take some action! It is essential that you take an active stance and do something, whether you change your environment or change yourself. Never fall into the trap of believing that there is nothing you can do about the stress in your life. This stance quickly leads to passive or minimal coping efforts, demoralization, and increasing stress. An extreme instance of passive coping is the alcohol or drug abuse of the impaired caregiver.[45]

The model of stress presented here has revealed the many negative consequences of avoidance, and, as a rule, the best antidote to avoidance is approach. Approach the problems you are confronted with, practice stress management skills, look for places where you can effectively take control—and do it. Because burnout usually results from the kinds of environments we are exposed to, it is critical always to begin stress management at Stage 1 of the stress response and to look for ways to change the actual demands or problems we face. This can include trying to affect organizational elements like staffing, job design, training and support, the mix of less demanding and more stressful work, and so forth.

Ask first, "Is there anything I can do to change this situation?" Try to focus on things that *can* be changed. In this regard, many stress experts have recognized the powerful wisdom of theologian Reinhold Neibuhr's serenity prayer:

> God, give us the serenity to accept what cannot be
>   changed;
> Give us the courage to change what should be changed;
> Give us the wisdom to distinguish one from the other.[46]

It is often difficult to discriminate between those situations in which problem-focused coping might eventually yield positive results and those in which it will not. If we think change is possible when it isn't, we persist too long in our efforts to change the situation, and growing frustration pushes our stress levels even higher. For example, residents of Three Mile Island who adopted a more problem-focused approach had more psychological symptoms than did residents who used distancing, avoidance, and denial as their primary coping responses after this nuclear accident.[47]

The merits of avoidance also increase if a stressful situation is overwhelming. Sometimes it is most helpful to retreat psychologically while attempting to come to grips with an event of this great magnitude. In the case of grief and serious illness, avoidance can help maintain hope and courage, and the ability to flexibly adjust our levels of denial when faced with these situations is an indicator of good, rather than poor, coping skills.[48]

The other error we can make is to think that no change is possible when it really is. Then we give up too soon and remain stuck in the stressful situation. Here is an exercise that will help you prevent making this second type of error. First, look over the list of stressors you generated earlier in this chapter and next to those you consider beyond your control write a "B." After you do this, go through your list a second time and put a "W" next to all the remaining stressors that are within your control. Now try to think of reasons for changing as many "Bs" to "Ws" as possible. Explore all the ways that you can possibly gain control, even if your stressors seem beyond your control at first glance. We often equate having control over an outcome with having total control when in fact having even an extremely small influence can significantly enhance our sense of control in that situation. Look for small things you *can* do that will help overcome your sense of powerlessness, even though these actions might not bear fruit immediately. The key is to do something actively. If you can't change the situation, do something that might improve your response to it, like exercising or talking to a friend.

Set Limits

You can reduce your stress by limiting your time and involvement with the people you help. Our contacts with clients and families can evoke our deepest sensitivity and empathy, and we often know that if we are not there for these people, probably no one else will be. In an effort to help, we can lose sight of our own needs. It is critical to monitor yourself and be keenly aware of any sense that you have gone too far. Try to keep the demands you face and the resources you have in dynamic balance.

One way to view your role as a helper is to see yourself as the choreographer who makes things happen for the other person rather than the one who is always in the spotlight. You can't be the number one psychosocial caregiver for everyone you work with. Taking the choreographer role also means that you must give up some of the gratification that comes from being perceived as the principal care provider. But there is really no other effective strategy if you want to continue doing this work for an extended period. If you don't set limits, you will find that emotional and physical overload will eventually make you less available emotionally to the people you care for. I have seen many idealistic helpers come into the work of caregiving, try to be a best friend to all the people they work with, and then leave the field in a year or less because they felt drained.

Compartmentalize

Stress from work can easily spill over into your personal life, and, conversely, your private life can be more stressful than your work life. In her research on burnout in women, Ayala Pines found that home pressures contributed as much to the stress of professional women as did out-of-home pressures.[49] Conflicts between career and family can be enormously stressful for women. At the same time, success in both roles can lead to tremendous satisfaction. To achieve this success, it is important to put psychological and physical distance between your work life and your home life.

One useful way of setting such limits is not to bring your work problems home. The way to do this is to create an environment and a routine in which you can decompress. Sometimes a small symbolic act or cue—listening to a favorite song or reading a note to yourself on your door—can help remind you that you are leaving one world behind and entering another. When you are at home, keep your mind off your work life; when you are at work, avoid thinking about the problems at home. Although not easy to do, coping with the conflicting demands of work and home and preventing difficulties in one arena from disturbing success and happiness in the other are essential to effective stress management.

Develop a Stress-Hardy Outlook

As discussed earlier, a key point in the stress cycle is the appraisal stage (Stage 2 in the model). Appraisal determines whether a stress response is activated and whether a challenge or a threat is experienced. In a series of studies, psychologist Suzanne Kobasa and her colleagues looked at different groups of professionals undergoing high levels of stress. She found that certain characteristics differentiated high stress/healthy people from high stress/health problem groups. The people who managed stress better and had fewer illnesses than their counterparts were more likely to have an attitude of *hardiness*. The defining characteristics of this stress hardiness included a sense of challenge, commitment, and control.[50]

Challenge

The stress-hardy person tends to see a challenge where others see a threat. It is easy to see how this somewhat optimistic stance can prevent many unnecessary stress reactions. For example, the individual who is always waiting for things to settle down and who is always threatened when things don't will be more stressed than someone who knows that change is constant and that the current crisis will only be replaced by another. If we can see a potentially stressful event as an opportunity for growth rather than as a threat, we are likely to cope much better with the demands confronting us. However, as discussed in chapter 6, some stressors, particularly life's greatest tragedies, have no redeeming characteristics. To tell a mother who has just lost her child to leukemia to look at this experience as a challenge is cruel, even though she may grow and develop because of it.

For us as helpers, the advice to turn threats into challenges contains unmistakable wisdom, but this modern homily can also lead to self-blame if we interpret it as meaning that a fearless kind of hope and mastery is always possible—if only you have the right attitude. We all know that it is not so easy to change the way we look at things and that even traffic jams, small losses, extra work loads, and other daily hassles are sometimes alarming for most of us. Similarly, when we say of a situation, "That was a good learning experience," the unspoken message is often that we would have gladly skipped the learning if we could have avoided the situation in the first place.

Commitment

The stress-hardy individual is involved in life and life's activities—work, family, friendships—and views these involvements as interesting and meaningful. There is also a sense of interconnection and interdependence with the people in his or her life. For most caregivers, your work itself is a major commitment in that you have a sense of purpose and believe in the work you do. Thus, the work itself buffers the stress you experience doing that work. However, this can be a double-edged sword: If you have too great a commitment to your work, this can lead to burnout. That is why you need to balance your work life with a satisfying life outside work.

Control

As noted earlier in this chapter, a sense of control is an excellent buffer against stress. Because loss of control is a central element of the stress experience, believing and acting as if life experiences are controllable and predictable can—within certain limits—markedly decrease our stress. A sense of control is also a central feature of many other important concepts in the stress literature, including the belief that one can perform successfully in a given situation (self-efficacy), an optimistic outlook, and a sense that one's world and its demands are comprehensible and manageable (a sense of coherence).[51]

Again, the tendency to perceive ourselves as competent and skilled affects the stress response at the stage of our secondary appraisals: We are more likely to conclude that we can cope with a situation because our resources meet or even exceed the demands confronting us.

If we are open to change, take responsibility for our lives, and have good skills and self-confidence, we will be more likely to cope successfully with the inevitable stress of helping.

A good sense of humor is another attitudinal dimension that can enhance our ability to manage stress effectively.[52] The ability to laugh at ourselves and to see things from a larger perspective can take the sting of stress out of many of the daily hassles we routinely encounter. If we can avoid becoming overly concerned with minor annoyances and small worrisome issues, stress management will be much easier for us. A colleague once asked a very elderly man what the key things were that he had learned about life. The man replied that his principle was not to worry about so many things because almost nothing he had worried about had ever come true. His advice certainly concurs with the stress management motto "Don't waste 100 dollars worth of adrenaline on a 10-cent problem."

Practice the Art of the Possible

The pervasiveness of self-doubt as an internal stressor for helpers is fueled by the enormous range of skills required in most helping contexts. For example, the typical helper will at some time confront at least some of the following problems in individuals and families: suicide, alcoholism and drug abuse, child abuse, marital conflict, complicated grief, or eating disorders. He or she will be forced to intervene in some way with highly disturbed couples, families, and individuals.

How many helpers have—or even could have—received thorough training in each of these problems? Not very many! For this reason, it is important to differentiate between a healthy recognition of one's skill limitations and an unhealthy judgment of low self-efficacy as a helper. We must accept the fact that sometimes we don't know what to do and then be able to go on from there to do *something*— whether this something is making a referral, enlisting additional support, or learning new skills appropriate to the situation. The key is to have a good sense of what you *cannot* do and then go on to practice the art of the possible.

Also, change—whether in an organization or yourself—usually comes in small doses. In life, dramatic moments of change are less common than incremental steps toward long-lasting changes. I often remind myself that things take time, whether this involves learning new skills, helping people heal, building a team, or changing an organization.

Try to keep an open mind as you go about dealing with the stressors in your work. If your client doesn't respond positively to one intervention, try something else. If your expectations of your co-workers aren't met, give them some feedback or try changing those expectations. Most of all, be patient and creative.

Although we tend to blame ourselves when things go wrong, it is also important to recognize that accurately acknowledging our mis-takes and real behavioral deficits is associated with better stress management. When we make a mistake or don't know how to do something that others in our position do know, we need to engage in honest self-confrontation—without any blame. Then it is important to resolve to learn new skills and get more feedback from others—in essence, to work toward changing our behavior.

Improve Your Communication and Conflict Resolution Skills

Many helpers report that they are often stressed when they don't know what to say to the people they are caring for. There is no lack of caring and compassion, just an inability to find the words and ac-tions that can communicate their caring. As noted earlier, conflicts and communication problems with coworkers are also a major source of stress for most caregivers. Solid training in interpersonal helping and communication skills would be an excellent antidote to these two sources of stress; these skills are the focus of chapters 6 and 7.

Change the Oil: Exercise, Relax, or Meditate

No matter what your coping strategies are like, stress is unavoidable. Thus, we often need to make stress-management interventions at a more downstream point in the stress cycle. Once you arrive at Stage 3 in the stress response cycle and stress hormones are already being released into your body, the best action to take is to get them out of your system. An analogy might be helpful here: The oil in your car constantly collects dirt and needs to be changed periodically. Aero-bic exercise, meditation, and relaxation are all excellent techniques for "changing the oil" in your stressed body.

Exercise

Walk, swim, run, hike, or do whatever gives your body a chance to unwind. After a particularly difficult day, a long run or a game of basketball palpably reduces the stress in my system—I feel less tired, and my head is cleared of the day's worries.

People who exercise regularly are much less susceptible to burnout. Why is this so? The documented physical benefits of aerobic exercise (e.g., walking briskly, bicycling, racquetball, jogging, swimming) include increased respiratory capacity and improved circulation, reduced cholesterol and triglyceride levels, increased energy, improved sleep, increased metabolic rate, and a slowing down of the aging process. There is also a similarly impressive array of psychological benefits: feelings of self-control and self-confidence improve, along with better body image and self-esteem, mental functioning, and alertness. There is also catharsis of tensions from interpersonal conflict and job stress and relief from mild depression.[53]

You don't need to be a marathon runner to accrue these striking benefits.[54] If you engage in any form of exercise that burns 200 or more calories an hour three to four times a week, you will notice some dramatic changes. Vigorous aerobic exercise where the heart rate is elevated to between 60 and 80% of the maximum capacity for one's age is recommended.

Physical exercise gives you more energy and stamina, and that makes you better prepared to handle stress. The key is doing it regularly—at least three to four times a week. And that can be hard, especially if you are like the person who said, "I tried exercise once, and that was enough." If you don't exercise now, consider trying it. Exercising with a friend or a group that exercises regularly is a good way to begin.

Relaxation and Meditation

An alternative approach to stress reduction involves quieting our nervous systems when we are caught up in the fight or flight response. We can do this by practicing any of a variety of established and scientifically proven techniques, including progressive muscle relaxation, Herbert Benson's relaxation response method (a Westernized version of transcendental meditation), self-hypnosis, and autogenic training.[55] It is less important which method you choose than that you practice it regularly. Many of the same benefits found for regular exercise, particularly the psychological ones, have also been demonstrated for relaxation and meditation techniques. When the sympathetic nervous system is quieted by these practices, muscle tension decreases, the heart rate slows, and a feeling of well-being often occurs.

Know Yourself

Managing your stress requires knowing yourself. This means being aware of your moment-to-moment feelings and catching important issues or conflicts as they develop. We react to people and situations physically before we recognize our feelings or thoughts about them. When you are in difficulty or some feeling isn't clear, focus on your bodily sense of it. Surprises may result. These surprises can be clues to what is stressing you and what you can do to make the situation better. Being friendly to these discomforting inner feelings is often extremely difficult. We must relate to ourselves in a gentle manner that is similar to the way we strive to relate to the inner lives of the people we help.[56] That means knowing and admitting when we are scared. Or recognizing tender spots where we are easily hurt. Agreeing with this notion is easy; doing it is tough. Stress-resilient helpers look at potential danger spots and try to understand what these spots mean in their work and in their personal lives (i.e., they stay current with themselves). Many helpers find that keeping a journal or seeking personal psychotherapy helps them develop this kind of self-awareness and process their inner experiences.

Maintain and Enhance Your Self-Esteem

A positive view of oneself is an excellent buffer against stress. People with high self-esteem have less fear when they are feeling threatened than people with low self-esteem do. Also, high self-esteem makes it more likely that you will perceive yourself as having skills adequate to deal with a threatening situation.[57]

Our good feelings about ourselves bolster our sense of self-confidence. We think, "I'm pretty good at most things, and I'll probably succeed at coping with this situation as well." What builds your morale? What makes you stay involved? Is it a thank-you from a family member, a surprise birthday card or flower on your desk, a compliment on your work, or an intimate conversation with a friend or colleague?

My "do good–feel good" hypothesis (see chapter 1) is that your helping can function as a kind of self-reward—you can feel good, do good, and then feel even better. Research shows that helping improves our moods and self-evaluations.[58] The significance of the work you do and the commitment you have to it can also enhance your self-esteem. In these ways, your helping journey is made easier and less stressful by powerful psychological forces that support your self-esteem and your ability to help others.

However, when our stress is at its highest levels, most of these self-esteem enhancers are unavailable to us: We might not have time for intimate conversations, our self-confidence is shaky, and we don't feel that we are doing well at doing good. In addition, our self-esteem is further undermined by thoughts that we are doing a bad job of managing our stress. Optimal stress management becomes another task we can fail in and leads to negative self-talk, epitomized by the view "If only I did all the things I know I should do, I wouldn't have all this stress." Managing stress can be stressful.

Strengthen Your Social Support

Social support can be a great buffer against stress because it affects so many elements of the stress response. Strong social support can enhance your self-esteem and make difficulties at work look less threatening. Encouragement, support, and feedback lead to a greater sense of optimism and confidence that the resources to meet current challenges are available. Sharing painful experiences and self-doubts with others doing the same work helps in two ways: It helps us re-define these difficult experiences as normal and human, and it leads to the identification of other coping responses. This kind of sharing can improve both your self-esteem and your sense of efficacy.

Receiving strong support from your coworkers, friends, and family is sometimes as difficult as it is important to do. Support from coworkers and peers is a crucial component of personal stress management. However, a secondary effect of not having enough time to do the work is not having enough time to offer and receive support for doing it. This is particularly unfortunate because only your co-workers and peers can provide the kind of empathy, feedback, and encouragement essential to you as a helper. The lack of support from these individuals can make a critical difference. For example, receiving inadequate psychological support at work is an excellent predictor of burnout in oncology clinical nurse specialists.[59]

Social support from family and friends can also be elusive. How do people in general react when you tell them what you do as a helper? If you work with highly distressed populations, like the terminally or seriously ill, it is likely that you receive one of two reactions. Either people put you on a pedestal and tell you, "I could never do that," or they look at you with a critical eye and give you the message that there must be something seriously wrong with you (e.g., you must be depressed or have a morbid interest in human suffering to do this kind of work). This kind of dynamic can lead to a situation where you go from the intense, often one-way intimacy of the helping encounter to a personal social life that lacks normal levels of intimacy and social exchange.

Family members can provide invaluable support to the stressed helper, but they can also be an additional source of stress:

Sometimes my family makes me feel morbid and "creepy" because they can't understand that working with the dying really means the privilege of helping the living.

It is common for many people to feel more appreciated and less stressed at work than at home:

Often my work gives *back* so much to me that I feel selfish doing it. At home I am rarely appreciated for what I do. I am appreciated in my work, and often I feel guilty that I *need* that approval and appreciation.

Stress at work can also affect one's home life:

I've put my heart and soul into my hospice program. It has taken most of my time and energy. My husband hates my work and the time it takes. It has nearly destroyed our marriage. In many ways, the hospice fills my cup more than my marriage, and I'm in constant conflict with myself.

I feel that I can be very caring and empathetic at work to the point that when I get home I want to be left alone. (This happens even on "good" days.) In turn I feel I neglect my husband and children in an emotional way. There are times that I find it hard to initiate a hug with any one of them, making me feel guilty. My husband has so often said, "You care more for your patients than you do for me." Maybe that is part of the reason I'm like this: I've heard it so much I'm proving him right. Drained at work, drained at home.

When conflicts at home become too difficult, the helper can avoid them by becoming more involved at work:

I would like to leave my husband in order to devote more energy to my work.

There are times when I get more out of my work than I do from having sex with my husband.

These poignant disclosures reflect the need to maintain balance in one's life as a caregiver and illustrate the destructive consequences of avoidance as a coping style.

An extensive support system is critical to preventing burnout. Unfortunately, many caregivers (like most other people) focus their emotional and support needs primarily on one person—usually a spouse or partner. Imagine a caregiver named Mary and her husband, John, a tax accountant. Today, Mary has just had an emotionally powerful experience. Her patient died while holding her hand and saying, "I love you! Thank you!" Her husband had lots of problems at the office and came home exhausted. He isn't interested in hearing any more "death and dying stories." When Mary struggles to get him to listen, he says, "Mary, let's not forget that there's death *and* taxes." So they sit silently at the dinner table, both of them feeling discounted and ignored.

Many of us with our limited support systems turn problems like these into catastrophes—we take them as just another sign that our partner doesn't love us—or that we are simply incompatible. Although some interest and concern in our work can be expected from those we love, when we look for it only there, we are stressing these relationships and probably keeping ourselves from other sources of support.

The encounter between Mary and her husband can teach us an important lesson about social support and how we should approach the task of increasing this important resource. People commonly think of support in a narrow way (e.g., as someone who listens and agrees with you). Although having someone agree is important, support is actually multifaceted.

Here is a list of six different kinds of support experts consider important.[60] As I describe each, think about the people who give you that support. Picture their faces. If no one comes to mind, think about someone who could do so.

- The first kind of support is our common sense version—having a good listener. It could be someone at home or at work—someone you can always talk to about anything.

- The second kind of support is technical appreciation. It comes from an expert who gives helpful feedback on your performance and appreciates what you are doing.

- A third form of support is technical challenge. A colleague who can challenge your ways of thinking and working is providing this kind of support. This may be the same colleague who offers you technical appreciation.

- Emotional support comes from someone at home or at work who is there for you, whom you don't have to pretend with, who knows you well, and whose support is unconditional.

- Emotional challenge is a form of support that comes from a friend or colleague who can catch you when you are sloughing off or working aimlessly—someone who can comfortably say, "Are you sure you're doing everything you can?" or "Are you pushing a bit too hard and trying to do too much?"

- The last kind of support—shared social reality—is simply having a person who agrees with you. He or she has similar values, views, and priorities. This form of support can be as simple as two people exchanging a knowing glance when they encounter someone or something they think is annoying.

Reviewing your support system and then finding new ways to build it up is one of the best ways to manage stress and prevent burnout. Chapter 7 focuses on this issue and takes a detailed look at how a support group can meet many of your social support needs as a caregiver.

Selye's Recipe for Stress Management

After 50 years as a pioneering stress researcher, Hans Selye offered the following recipe for reducing the stresses of life:

The first ingredient . . . is to seek your own stress level, to decide whether you're a racehorse or a turtle and to live your life accordingly. The second is to choose your goals and make sure they're really your own, and not imposed on you by an overhelpful mother or teacher. And the third ingredient to this recipe is altruistic egoism—looking out for oneself by being necessary to others, and thus earning their goodwill.[61]

Selye's recommendations make good sense. We all need to carefully determine our own speed and work level. If you are one of those people who thrive on work, don't worry. If your goals and your energy levels are such that you will be extremely active, don't create stress where there needn't be by worrying about being this way.

Selye's advice to work toward your own goals, not those of anyone else, is closely related to the view of stress developed in this chapter. This view is that stress occurs when our personal goals are frustrated. But setting realistic goals in our work and in our private lives is not easy. It is often difficult to develop a clear image of where we would like to be and what specifically we must do to get there.

Small positive steps are what eventually will lead to success in achieving your goals. As the ancient Chinese proverb advises, "A journey of a thousand miles must begin with a single step." At each step we need to be clear about whether our efforts are making tangible progress toward our goals. This principle applies in our helping work as well as in our personal lives. Avoid setting goals that are so big and so general that you are never able to give yourself credit for meeting them, and regularly monitor your progress.

It can also be helpful to discuss your goals in a group setting such as a support group or team meeting. If others know what your goals are, they can share similar feelings and situations in their lives and can offer encouragement and good ideas.

Selye's third recommendation is to practice altruistic egoism. What he means is that we should try to earn the goodwill of the people around us because if we do that we will have more support and thus less stress. This reminds us that our caring connections with others are at the heart of our helping journey.

CONCLUSION

Stress is an intensely personal experience. Our encounters with it involve the deepest parts of ourselves—our self-esteem, our self-concept, our fear of loss, and our courage to confront it. When the demands we face exceed our resources, we feel distressed, and we tend to fall into the Helper's Pit. The natural unfolding of helping—and our progress toward realizing our personal vision of helping—becomes obstructed, and our stress increases.

Reducing stress requires that we take actions to change our external and internal worlds. It also requires that we open our hearts to ourselves. Some of the same openness and compassion that we give to the people we care for must also be turned inward. And then, somehow, we must find the courage to bring these difficult experiences of self back into the world with us and to share them with others. The decision we make at this point, whether to conceal or to reveal these secrets, may be the most important we make as helpers—and as human beings.

4

Everything secret degenerates.[1]

Lord Acton

How does it happen that the deeper we go into ourselves as particular and unique, seeking for our own individual identity, the more we find the whole human species?[2]

Carl Rogers

Secrets: Concealment and Confiding in Helping

TO TELL OR NOT TO TELL

Early in life, I learned a basic truth that I have spent most of my adult years trying to understand more fully. This twofold truth says that keeping threatening personal information concealed from others can be damaging to your health and that confiding these secrets to people who care about you can have a healing effect.

My first encounter with secrets began with a surprise eye examination administered in the first grade. When the nurse gave me a yellow slip to take home to my parents, I knew what it meant: I was slated to become a "four eyes." This was a horrible fate from the perspective of a self-conscious young boy. I felt embarrassed, afraid, and somehow inadequate. I decided that the best way to manage these fears would be to hide the yellow sheet in my bookcase and say nothing to my parents.

At first, I felt scared every time I looked at my bookcase. I was definitely doing something wrong and was afraid of my parents' reaction. Still, the alternatives were even more forbidding, so I kept my secret.

After a few months, I would forget the yellow sheet for weeks at a time. Yet my problem wasn't really solved because back at school I struggled to read the blackboard. At my eye examination the next school year, the nurse asked why I hadn't gotten eyeglasses the previous year. The jig was up. I did get the glasses, and my parents didn't punish me, nor did my classmates ever tease me (at least not within my earshot). I learned that I could hurt myself by keeping secrets, and as a result I became more trusting of other people's responses.

As a young Catholic boy, I also negotiated secrets in the confessional. What to tell and what not to tell? I didn't, for example, tell Father Francis about my masturbating. Instead, I gave him the same litany each week: "I used bad language five times," "I tipped over someone's garbage can on Halloween," "I didn't obey my parents four times." The litany was carefully calculated to elicit an optimal penance—something like five Our Fathers and five Hail Marys. If I really got into trouble during the week, I usually confessed it, and on those days my penance skyrocketed to an entire rosary. Despite my less-than-always-truthful approach, confession usually felt good. I could share some of my secrets with a listener who didn't make harsh judgments about my everyday life.

I also remember some wonderful secrets as well: kissing Janet Page at age 6, stealing away with some older kids to have my first cigarette, hiding from my parents in a secret spot behind my sandbox, developing a secret code for communicating with my friend in math class, and soaping my second-grade teacher's windows. These experiences taught me that secrets can also strengthen one's sense of identity and add a sense of excitement to life, as the Swiss physician Paul Tournier noted when he said that every child is proud of having a secret.[3]

As an adult, I have continued to learn about secrets. During the past 10 years, I have explored secrets in many different professional contexts—with my psychotherapy clients, in my research on normal and traumatized people, in the classroom, and as a consultant working in different health care settings. I am not alone in my fascination with secrets; they have captivated the interest of humankind throughout history. The works of countless poets, playwrights, and philosophers have explored the psychological significance of secrets. The act of keeping distressing thoughts and feelings secret from others and the psychological consequences of doing so are also longstanding concerns of psychologists—from Freud's pursuit of the pathogenic secret to modern day family therapy's focus on family secrets.

Some great thinkers have expressed the view that humans aren't very good at keeping secrets. Benjamin Franklin remarked, "Three may keep a secret if two of them are dead" and Petronius, the Roman satirist, observed, "Sooner will men hold fire in their mouths than keep a secret."[4] Yet when we consider personal secrets, particularly those concerning information that is highly threatening to our self-esteem or well-being, the Latin saying that "small sorrows speak, great ones are silent" seems more accurate. These silent sorrows can include being molested as a child, a failed marriage, unexpressed grief, a serious illness, or any other great personal trauma. Most helpers have seen how major traumas, especially those with some social stigma attached to them, can lead to tightly held secrets. And they know that much of the work of helping involves being a companion to the person as he or she confronts these painful secrets.

In a series of classic psychology experiments, social psychologist Stanley Schachter found that when people are told they will soon be subjected to frightening experimental conditions, they prefer to wait with people who share a similar fate.[5] But when other researchers later added a condition in which subjects were told they were about to perform an embarrassing task, like sucking on rubber nipples or holding baby bottles, they found that their subjects tended to avoid people who were in the same circumstances.[6]

The person in distress, who must decide whether to reveal or conceal his or her difficulties, may experience both of the conflicting motivations identified in these experiments. There is often an ambivalent, approach-avoidance quality to our experience in these moments—one part of us would like to reveal our pain, to gain some acceptance of it, or to learn from others who have had similar experiences. Another part of us cautions against doing so and wonders, "Will they think less of me, maybe reject me, if they know this about me?"

At the core of this distress-disclosure dilemma is the desire to maintain one's esteem in the eyes of others. Our fear is that we might present people with an image of ourselves that we don't really want to project. Though we long to be known and cared for by another, self-protective urges caution us not to make ourselves more vulnerable than we can tolerate.[7] Our decision to conceal or reveal a particular secret reflects our feelings about the other person and the relationship, our trust in the other's discretion, the level of intimacy and empathy that already exists between us, and our personal proclivities.

The concern that others will evaluate us negatively and withdraw their support if we talk about our problems is not unfounded. There is a great deal of evidence that distress disclosure can lead to unfavorable reactions, rejection, and the loss of social support.[8] As psychologists Dan Coates and Tina Winston observe, "People who keep their negative feelings 'bottled up' and who turn out to be more sick ... may have begun as individuals who talked about their troubles but painfully learned that no one wanted to hear about them."[9]

For example, when cancer patients reveal the fact of their disease, they often feel that friends and family members misunderstand them and explicitly or implicitly encourage them to avoid this difficult topic, with the rationale that focusing on it is a sign of poor adjustment.[10] The solution to the distress-disclosure dilemma, according to Coates and Winston, is to surround ourselves with people who can continue to be supportive while allowing us to fully reveal our troubles.[11]

THE JOHARI WINDOW

The Johari Window is a helpful tool for thinking about our degree of openness in revealing ourselves. It was developed by Joseph Luft (Jo) and Harry Ingham (hari).[12] This simple and elegant graphic model identifies four different kinds of information about yourself. Think about the diagram as representing your total self as you relate to other people. The four panes of the window represent different aspects of your total self in relation to others and reveal several facets of what is happening at both the individual and interpersonal level. You can draw a window to describe specific relationships, or you can create one that illustrates how you generally relate to other people and yourself in terms of the secrets in your life.

The Johari Window

	Known to self	Not known to self
Known to others	I Open	III Blind
Not known to others	II Hidden	IV Unknown

Quadrant I represents those behaviors and motivations that are known to you and others. This is your public self. Quadrant II is the hidden area of the self. This area includes all the personal information you are aware of but others aren't. If you are just meeting a new person, this quadrant is very large, and it shrinks as you share your feelings and other information about yourself over time. Quadrant III is a blind area, representing behaviors and motivations that you don't know about but that are apparent to others. For example, you may have a mannerism or a bad habit that you are not aware of but that is perfectly obvious to other people. (This quadrant is some-times called the "bad breath" quadrant.) Quadrant IV, the unknown area, includes information that neither you nor other people are aware of. Our unconscious motives and feelings reside in this quadrant.

The Johari Window can also help us chart our personal growth and change. Luft and others argue that personal growth and psychological health are achieved as Quadrant I expands and the other three quadrants become correspondingly smaller. For example, when I help a client cope with her grief, I discover more about her feelings and her experiences, thus expanding her Quadrant I. In this process, Quadrant II also shrinks because fewer of her thoughts and feelings are concealed. As I continue to give her feedback, her blind area (Quadrant III) also shrinks as she learns new things about herself that others can see but she cannot. Once these are in her awareness, they can move into Quadrant I, expanding it even further. In our work together, the extent of personal information formerly unknown to her and unknown to others (Quadrant IV) also shrinks as she grows and learns new things about herself.

Try this experiment: Imagine that 100 points represent your total self. How much of this total self would you say is public—that is, known to others—and how much is private, or unknown to others? Distribute your 100 points in Quadrants I and II. Be sure your total adds up to 100. In this exercise, people typically assign about 60 points to the public area and 40 points to the private area. How do your figures compare with those?

Now look at the number you assigned to the private category. This category would include your secrets because your secrets are unknown to others. What percentage of your private self is currently represented by your secrets? Most people say that about 20% of their private selves is secret. Is your estimate of your secret self higher or lower than the average figure?

SELF-CONCEALMENT: WHAT YOU DON'T SAY CAN HURT YOU

Your estimate of how much of your private self you keep secret is an informal assessment of what I call self-concealment. Self-concealment is a familiar human experience. Most of us have uncomfortable feelings, thoughts, and information about ourselves that we avoid telling others. These secrets can range from mildly embarrassing to highly distressing.

Although we sometimes conceal positive information about ourselves, such as inheritances or awards, we most frequently conceal personal information that we perceive as negative. This kind of self-concealed negative personal information is consciously accessible to us, as distinguished from the "unconscious secrets" that result from repression or denial in the Johari Window's Quadrant IV. We actively keep these secrets from the awareness of others; sometimes we tell them to only one or two persons, and sometimes we don't share them with anyone at all.

My research, helping, and personal life experiences all confirm that some individuals tend to self-conceal more than others and that the most painful or traumatic experiences are often concealed (e.g., sexual abuse as a child, rape, strong negative thoughts about oneself, unhappiness in relationships, family secrets, grief, and medical conditions such as herpes or HIV infection.[13]

I have developed the scale on the next page to measure the different facets of self-concealment.[14] Before I describe self-concealment in more detail, answer the 10 items on this scale for yourself, using the rating scale provided. Add up your ratings. (Most people score about 26 on this scale.)

Self-Concealment Scale

1	2	3	4	5
Strongly disagree	Disagree	Neutral	Agree	Strongly agree

1 2 3 4 5   I have an important secret that I haven't shared with anyone.

1 2 3 4 5   If I shared all my secrets with my friends, they'd like me less.

1 2 3 4 5   There are lots of things about me that I keep to myself.

1 2 3 4 5   Some of my secrets have really tormented me.

1 2 3 4 5   When something bad happens to me, I tend to keep it to myself.

1 2 3 4 5   I'm often afraid I'll reveal something I don't want to.

1 2 3 4 5   Telling a secret often backfires and I wish I hadn't told it.

1 2 3 4 5   I have a secret that is so private I would lie if anybody asked me about it.

1 2 3 4 5   My secrets are too embarrassing to share with others.

1 2 3 4 5   I have negative thoughts about myself that I never share with anyone.

One recent study found that high self-concealers tended to report more depression, anxiety, and physical symptoms than did low self-concealers.[15] These findings were striking but not surprising; the idea that hiding significant aspects of the self can result in psychological or physical illness is a very old one.

William James, the father of modern psychology, seemed to sense this connection when he described secrets as "pent-in abscesses":

> For him who confesses, shams are over and realities have
> begun; he has exteriorized his rottenness. . . . One would
> think that in more men the shell of secrecy would have
> had to open, the pent-in abscess to burst and gain relief,
> even though the ear that heard the confession were
> unworthy.[16]

Henri Ellenberger has traced the historical importance of the concept of the pathogenic secret in the development of dynamic psychotherapy.[17] The procedure of extracting concealed and intolerable experiences appears in the confessional practices of Catholics, the "Cure of Souls" tradition among Protestants, and the healing rituals of animal magnetism and hypnotism.[18] These were, Ellenberger argues, precursors to the application of this concept by Freud, for whom the pathogenic secret was at the root of mental illness.

Psychotherapist Carl Jung considered secrets a kind of "psychic poison" that estrange us from the larger community, but he also saw the role that keeping certain personal information private can play in growth and individuation:

> The first beginnings of all analytical treatment of the soul
> are to be found in its prototype, the confessional. . . . Once
> the human mind had succeeded in inventing the idea of
> sin, man had recourse to psychic concealment; or, in
> analytical parlance, repression arose. Anything concealed
> is a secret. The possession of secrets acts like a psychic
> poison that alienates their possessor from the community.
> In small doses, this poison may be an invaluable
> medicament, even an essential pre-condition of individual
> differentiation.[19]

Note here that Jung doesn't distinguish between self-concealed personal information, which is available to our awareness, and repressed information, which isn't.

Modern psychologists have also expressed this view. Erich Fromm considered the inability to disclose oneself as a core reason for the alienation of the modern individual from self and others.[20] O. Hobart Mowrer believed that concealing one's misdeeds leads to neurosis and encouraged clients to disclose these behaviors to significant others.[21]

Sidney Jourard, who has conducted pioneering work on self-disclosure, explicitly relates self-concealment to stress and illness:

> Selye proposed the hypothesis that illness as we know it arises in consequence of stress. Now I think unhealthy *personality* has a similar root cause, one which is related to Selye's concept of stress. Every maladjusted person is a person who has not made himself known to another human being and in consequence does not know himself. Nor can he be himself. More than that, *he struggles actively to avoid becoming known by another human being.* He works at it ceaselessly, twenty-four hours daily, and it is work. In the effort to avoid becoming known, a person provides for himself a cancerous kind of stress which is subtle and unrecognized, but none the less effective in producing not only the assorted patterns of unhealthy personality which psychiatry talks about, but also the wide array of physical ills that have come to be recognized as the province of psychosomatic medicine.[22]

In a series of studies, James Pennebaker and his colleagues examined what they call the confiding-illness relation or the inhibition-disease link. They found that not expressing thoughts and feelings about traumatic events (divorce of one's parents, death of a spouse, death of a parent, and sexual traumas) leads to long-term health effects.[23] Surveying his own and other findings, Pennebaker arrives at this extraordinary conclusion: "The act of *not* discussing or confiding the event with another may be more damaging than having experienced the event *per se.*"[24] Pennebaker explains these effects much as Jourard does, saying that they result from increased physiological and psychological work accompanying the concealment of the traumatic events.[25]

Another possible way self-concealment affects health is that by self-concealing we disconnect ourselves from whatever help might be offered by family, friends, and caregivers. If other people don't know that we are distressed about something, there is no possibility that they will offer us assistance. In this way, self-concealment obstructs helping by stopping it at its first stage: a potential helper's awareness of our distress. Because no help is offered, our distress increases, and our psychological and physical health worsen.

PEOPLE'S BIGGEST SECRETS

What is your biggest (i.e., most difficult, burdensome, or painful) secret? I once asked this question of over 300 human services workers and graduate counseling students participating in a questionnaire survey.[26] I also asked this largely (91%) female group to describe what keeping this secret was like for them. Because of the highly intimate nature of the questions asked, extreme care was taken to protect the confidentiality of respondents. All subjects were told not to put their names anywhere on the questionnaire.

Here is a small sample of the heart-rending disclosures given in response to these two questions:

The secret: I had a little girl who was born severely brain damaged. I was young and just starting my career. For many months I tried caring for her but was "going under" fast. I eventually gave up all rights and responsibilities through the courts, and have felt guilty, sad, and terrible.

What it's been like: I feel dishonest when others are describing similar situations and I can't talk about mine.

The secret: I had sex with my younger brother when I was 17. I was drunk. I have never talked about it since, nor have I talked to him about it.

What it's been like: It's terrible. This is the first time I have been able to even come close to talking about it. It has tormented me for years. There is so much guilt. I can't begin to describe it.

The secret: I have this very strong feeling (always present, in retrospect) that I am not fulfilling my purpose in life, that when the record is written, I will not have been all that I could and should have been.

What it's been like: Causes me to be dissatisfied with myself regardless of what others might consider my contribution to life to be.

The secret: I'm not in love with my wife anymore. I care about her, and she's my dearest friend, but I'm very lonely for a passionate man/woman relationship.

What it's been like: I'm crying on the inside, but I can't let it out. I feel very tight and can't experience happiness or enthusiasm for life.

The secret: I was young, naive, and trusted the clergy[man] where I worked part time as office church secretary. I was sexually abused and raped by him, yet the biggest hurt and pain was when no one would believe me because I was from a poor family and he was held in high esteem in the community.

What it's been like: Prior to sharing it with my spouse, it caused us much frustration and distress in our sexual relationship.

The secret: Homosexual experience when I was 26 or so. It lasted for 6 months or so and was a very rewarding relationship which filled needs I had at that time. I then moved back to heterosexual relationships and remarried.

What it's been like: At the time the relationship was going on I was very concerned that coworkers and friends would find out. A lot of guilt feelings since my family would have had a very difficult time understanding the relationship. Now that it is long past it's no problem, except that I sometimes would like to share it with my spouse, but know he'd never understand.

The secret: I have something to share, for which I require no response from you, except for you to listen. Maybe by your listening and my telling it, it will help me get rid of the guilt I carry. When I was 21 or 22 I allowed my father to fondle and caress me. I didn't let him have sexual intercourse; I feel that God stopped it before that.

What it's been like: I don't think of it much. I've buried it. It just reminds me of the humanness we all share (weak spots in our personalities).

The secret: Failure of marriage. I feel rejected, denigrated, demeaned. I feel that it must be my fault but can't put together the whys. It is a loss that fades slowly but will never go away entirely.

What it's been like: It imposes a feeling of sadness. I can compensate for it by making others feel happy; my job and clientele make this possible. I have lost any confidence that I might have any future meaningful relationship with another, and so I don't try. I don't want to. I feel lonely and try to assuage the feeling by working, reading, etc.

The secret: I had an affair. My son is not my husband's child.

What it's been like: A very trying experience for many years, but now it's faded in importance. Keeping the secret was easy because my parents would have been destroyed, particularly my father.

The secret: Concern that I was an inadequate parent to one of my children because I seem to have few feelings about that child. I don't like to have him around me.

What it's been like: Scary, mostly in terms of the damage I might have caused to his emotional health.

By coincidence, another person's secret complemented this parent's concerns:

The secret: I have never been sure that my parents loved me. At times I feel my father has cared for me. I never will know about my mother as she died 21 years ago. Can't remember ever hearing her say, "I love you" to me. I feel like a baby to be 40 years old and be so insecure about this.

What it's been like: It was very hard to even verbalize. Seems like by the time you are my age, a person should know whether they were loved or not. I think it was a cause of my insecure feelings. Parental love is our base. It's hard to love ourselves if we aren't sure about our parents. I feel this secret has influenced my personal relationships.

I was stunned by the fact that 20% of my subjects had not confided their biggest personal secrets to a single other human being! Some of their major reasons for not disclosing their biggest secrets were that they saw them as too personal or embarrassing, they feared others' reactions, they were afraid of hurting or burdening others, or they felt that it was nobody else's business.

But what happens when the secret is divulged? In another question, I asked about interactions in which a personal secret was revealed to another person. One woman said:

I told my best girlfriend that I had an abortion. Though she personally would never abort a pregnancy, she knew how devastatingly painful this experience was for me. She gave me total support. That was 7 years ago. We've gone through

the deaths of both of our husbands since then. Our relationship has grown only stronger as the years have passed.

A positive effect on the relationship was described by more than
90% of the respondents; they used phrases like "our trust became
stronger," "it brought us even closer," "it strengthened our relationship," "the best conversation I'd ever had with her," and "she knew
my pain and still believed in me." One woman wrote, "I remember
being amazed that she could know the worst thing about me and still
want to have me for a friend."

The positive effects of these exchanges on relationships seem to
have positive effects on health as well, especially when stress levels
are high for the discloser. Several studies have looked at the health
protective functions of having a confidant following a stressful life
event. The findings are striking. Women who had severe life events
and who lacked a confidant (defined as a person with whom the
woman had a close, intimate, and confiding but not necessarily sexual relationship) were roughly 10 times more likely to be depressed
than women having such a relationship.[27] Women reporting the lack
of an intimate confidant had more psychological symptoms than
those who did report such a relationship.[28]

Based on my research, my clinical experiences, and my personal
life, I have come to the simple conclusion that we all need to have at
least one significant other we can confide all our troubling thoughts
and feelings to. I also believe that we need to disclose all these
distressing thoughts to at least this one confidant. If we don't, our
self-concealing behavior tends to influence our attitudes toward ourselves, and we conclude that there is some part of ourselves that is
in fact unlovable, or else we would reveal it. The only way out of this
vicious cycle is through disclosure to a caring and empathic confidant. T. S. Eliot expressed this idea eloquently:

> If a man has one person, just one in his life,
> To whom he is willing to confess everything—
> And that includes, mind you not only things criminal,
> Not only turpitude, meanness and cowardice,
> But also situations which are simply ridiculous,
> When he has played the fool (as who has not?)—
> Then he loves that person, and his love will save him.[29]

SECRETS OF PEOPLE FACING
LIFE-THREATENING ILLNESS

My professional interest in secrets developed from my clinical work,
particularly my work with people facing terminal illnesses. Working

with people whose deaths are imminent ushers us into a world where efforts to encourage honesty and genuineness are often frustrated. Secrets are held by many patients, their families, and their helpers as well. People are often "protected from the truth," and difficult feelings are kept hidden.[30] Some secrets are vigorously concealed by their holders; others are loosely held and readily revealed to a receptive listener. The secrets range from information concerning diagnoses and prognoses to confidences shared in tender moments, from disturbing family secrets shared with the proviso "Promise not to tell" to unspoken anger, shame, guilt, and hope.

For example, from a self-concealment perspective, AIDS is nothing less than a nightmare, an ordeal made worse by the secrecy that so often accompanies it. At each stage of this disease and its treatment, tough decisions concerning whether to conceal or to reveal difficult personal information add to the suffering of persons with AIDS, their caregivers, and their professional helpers. These decisions begin with the dilemma of whether or not to be tested for the virus, multiply with a positive test result, and continue throughout treatment: "Whom can I tell about this?" "What will my employer, co-workers, friends, family, or lover think?" If the person is gay and has concealed this fact from family and friends, disclosing this disease is made even more difficult: "Whom should I tell about my treatments? . . . my feelings? . . . my grief?"

Concealment in this kind of circumstance is not irrational. Tremendous stigmatization and discrimination are directed toward people with AIDS, and the disclosure of personal information must be carefully managed.[31] This situationally induced self-concealment makes coping with the disease even harder. Its pressure compounds the physical and psychological stress of the disease, its treatments, and the multiple losses so often experienced by persons with AIDS and their primary caregivers.

The helping professional or volunteer who cares for people with AIDS can also be thrown into a self-concealment pressure box: "Whom should I tell that I'm doing this?" "Whom can I turn to for support?" Many caregivers tell me that friends and family members either ask or demand that they not work with persons with AIDS. Ironically, at a time when these dedicated and committed helpers need support the most, it often disappears.

Faced with life-threatening illness and loss, family members sometimes make a bad situation worse by adding the burden of secrecy. Usually well intentioned, they seek to prevent pain, but their actions often increase it. I once worked with a Chinese American family in which the patriarchal grandfather prohibited the family from telling his enfeebled 94-year-old wife that her daughter had died. Younger members of the family refused to attend the family's Chinese New Years party—a very strong statement in their culture—because they were not allowed to acknowledge her death. In their words, "To deny her death was to deny her."

Family members can also conceal medical information from the patient. A nurse once described the following scene: She and the rest of the medical team were at the door of a patient's room. Inside the room, the patient looked up from bed and said, "What's this?" pointing to the large tumor that now protruded from his abdomen. At this same moment, the patient's wife stood behind him, waving her arms, commanding the caregivers not to talk with her husband about the tumor.

In situations like these, it often seems as though there is an elephant in the room, but no one can talk about it. Everyone knows what the truth or issue is, but no one feels comfortable directly addressing it. Caregivers in these situations must become experts at secret management—the keeping or uncovering of secrets. They must, as philosopher Sissela Bok puts it, "navigate in and between the worlds of personal and shared experience, coping with the moral questions about what is fair or unfair, truthful or deceptive, helpful or harmful."[32]

These choices are never easy for the caregiver, but sometimes we know that we have made the right one:

A dying patient's wife said, "Don't talk to him about dying. He's a private person—doesn't talk much and doesn't want to talk about death." I went into the room without the wife, and he seemed so in need of talking, I asked, "What would you like to share in the time you have left?" He held my hand and poured out his heart for 2 hours and talked of fears of dying.

Deep disclosures can bring healing and closure to one's life:

One of my patients opened up and told his family through me about a whole lifetime of experiences which he had never shared before. I had wondered when I first saw him how I could possibly help him—he was followed for months by other nurses, and there had been no changes and no real problems to solve. Shortly after he shared his secret stories he died, his work done. I felt overwhelmed with gratitude that I could be the helper for this final work of his.

A colleague of mine once related a similar story. An elderly dying woman was visibly agitated, and he stopped to talk with her. After several minutes of solid attention, she began to tell him a secret from her childhood. She had stolen her parents' silver setting and had never told them. This secret had haunted her throughout her life. My friend stayed with her for a bit longer, and she seemed much relieved. Late that night she appeared at the nurses' station and gave the nurse her Bible and her false teeth, saying, "I won't need these anymore." She went back to her room and died in her sleep.

In this deathbed scene, a daughter's ambivalence toward her dying mother is explained by her lifelong secret:

> We cared for a 65-year-old mother who was dying. A very
> pleasant, jovial daughter who was caring for her seemed
> so unsure of what she wanted to do for her mom. Her
> feelings swung from one day wanting to do a great job
> (which never quite happened) to the next day seeming
> disinterested. It was easy to wonder what kind of daughter
> was she. The last few hours of her mom's life she disclosed
> that she had been sexually abused as a child by her mom's
> boyfriends, and how her mother had just looked the other
> way. I wondered how often I had come to conclusions
> about people and situations. I realized how little we really
> know about some of the people we care for, and I felt
> guilty because I sometimes judge them even when I try
> not to.

HELPER SECRETS

The demanding and emotionally complicated nature of caregiving can trigger self-doubts and arouse strong emotions that may be embarrassing or even mortifying. All helpers probably have some troubling thoughts and feelings related to their work that are difficult to share with others. When these troubling thoughts and feelings are kept inside and not confided, they can become invisible, internal stressors, which I call helper secrets.[33]

It often feels inappropriate to admit one's limitations, vulnerabilities, ignorance, and problems, particularly in one's work. As professional or volunteer caregivers, we expect ourselves to be knowledgeable, strong, successful, and in control. When problems do arise, most caregivers feel that they are at fault and hide them from others; they assume that everybody else is coping effectively and that they alone are failing. The result is what social psychologists call the *fallacy of uniqueness* or *pluralistic ignorance* (i.e., the individual falsely assumes that he or she is the only one feeling this way).[34] Although individuals with a greater propensity for self-concealment would be more likely to hide these experiences, all helpers do this to some degree.

As a consultant to health care teams and organizations, I discovered many years ago that when caregivers revealed these kinds of personal thoughts and feelings, they always felt that theirs was a unique experience. Yet my cumulative experiences taught me that these helper secrets also have a universal quality—the specifics change, but the larger themes they reflect are repeated over and over, both within and across helping organizations.

My subsequent research on helper secrets confirmed this view. I have studied many thousands of helper secrets that I have collected from nurses, clergy, physicians, social workers, home health aides, volunteers, and other caregivers. In my formal studies of helper secrets, I have used content analysis procedures to identify the major themes and issues repeatedly reflected in these disclosures.

As you encounter the helper secrets that follow, keep in mind that these are, in fact, secrets—they are uncomfortable and embarrassing personal information. Only some serious soul searching and the assurance of anonymity permitted their disclosure. So, these self-revelations must be approached with compassion and respect; they reflect the inner struggles of caregivers as they strive to be competent and caring helpers.

"I've Distanced Myself From Patients and Families"

In a study of helper secrets I conducted involving nearly 500 nurses, more than one out of five responses contained descriptions of participants' wanting to or having actually emotionally or physically distanced themselves from patients, patients' families, staff, or their own family members.[35] This distancing took many forms: "becoming emotionally distant," "ignoring patients' needs," "avoiding visiting the difficult patient," "holding a part of myself back," and "feeling cold and unsympathetic" are just a few examples. This theme is also pervasive in the helper secrets of other caregiver groups.

Can you think of a way in which you have emotionally or physically distanced yourself as a caregiver? How did this make you feel about yourself? Chapter 3 offered a close look at how avoidance leads to lowered self-esteem and gave some examples of avoidance in caregiving. These experiences might be placed at the low-involvement end of the continuum of emotional involvement, as discussed in chapter 2. The difficulty for the helper in attempting to achieve emotional or physical distance is that these efforts actually raise, rather than lower, stress levels because they lead to feelings of self-doubt, guilt, shame, and personal and professional inadequacy. They augment distress and in doing so make this an untenable long-term stance.[36] This stress–avoidance–guilt sequence is reflected in the following disclosures:

> I have "distanced" myself deliberately from some patients and families as a form of self-protection when I've felt emotionally overloaded—even though I felt they needed emotional support themselves.

> I feel guilty that my caregiving has become more emotionally distant. Seems I'm protecting myself. I don't want to give so much of my energy to others' lives or my work.

> I feel cold and unsympathetic when a coworker tells me the same old problem.

> I often say I'll be right back when I have no intention of coming back.

> I have always tended to avoid saying good-bye to my patients. I sometimes make myself do it but am glad if they slip into a coma before I make the time to tell them how I feel about them.

> Sometimes the last thing I want to do is care about the person. I just want them to get away, at the same time I realize I care. I don't know which feeling to respond to. I just need to get away.

> Right now I feel as though I don't want to commit myself to a new patient. I'm not sure I want to take time away from my family, which is very emotionally satisfying at this time. I feel guilty about this.

> I became friends with one of my patients, and we often had lunch together and talked on the telephone. Then her doctor told me that she was terminal. I went on vacation, and when I came back I never called her or returned her calls. That was over a year ago, and I wonder now whether she is dead. Her doctor does not know because she changed to a doctor who is with a different hospital. A week ago, I called her number—no answer. Is she dead? I feel guilty.

"I Feel Inadequate"

Concern about one's competence and effectiveness as a caregiver is another frequently occurring theme in helpers' secrets:

My inadequacy is my most personal secret, and it is very frustrating to be constantly in the company of so many talented, capable people.

I wish I had more confidence in myself. I feel everyone is smarter and more knowledgeable than me.

I often feel inadequate to say those wise and empathetic things that can be so comforting. I wish I could say those special words/phrases that are "just right."

I'm always scared I won't have the technical skills to handle the patients' needs. This makes me really feel like an incompetent, bad nurse. Everyone sees me as capable, but I am afraid. I seem to do OK when faced with new situations, but I panic inside. I'm afraid of being seen as incompetent by patients—that's where it hurts most.

The prevalence of this kind of helper secret is not surprising. Feelings of inadequacy and incompetence are frequent themes in the secrets of nonhelper populations as well.[37] These kind of concerns and self-doubts seem to be invisible stressors affecting all helper populations. In one study, for example, psychotherapists reported that doubts about the efficacy of their helping were their number one stressor.[38] Also, feelings of inadequacy and strong self-doubt are understandable given the many challenges facing today's caregiver. The relentless demands of ever-changing technologies, treatments, and psychosocial complexities can create the "terror of error" experiences described in chapter 2.

"I'm an Impostor"

Feelings of inadequacy and self-doubt are common and often take the form of feeling like an impostor—someone who is posing as a competent caregiver but who really lacks the expertise to do the job. There is a strong fear of being exposed as a fake and a fraud:

I feel I've really fooled the world. That I'm in this position and people think well of me. I've fooled them! I'm not that great.

Even though I have been a nurse for many years and am now a nurse administrator, I'm sure I couldn't pass state boards today.

Deep down inside I feel that I am fooling everyone—I'm not as bright or competent as people think I am. What if I fail? What should I do?

I feel that I'm a fake. Someone else would be more effective. I frequently feel like I'm flying by the seat of my pants.

I feel like I am an impostor—at work everyone looks up to me for the "latest" or "how to do it best" information. So far I have been able to wing it or come up with an acceptable answer, but I live a lot with the fear of making a big mistake in front of everyone.

I am really uncomfortable—I've been put in charge of developing a hospice program; I don't think I know enough about it; I feel like a fake trying to pull off a bubble about to burst. On top of that, if the bubble did burst, and I was exposed as a fake, I would deserve to be ridiculed, laughed at, scorned, fired, burned at the stake.

I'm afraid that if anyone found how much I don't know they'd head for the door.

"I'm Angry!"

Unspoken anger, frustration, and impatience—with patients, family members, coworkers, and administration—is a frequently occurring theme in the helper secrets I have gathered:

There are times when I'd like to shake some of the people I work with until they scream and cry. I hate detachment as a coping mechanism. I can't reach them and I don't feel like they can *hear* me. . . . So how on earth can we deal deeply with patients, family, and each other?

There are times when I feel like screaming or kicking or hitting something—like I'm about to lose control—but I usually just make tight fists, breathe, and then return to the situation looking and hopefully acting calm, in control, and like a nurse.

A couple of weeks ago, I was feeling really burned out and I had a newborn who wouldn't eat, and when I gavaged (tube-fed) him, he spit all the formula back up, and I gritted my teeth and became so angry at the baby, it really scared me because I felt like I could have hit him for not eating. I waited 15 minutes and then tried to feed him again, feeling much better, but I felt guilty for a *long* time.

Sometimes when an AIDS patient is very difficult, demanding, and obnoxious, I would like to tell them they deserve what they got.

Sometimes I feel like I'd really like to tell a few certain arrogant doctors to stop feeding their egos through their ill patients and that their patients aren't the only sick patients in the hospital.

I hated the husband of a patient because he wanted her to die and did not want to care for her or be with her. I couldn't be totally effective because of my antipathy. He was selfish and I didn't help him through the crisis as I should have.

This last disclosure reminds me of conflicts I experienced while working with a particular family. Jane was a 50-year-old woman with metastatic breast cancer. As she became more seriously ill, I met with both her and her husband. She didn't want to be told how long the oncologist thought she might live; although she was aware that her condition was terminal, she preferred not to have a "death sentence" hanging over her, and she expressed this desire clearly to me and to her husband, Ray.

On a rare day when Ray accompanied her to the oncologist, he remained alone in the office and insisted that the oncologist give him an estimate of how long Jane would probably live. After extracting this prognosis from the reluctant physician, Ray immediately went out in the hallway and delivered this information to his wife, something akin to passing her an emotional hand grenade. Later, Ray also pointed to a drawer where he kept a revolver and said to Jane that if he were in her situation, he knew what he would do. He also refused to comply with Jane's request that her deathbed be moved to the room looking out at the flower garden she so dearly loved.

Knowing the agony he caused Jane, I hated Ray, and I often thought that if the world had an ounce of fairness in it he would be in that deathbed, not Jane. I somehow persevered and helped with Jane's dying, but I could not bring myself to have any further contact with Ray after her death. I didn't help him with his grief and felt guilty about it for a long time.

"What About Me?"

One-way giving is built into caregiving. Of course, there *are* moments of reciprocity—a deeply felt thank-you, an award, unsolicited caring from a coworker—but these events do not change the fundamental reality that in caregiving the focus is on your patients or clients, and there is no guarantee that you will receive anything more in return for your services than a paycheck, the intrinsic satisfaction of helping others, or both.

A small but significant group of helper secrets contain direct expressions of a desire to receive—as well as to give—caring and appreciation from patients and their families, coworkers, and the administration. Although these secrets represent only a small percent of the total number of secrets, they poignantly highlight an important stressor in caregiving:

> Sometimes I wish I weren't a nurse—because I don't want to give anymore and don't want to have to keep constantly learning. I resent it. I want to be taken care of—me.

> Sometimes I get angry and disgusted with myself for being afraid to discuss my feelings or communicate intimately and effectively about things in my life that really bother me. I always give in and never insist on being heard and cared about. I never think my feelings are as important as other people's.

> I sometimes get to the point where I can't pick up a baby and hold him/her because I can't "give" any more. I'm the one that needs to be held and rocked!

This next secret contains the themes of distancing, feeling like an impostor, and one-way giving:

> I feel like such a fraud. All my life people have considered me so strong, and I'm not. I badly need to have someone to talk to about things that happen in this work, and it never seems to occur to anyone that I need support too. The thing that weighs heavily on me is that I make deep personal contact with about one patient in five, and I feel so guilty about the other four.

A desperate need for more nurturance and self-care is reflected in this ominous secret:

> Sometimes I wish that I would come down with a semi-serious illness so that *I* could be taken care of for a while.

These secrets usually include an inner voice that is asking, "What about me?" and critical feelings toward oneself for not being assertive enough in getting one's own needs met. Helpers holding these secrets are fighting against the tendencies that psychologist Christina Maslach identified in describing the burnout-prone individual: "This person is often unable to exert control over a situation and will passively yield to its demands rather than actively limiting them to his or her capacity to give. It is easy for this person to become overburdened emotionally, and so the risk of emotional exhaustion is high."[39]

"I'm Overwhelmed"

Another theme, one closely related to that of one-way giving, focuses on difficult feelings associated with emotional and physical demands at work and at home:

> Sometimes I feel like too much is expected—janitor, counselor, maid, mother, sister, etc. It makes me feel like I'm being manipulated and drained. I feel resentful.

> I resent being the everlasting strong cheerleader and eternal caregiver and having the staff think that when I call for help—verbally and/or through body language (drooping posture, face) I'm doing it to be one of the gang. Short version: I feel misunderstood. I'm human, too!

> Too many demands are killing me.

> I had a patient who I felt was very selfish and demanding, and the family seemed very selfish and demanding—and I gave in to their demands when it didn't seem necessary. But I had demands in my life that didn't get taken care of, so some important things in my life fell apart (I lost a lover), and I'm still mad at myself and them.

> I feel like I could manage part of my job very well, but there are too many different aspects for me to do all of them well. Some days it seems that the demands are overwhelming. But I'm afraid to admit I can't handle it all.

> Trying to be supermom, supernurse, and superwife sometimes burdens me so. When I fail in one area, there is a domino effect. I hate to fail.

These self-disclosures underline the fact that even the most common stressors encountered by caregivers, such as being overburdened by multiple roles at work and at home, have the potential to create a sense of inner turmoil that is then concealed. Most helpers would probably feel relatively comfortable confiding in someone about the excessive demands they face, but they still might hide some of the deeper experiences related to those demands: the pain they feel when the "domino effect" occurs, "hating to fail," "feeling manipulated and drained," and "resentful." As noted in chapter 2, these kinds of demoralizing experiences can be key contributors to burnout.

"I Wish He'd Die"

Life isn't tidy, and death doesn't always come at exactly the right moment. Caregivers working with the terminally ill often confront situations in which their deep caring and compassion lead them to wish for the death of a patient. I remember that I felt this way about my grandmother, who had severe Alzheimer's disease.

Patients whose pain cannot be controlled or who, suffering greatly, ask with their eyes or with their words for assistance with their dying can trigger many difficult feelings in caregivers. An extremely common secret of caregivers working with the terminally ill is the unspoken wish that a patient would die to end that patient's agonizing suffering:

> Sometimes I pray that God takes this patient because he's suffering so much. I hope he dies soon. I feel guilty.

> I've wanted to help a terminally ill patient to die before things got worse. That is to say, I've wanted to give or encourage them to take too much pain medication so that they would die peacefully without further pain or suffering.

> I wish I could pull the plug on someone I know will have a poor quality of life.

> A patient wants to commit suicide so she will not suffer too much and will not continue to be a burden to her family. I find I have very ambiguous feelings about what to say to her. How can I say she should continue to suffer? How can I possibly understand how she feels? She only has a short while to live anyway, and it will be very painful.

> He was in constant pain, unable to move, unable to control bodily functions. I straightened his bed and I held the pillow. I wanted to cover his face. I didn't. He died 4 painful days later.

One caregiver disclosed an actual assisted death:

> The patient I grew to love deeply in a short time—I
> euthanized her, before the very end—she requested it, but
> I didn't have any experience in doing a proper job and
> screwed up terrible. She awoke and said to me, "We goofed
> up, didn't we?" I had to tell her yes and acknowledge the
> added pain and discomfort I caused her. The second time
> I gave it a try, it worked.

Discussions of the pros and cons of assisted euthanasia are increasing in the United States and Europe. Dame Cicely Saunders of St. Christopher's Hospice offers these thoughts on the implications of offering assisted euthanasia as an option:

> We would present people with an intolerable dilemma
> when they need support to take courage and trust us
> never to think they are a burden. Those most experienced
> in meeting the difficult medical, nursing, and above all,
> personal and social problems that are now referred to
> hospice teams are the very people who see the most
> compelling arguments against euthanasia, understood
> as the deliberate shortening of life. We know something
> of the potentials in treatment—and are learning all the
> time—and we believe in personal growth, even to the end
> of life, however diminished it may look.[40]

Saunders's comments remind me of the aphorism that you only get to see the light from your star when it gets dark. The darkness of night is terrifying. The stars come out slowly. If we don't find the courage to journey into the darkness with our patients, we may be abandoning them to a starless night.

REAL VERSUS IDEALIZED IMAGES
OF SELF AS HELPER

Avoidance, self-concealment, unrealistic expectations of self, the tendency toward self-blame, and the fallacy of uniqueness all foster the development of helper secrets. Another key, related element is the discrepancy between the caregiver's real and idealized images of self as helper.

As caring and altruistically motivated helpers, we ask ourselves, "I am a caring and giving person. That's why I got into this work in the first place. How can I ignore patients' needs? Why do I distance myself and wish that patients would die? Why do I feel so angry toward the people I'm caring for?" We ask, "Is there something wrong with me?" and then our self-esteem begins to plummet. This negative self-talk becomes an internal stressor that can make even the brightest of helping flames flicker, if not burn out completely.

When our self-expectations are not realized, we tend to experience guilt and anxiety, then resentment, anger, and burnout.[41] This discrepancy between our idealized images of ourselves as helpers and our day-to-day experiences creates inner turmoil and promotes the development of helper secrets.

Where do these idealized images of self as helper come from? Claude Steiner suggests that the idealized self-images of nurses can be traced to the "script" they are assigned by society: "Take care of others first" and "Don't ask for what you want."[42] These injunctions conflict with many of the strong feelings that are reflected in helpers' secrets, thus explaining why the latter are concealed and not openly confided.

Another source of problematic idealized self-images for female caregivers in particular is the training in being overly responsible that they receive in our society. Women are taught from an early age to be responsible for managing relationships and making them work; this training can make women caregivers more vulnerable to overextending themselves and to blaming themselves when their helping fails. But this overresponsibility is not a sign of sickness and should not be pathologized and given labels like codependent caregiving; rather, as Jo Ann Krestan and Claudia Bepko put it, it is a positive impulse gone awry and simply needs to be balanced with a sense of responsibility to self.[43]

We all had parents, teachers, and other helper role models in our lives who shaped our idealized image of self as helper. But I think we can also gain some insight into these idealized images—these schemas or mental blueprints we have for helping and helpers—by carefully looking at some of the helping heroes we have been exposed to. Mother Teresa, Albert Schweitzer, and Florence Nightingale are just a few of the most famous and influential helpers who may have inspired us. The model they all reflect is that of the selfless caregiver working tirelessly in the most adverse of circumstances.

We also need to look to our popular culture. As a child, my favorite fictional characters were the Lone Ranger, Batman, and Superman. Vicariously participating in the adventures of these valiant helpers always made me feel good because, in retrospect, I think it affirmed my altruistic self.

As helpers, these fictional characters had several striking features in common: First, their true identities were hidden from others.

Second, a traumatic loss preceded each of their careers as a helper: Superman lost his entire family and was orphaned; the Lone Ranger was a Texas Ranger attacked and left for dead by bandits (his brother was killed in the attack), who was rescued and revived by Tonto; as a young boy, Batman witnessed the brutal murder of both of his parents. We sensed a profound connection between these painful events and our heroes' passionate commitment to doing good. Third, their helping was, it seemed, purely altruistic. These were people who selflessly did good for others. They rode, flew, or drove off before anyone could even thank them, let alone ask about their own needs: Who was that masked helper? Fourth, each seemed, in the end, invulnerable. Although there were some close calls with kryptonite, we knew that when we looked up in the sky, Superman would always be there. Fifth, these superhelpers all had unhappy personal lives—they were wounded healers.[44] Bruce Wayne had an unending string of failed relationships—Julie Madison, Vicki Vale, and the Batwoman. Clark Kent desperately sought real intimacy with Lois Lane but was brutally beaten by a bully when he shed his super powers to attain it. Finally, they *never* failed. They always came through, no matter what the odds against them were.

During the endless hours I watched these helping icons, I vicariously felt that good feeling that comes from helping others—the do good–feel good effect. Unfortunately, I also learned that helpers can't be fully authentic, don't seek help in dealing with their traumatic pasts, never accept any appreciation for the good work they do, have miserable personal lives, and always succeed. Now, when I sometimes fail or feel vulnerable or have a need for appreciation or greater authenticity as a helper, I feel uneasy because these experiences don't match with my mental blueprint of the "great helper."

A key antidote to this insidious source of stress is to develop a more balanced, less perfectionistic, and more realistic ideal image of yourself as helper, and to do this without sacrificing your vision.

THE HELPER SECRETS EXERCISE

The best way to relieve the stressful effects of helper secrets is to disclose those troubling thoughts and feelings to a trustworthy confidant. Before I explain why this is helpful and how best to do it, let me emphatically state what *not* to do with your helper secrets: Do not indiscriminately share them. Nothing could be more hurtful to yourself. Both research and our informed intuition suggest that the choice of confidants and the context for this self-disclosure are critical considerations. You have to find a trustworthy confidant who is able to respond openly and nondefensively to your inner experience. Friends, family, and other members of your social support network can provide one arena for these disclosures. But perhaps helper secrets are best shared with a colleague who does the same kind of work (i.e., someone who can have "instant empathy" with these difficult feelings).

Revealing difficult inner experiences is not something you want to leave to chance and to the conversational patterns of everyday life, where interruptions, quick advice, veiled judgments, and other unhelpful responses are common. When I have given workshops or led retreats, I have found that the following highly structured exercise can be an excellent vehicle for caregivers to disclose their helper secrets and get a caring, helpful response from others.

I ask the caregivers to write their helper secrets on identical index cards or sheets of paper.[45] I ask them to exclude any personally identifying information in their secret descriptions. The secrets are then gathered and randomly redistributed in the group. (If someone gets his or her own secret, that will still work because the rest of the group won't know this.) Of course, if members of the group know one anothers' handwriting, extra precautions, like having a person outside the group type or transcribe the secrets, should be taken to preserve anonymity.

The secrets are then read aloud, and I ask the other participants to share experiences similar to those expressed in the secret being read—what psychologist Gerald Goodman calls "me-too self-disclosures."[46] These me-too self-disclosures are directed toward the person who is reading the secret, and that person simply listens to the responses of others as a kind of surrogate receiver for the actual secret holder. Here is a sample of the kind of dialogue that can occur in these sessions:

Secret: There was a young mother of three I cared for dying from ovarian cancer. We were giving her a big dose of IV morphine every 1 to 2 hours. After one of the doses I gave her, she quickly stopped breathing. One of the family members asked me if I killed her with that last dose.

Response: I was really close to a family and followed the patient for 3 years, it was a baby, from birth, and gave him his last dose of morphine, and that's exactly what the mother said to me—"You've killed my baby." But to this day she still has contact with me and calls me. But it's still . . . it's right here *(tears in her eyes as she touches her heart).*

In nearly a decade of doing this exercise, I have found that the listening group members can almost always find some part of the experience conveyed in the secret that they can identify with and be self-disclosing in response to. Sometimes the entire room is filled with nodding heads, but everyone is a bit reluctant to respond verbally because the secret shared is reminiscent of the participants' own secrets. Other times, nearly everyone makes an empathic self-disclosure. For the deeper revelations, it might take quite a while—certainly more than a few minutes—until someone gets in touch with a similar experience, so you might need to give more time.

After all the secrets are read and responded to, there is usually a tremendous sense of relief in the room that comes from knowing that one is not alone in having these thoughts and feelings. Many people have said that what had been a well-kept secret became something that they could freely discuss with others. Even though their secrets remain anonymous, they experience the feeling that a formerly secret part of themselves is now known to others (i.e., Quadrant II of the Johari Window has gotten smaller), and the responses they have received make them feel differently about these formerly secret parts. I believe that this profound change in stance toward one's inner world is a key element in helping and psychological healing.

You don't need to participate in a helper secrets exercise to experience this kind of shift. You might not even need to communicate these difficult experiences to anyone else. The simple act of writing about our secrets can have a positive effect on our stress levels.[47] This is one reason I encourage caregivers to keep a diary of their helping experiences.

What you can't fully achieve through writing alone is that sense of "being in the same boat" with other caregivers—the deeper knowing that others have some of the same difficulties with the stressful situations you encounter. You might know this at a cognitive level—for example, as a result of reading this book—but real knowledge at a deeper level can only occur when you actually hear and respond internally to the disclosures of others like yourself.

The best antidote to helper secrets is to talk about our stress and to learn to see it as a common part of our work. When these difficult feelings are shared and worked through, they can be normalized, the natural bias toward self-blame can be corrected, and your energies can be directed toward developing better coping and problem-solving skills and strategies.[48]

In your work, you naturally value and promote honesty, openness, and revelation; your courage and skill, applied in a timely and strategic manner, allow painful experiences to be safely confronted and the burdens of patients and families to be lifted. Yet in this role of midwife to open communication you may sometimes forget that your longevity as a helper also requires maintaining an open and friendly stance toward *yourself* and the inevitably difficult experiences you have as a caregiver.

Helper secrets alert us to our inner crises as helpers. The Chinese pictograph for crisis is composed of two characters, one signifying danger, the other opportunity. Helper secrets have a similar twofold nature. Though frequently highly painful, they contain information vital to your survival as a helper; they point to difficult areas of experience that demand greater attention. When they are concealed, helper secrets can corrode you from within; when revealed to empathic others, they can strengthen your support network and enhance your personal and professional growth.

CONCLUSION

In *The Great Turning,* Craig Schindler and Gary Lapid point out that the single-celled organism differentiates between "me" and "not me" and adjusts the flow of information across its boundaries accordingly:

> A primitive single-celled organism can be observed to
> move toward that which nourishes it and away from
> noxious stimuli that threaten it. In a nourishing
> environment, the organism becomes more porous and the
> flow across its cellular membrane is enhanced. In toxic or
> less supportive environments, the organism reduces its
> porosity and the flow across the cell wall is diminished.
> The single-celled entity therefore spends a great deal of its
> life moving toward "friendly" environments and away from
> "unfriendly" ones.[49]

Creating friendly environments that facilitate a caring sense of connection and encourage the free flow and exchange of information crucial to the health of all living systems is a challenge that pervades all our work as caregivers.

One experience on my own helping journey taught me a great deal about the healing connections that can rapidly develop when a friendly environment is offered to people in emotional pain. Let me describe this situation as if we were there: We are at a rustic retreat site in California. Sunlight is streaming through tall cathedral-like windows, warming the chilly meeting room. I look out at the expectant faces of the retreat participants. The diversity of the group is striking. The more than 70 cancer patients and family members attending this We Can Weekend program span different ages, races, and nationalities.[50] But, as we will soon discover, the differences among group members will be dwarfed by their common experience of cancer.

It is the first morning of our retreat. We have just completed some ice breaker exercises that helped us introduce ourselves. Now red pieces of paper are distributed, and I am asking participants to write their secret fears on one side and their secret hopes on the other side. Quiet fills the room. I begin to worry about what will happen. Perhaps this is too threatening for the group. This exercise is my addition to the We Can Weekend curriculum, and I fear I might regret it. Only hours ago these people were complete strangers, and now I'm asking them to disclose some of their deepest feelings. When everyone is finished writing, the papers are exchanged randomly several times to ensure anonymity, and we slowly begin reading our fears:

Being totally dependent on others.

That I will not be there when needed most.

I'll die a painful death.

Giving up.

Having to say good-bye.

My dad dying.

That I might get cancer when I grow up.

The loss of my closest, most understanding friend
and supporter.

That I will die without coming to peace with my life.

Many participants are trembling as they read their secret fears. Others begin to cry. Their hands and arms are extended to virtual strangers. Tears stream down my face, and a look of awe is on the face of a colleague. A kind of emotional contagion spreads through the room: A fear touches one person, then someone else. To an outside observer, it might seem that we have jumped into the Helper's Pit together. But for us, it feels more like we are scaling the walls of the pit together, reaching out to hold on to one another as we climb.

After a pause, they turn the papers over and begin to read their hopes:

That I will be able to see my grandchildren.

To be able to keep laughing at this.

My brother gets well soon and we can be a family
together again.

That my wife is successful in combating and overcoming
her cancer. That she and I will remain together until the
end of our lives.

That I can give the emotional support that is needed
throughout this ordeal.

That I beat this.

Communication, openness, forgiveness, patience,
and that there is hope.

That my mom will not suffer.

I hope for courage—and lots of it.

The change in mood in the room is palpable. The connection between us—that almost sacred sense of we-ness—is something I will
always remember. When things get tough, it is a real source of
strength for me.

An extraordinary level of trust and openness prevailed during
the remainder of the weekend. A group of strangers had become intimate and supportive friends, and many of these relationships continued long after the retreat.

It is often forgotten that in the Greek myth of Pandora's Box, after
the Furies escape, one entity remains: Hope. Perhaps the key to our
success was that we kept the lid open long enough for Hope to
emerge. We might have closed the lid too soon, or never opened it, or
tried to beckon Hope without her terrifying companions. The lesson
here—which applies to both personal and helper secrets and which
is the focus of the remaining chapters in this book—is that hope can
emerge triumphant, replacing denial, avoidance, and fear, when it is
sustained by caring, empathy, and support.

PART TWO

The Interpersonal Challenge

The practice of medicine is an art, not a trade; a calling, not a business; a calling in which your heart will be exercised equally with your head.[1]

Sir William Osler

The question now is what have you known about being human that you can translate into usefulness to other people, to those you intend to help? How can you "relate"—which is to say, so act in the helping interchange—that the person you assist may experience some sense of being cared about by another human being and of being allied with him? He will not be asking you for a relationship. He is likely to be asking you for some plain, ordinary, necessary life-sustaining thing like money, like medicine, like advice, like action in his behalf. But what he gets from you, whether in material or psychological form, will be "twice blessed" when it is conveyed in such a way as to affirm his personal worth and his social linkage.[2]

Helen Harris Perlman

The Helping
Relationship

QUALITIES OF THE EFFECTIVE HELPER

If you needed to explore an unpleasant aspect of yourself, or were contemplating a divorce, or were suddenly diagnosed with a life-threatening illness, what kind of person would you feel most comfortable sharing these experiences with? How would you describe the relationship you would like to have with this helper? Would this person be caring . . . empathic . . . flexible . . . a good listener . . . encouraging . . . friendly? Someone you could trust and tell your secrets to? Would he or she express interest in you? Believe in you? Would you like your relationship with this helper to be one of equality and mutual participation?

These are probably some of the qualities that come to your mind when you consider seeking help for yourself. That isn't really surprising because these same qualities are among those identified in hundreds of research studies as the defining features of successful helpers and helping relationships.

Notice that your first thoughts probably weren't about the professional training, credentials, theoretical orientation, or technical expertise of the helper you would seek out. These considerations might enter into your decision making later, but the initial concern you and other people in distress usually have is finding someone who can offer you a supportive and caring relationship.

This particular set of priorities in help seeking is the same one that recent scientific findings would argue for. For example, Joseph Durlak reviewed 42 studies comparing the effectiveness of professional therapists and paraprofessionals and concluded that paraprofessionals perform as well as or better than highly credentialed professional helpers.[3] Psychiatric aides, medical personnel, untrained college students, and lay adults having no professional mental health education consistently achieved clinical outcomes equal to or significantly better than those obtained by psychologists, psychiatrists, and clinical social workers. Other outcome studies show that when different schools of therapy are pitted against one another, no one brand of therapy is more effective than another.[4]

Surveying these findings, psychologist Thomas Wills said:

> It was traditionally assumed that client improvement in
> therapy depended on the application of specific technical
> skills, derived from a theoretical system of psychotherapy
> and implemented by a trained professional. However, the
> evidence just considered makes this seem unlikely. Here
> it is taken as a given that therapeutic gain, broadly
> construed (namely, increased self-esteem, self-control, and
> ability to deal effectively with social situations), is based
> on a significant relationship with another person,
> characterized by feelings of mutual respect, acceptance,
> and liking or positive regard.[5]

Given these results, Wills suggests, anyone in the top 25% of all people on psychological maturity, personal security, and social skill could be expected to be a fairly effective counselor.[6]

Are most of your personal and helping relationships characterized by feelings of mutual respect, acceptance, and liking or positive regard? If you answered "yes," then you very likely qualify as a member of the top 25% of people Wills describes who could be reasonably effective therapists without any training in psychotherapeutic methods.

Let's assume that you *do* possess these qualities, and to them add your idealism, altruism, and capacity for empathy, as discussed in chapter 1. What can you conclude about yourself as a helper? You might conclude that you have enormous potential as a caregiver, that you will be very successful in your work.

But too often we come to just the opposite conclusion and underestimate our helping potential and impact. I see this often in volunteer caregivers and nonprofessional counselors (professionals from fields other than counseling and therapy—e.g., nurses, physicians, lawyers, and other helpers—who are often the first or only caregivers on the scene and who routinely offer much-needed counseling and therapeutic supportive care to their patients and clients). They compare their own helping efforts with those they imagine highly trained mental health professionals would make and conclude that they aren't making the kind of difference that these mental health experts would make in the same situation. The therapeutic and healing value of a touch, a hug, a discussion of a problem, or a brief, encouraging conversation or phone call are dismissed with statements like "I'm only a volunteer," "We just talked," or "I didn't really do anything." Often we don't really appreciate that in dealing with most emotional problems, as Eugene Kennedy and Sara Charles observe, "a little bit of help is a lot of help"[7] and that simply being there with our clients can have a healing quality.

THE HEALING POWER OF HUMAN PRESENCE

I truly believe that the healing power of helpers and helping relationships is bolstered by the invisible contributions of simple human presence. The difference between no human contact and the presence of another is a significant yet little-studied psychological phenomena. Indirect evidence for this hypothesis is provided by Schachter's studies (reviewed in chapter 4), which show that, as long we don't feel ashamed by our circumstances, we tend to seek the presence of others when we feel threatened and that we are comforted by their presence. We also tend to have better health if we have solid social support (see chapter 1). Human presence might be a key component of social support contributing to these positive health effects.

An impressive study done by physician John Kennell and his colleagues has looked at this phenomenon more closely. These researchers examined the impact of the continued presence of a supportive companion during labor and delivery for more than 400 women in labor in a public hospital in Texas.[8] At this teaching facility, companions are not routinely permitted to be with a woman during labor and delivery because there is insufficient privacy on the ward to allow visitors.

The experimenters trained a group of doulas (*doula* is the Greek word for an experienced woman who guides a new mother in her infant care tasks) and assigned them to the women in the supported condition. The doulas stayed at the bedside from admission through delivery, soothed and touched the laboring woman, and gave her encouragement. They also engaged in some patient education and explained what was occurring during labor and what might happen next.

Patients in the observed condition did not have a doula assisting them but instead had an observer in the room at all times. This observer kept a record of what was happening in the patient's room without speaking to the laboring woman, remaining as inconspicuous as possible in the crowded and hectic labor room. There was also a control group that was neither supported nor observed.

The three groups were compared on a variety of medical outcomes, including oxytocin use, duration of labor, type of delivery, and neonatal outcome. The doula intervention significantly reduced caesarian section rates, forceps deliveries, the need for oxytocin, and use of epidural anesthesia. Also, labor was shortened and the incidence of maternal fever was decreased.

More striking, the presence of an observer also had a significant effect on obstetrical outcome measures—compared with the control group, the women who had an observer used less oxytocin and had shorter labors. For those who had spontaneous vaginal deliveries, epidural anesthesia was used in 7.8% of the women in the supported group, 22.6% of the women in the observed group, and 55.3% in the control group. In other words, the observer alone had significant impact on many outcome measures, and when caring responses like giving information and touching (the doula condition) were added, the effects were even greater.

The researchers discuss the results:

> The fact that an observer who stayed in the labor room at
> some distance from the mother during the entire labor had
> a significant effect on obstetrical outcome measures even
> though she did not speak with the mother may provide a
> clue to the needs of a woman during labor. In trying to
> dissect the process by which the "doula" has an effect on
> labor, it is impressive that part of her effect *may be solely
> her presence* [italics added], without intimate interactions
> such as talking and touching.[9]

The healing power of human presence is an integral part of helping, a part of the "social linkage" that when directly felt makes our helping "twice blessed," as the quotation by Helen Harris Perlman at the beginning of this chapter makes plain. The "low tech, high touch" aspects of caregiving are not just components of a pleasant bedside manner; they are critical to the treatment and can affect both psychological and physical outcomes in a positive manner.[10]

EMPATHY

The caring qualities and behavior that we bring to the helping relationship extend the therapeutic effects of simple human presence. As effective helpers, we are first of all empathic. Empathy requires freeing yourself to see, understand, and experience life through another's being. The English word *empathy* is the equivalent of the German word *Einfühlung*, literally translated as "feeling into." When first introduced at the turn of the century, the term was used primarily to refer to aesthetic experience of various art forms—the feelings you might have when listening to a work by Mozart or when viewing a masterpiece by Michelangelo.[11] Being empathic means feeling your way into the consciousness of the other person and seeing the world through his or her eyes.

In empirical research, empathy is consistently identified as the most important element of successful helping relationships.[12] Carl Rogers offers this description of empathy:

> It means entering the private perceptual world of the other
> and becoming thoroughly at home in it. It involves being
> sensitive, moment to moment, to the changing felt
> meanings which flow in this other person, to the fear or
> rage or tenderness or confusion or whatever, that he/she
> is experiencing. It means temporarily living in his/her life,
> moving about in it delicately without making judgments,
> sensing meanings of which he/she is scarcely aware, but
> not trying to uncover feelings of which the person is totally
> unaware, since this would be too threatening. It includes
> communicating your sensings of his/her world as you look
> with fresh and unfrightened eyes at elements of which the
> individual is fearful. It means frequently checking with
> him/her as to the accuracy of your sensings, and being
> guided by the responses you receive. . . . To be with
> another in this way means that for the time being you lay
> aside the views and values you hold for yourself in order
> to enter another's world without prejudice. In some sense
> it means that you lay aside your self and this can only be
> done by a person who is secure enough in himself that he
> knows he will not get lost in what may turn out to be the
> strange or bizarre world of the other, and can comfortably
> return to his own world when he wishes.[13]

The empathic helper is aware of the client's private, inner world of perceptions, conscious and blocked feelings, and the meanings ascribed to these perceptions and feelings. Empathy is at the heart of our helping work, for without the deep understanding it generates, we can't know what people need or how to assist them.

Note that Rogers's definition of empathy includes communicating your empathic understanding to the other person. For Rogers, empathy involves seeing the problems of the other person from his or her perspective, feeling them with him or her, and then delicately checking out the accuracy of your sensings by describing them to the other person. Thus, empathy requires both role taking and emotional responsiveness.

Empathy begins with listening. When asked to summarize the basic personality and professional requirements of a psychotherapist, renowned psychoanalyst Frieda Fromm-Reichmann said, "The psychotherapist must be able to listen."[14]

I like to think that as listeners we are always trying to get to the crux of what someone is saying. To do this, we must respond to the nonverbal and the verbal aspects of his or her message. Good listening requires absorbing the mood of the other, noticing a puzzled look, seeing a small sigh or a hand that becomes a fist. These nonverbal cues are often the best signals that good listening will be highly productive. There is a sense of poignancy or possibility in these moments, a sense that something important may emerge. Reputedly, Freud once summarized his therapy in a single word: *surprise*. Good listening leads to surprise—it is an enriching process of discovery for both participants.

Listening requires deep attention to our innermost experiences. Theodore Reik spoke of "listening with the third ear," emphasizing that our deepest understanding of the people we help draws upon our intuition as well as upon logic and inference.[15] This kind of intuitive listening is rooted in a genuine desire to know the inner experience of the other, and, as psychologist Robert Katz puts it, it "depends on the wish to be of loving service and a readiness to be lovingly touched by the sufferings of others."[16]

This is what listening is like for me. When clients discuss emotional issues with me and seek understanding and involvement, I direct all my energies to the tasks of listening and responding to them. I begin by focusing my attention on exactly what my client has been saying. What words is he or she using? Are there any feelings explicitly or implicitly being communicated in this message? I take the message in and replay it inside myself, mentally taking his or her position and thinking what it would be like to say or feel this. For example, if I hear a self-defeating statement, I take it inside and feel the pain that goes with viewing oneself that way.

I might also see a connection between this current message and something shared with me at an earlier time. In this way, previous conversations inform my understanding and deepen the quality of my "what this is like for him or her" approximation. In a way, I take the feelings inside me (a kind of identification) and then relate to them, with my own feelings and my understanding of them resonating with this internalized other.[17]

Then there is a phase when I step back from this inner dialogue and try to make sense of—and give words to—what is occurring. This is a more analytic phase; perhaps it is the "detached" component of detached concern, as discussed in chapter 2.

When my clients rush from one topic to another, I try to return us to the present moment by reflecting my current understanding of what they are communicating. As I attempt to accurately capture some of their inner reactions, they take my reflected message and check it against their internal sense of what they are saying. If my message fits for them, they move forward in their experiencing. In a way, I am facilitating a deepening of their own empathy with themselves.

One way of describing this is that you are helping the person to experience his or her experience more fully. This sounds like a tautology, but it makes good psychological sense. When we have problems, we feel stuck. Some aspects of our inner reactions are felt as unacceptable or "not me," and we are hesitant to disclose or even acknowledge these parts of ourselves.

A deep sense of empathy can enable us to truly inhabit our experiences and thus free us to achieve a different orientation toward our feelings and to allow them to serve us in a more constructive fashion—in essence, to engage us in the process of change, as Leslie Greenberg and Jeremy Safran depict here:

> The process of acknowledging previously unacceptable feeling is experienced as a stamping of that feeling as OK, as mine, as legitimate, and almost desirable because it is what I'm experiencing. One feels a type of relief or recognition, "Oh, this is what it is"; allows it, "I feel really sad, lonely, ashamed, angry, or whatever"; and accepts it, "Yes, this is what I feel, and I accept this as part of my experience without censure or punishment." Often the feeling first accessed is pain, which has been assiduously avoided not only for fear of the pain itself, but of its meaning and of being out of control if I let in that experience. When one faces the pain, however, certain feelings and meanings emerge that had been previously avoided. Accepting these feelings as truly occurring tends to deepen the individual's awareness of what is occurring, and informs them of what they want, are missing, or wish for; that is, the feelings are information that tells them in a very direct fashion of their desires. The hitherto disclaimed is thus claimed as one's own.[18]

In these moments, empathy is not just an abstract understanding of the other's experiencing—it is part of a caring connection, part of feeling and being with the other. There is a sense of we-ness, a kind of communal orientation toward the other.[19] In Martin Buber's terms, you establish a kind of I-Thou relation with the other in which there is a sense of unity while at the same time a real separateness.[20] Other feelings that are not specific to the person you are helping are frequently part of this empathic process: warmth, tenderness, concern, and compassion. These sympathetic responses are also a vital part of the caring connection.

This caring connection is your most indispensable tool as a helper. It sustains and guides your helping and connects the deepest and best parts of yourself with the person you are helping. In this way, empathy and caring serve as a bridge between your innate altruism—your own humanity—and your helping. No matter what else you do for the suffering person, it will indeed be "twice blessed" if your actions are grounded in a compassionate understanding and experiencing of the other.

It might be useful for you to think of helping as analogous to driving a car. As psychologist Eugene Gendlin has observed, listening and empathy are like watching the road while you are driving.[21] You do lots of other things along the way, but if you take your eyes off the road, you can never get to where you are going, and you might have a major accident. When you are empathically attuned to the person you are helping, you will avoid making irreversible errors. Your helping will also be guided toward positive and creative directions, even in situations where you don't immediately perceive what the best direction to go is.

Here is one illustration of this point from my work as a helper: Pamela died 18 months ago. I was talking with her parents, Nick and Marge. Pamela died on their wedding anniversary and was buried on her mother's 60th birthday. Nick and Marge were telling me that their anniversary can never again be a happy day. Marge doubted that she could ever feel happy again; the thought of being reunited with Pamela in heaven was her only respite from the pain of losing her beloved daughter.

I was Pamela's counselor during her treatment for Hodgkin's disease. Her cancer returned on the eve of her 2-year remission milestone. Sadder still, the recurrence was diagnosed 2 weeks before her long-awaited wedding. She and her fiance decided to go ahead with the wedding anyway.

I loved Pamela and her incredible fighting spirit. I still grieve for her. And I felt Nick and Marge's deep pain. As I listened to them, I recalled conversations with Pamela about life and about her relationship with her parents. I remembered the deep feelings of love she expressed for her parents.

In the midst of our conversation, I began to tell Marge and Nick what Pamela had said. This wasn't a carefully planned intervention, and I don't know why I remembered these conversations from several years earlier. I had tears in my eyes as I spoke. I felt like a messenger delivering a gift from someone far away. I saw the pain on their faces ease, the guilt they felt about not having done enough lessen. Their healing moved one small step forward.

EMPATHIZING WITH YOURSELF

There has been considerable debate concerning the origins of empathy and whether or not it is a skill that can be taught. The most accepted conclusion is that the skill of communicating our empathic understanding of our clients can definitely be taught and that our capacity to be empathic can be enhanced through different kinds of experiential learning.

Much of our everyday empathizing involves responding to others' anxiety, anger, depression, and other forms of emotional distress that result when separation and loss threaten the relatedness and attachments that are so vital to everyone's well-being.[22] Consequently, our capacity for empathy is rooted in our own emotional knowledge of loss. This kind of knowledge is an unavoidable part of the human condition, but some individuals are better schooled than others, as psychiatrist Alberta Szalita observes:

> But it is perhaps through personal suffering that we learn
> most about empathy. . . . Suffering is not a guest we have
> to invite; it comes unasked and may even become an
> inseparable companion. Suffering per se does not lead to
> wisdom, as some people maintain. Wisdom is more readily
> acquired when we gradually emancipate ourselves from
> narcissistic preoccupations. Empathy becomes more
> accessible as we come to grips with fears of death.
> Confrontations with sorrow, grief, and bereavement are
> always painful, but often engender a more compassionate
> attitude toward others and a commitment to life. It little
> matters how imaginary or insignificant are the concerns
> we confront in ourselves or others. One person may react
> to petty grievances as intensely as another person reacts
> to a great tragedy. The test of one's empathy is the
> capacity to relate to the sensitivity of the sufferer rather
> than to the magnitude of the misfortune.[23]

Rilke might have had this idea in mind when he wrote the following words:

Do not believe that he who seeks to comfort you lives
untroubled among the simple and quiet words that
sometimes do you good. His life has much difficulty and
sorrow and remains far behind yours. Were it otherwise, he
would never have been able to find those words.[24]

Our sensitivity to others reflects how we relate to our own loss
and pain. Empathy requires that we find the courage to look openly
and courageously, as Rogers noted, "with fresh and unfrightened
eyes at elements of which the individual is fearful," in moments when
the reminders of our own pain can push us toward avoidance or into
the Helper's Pit. Another way of saying this is that if we listen in an
open and compassionate way, we help our clients become friendlier
toward their inner lives.

In a captivating clinical case history, child psychoanalyst Selma
Fraiberg and her colleagues illustrate how we cannot hear the pain of
another until we have listened to our own.[25] A 5-month-old infant,
Mary, was showing dramatic signs of lack of care: She rarely smiled,
showed little interest in the outside world, and, even when she was
suffering, didn't reach out for her mother. Mrs. March, described by
others as a "rejecting mother," was depressed and "seemed locked
away in some private terror, remote, removed."[26] Mrs. March would
make only minimal efforts to comfort Mary while Mary screamed
hopelessly and the clinicians looked on incredulously. The therapists
quickly framed the key diagnostic question as "Why doesn't this
mother hear her baby's cries?"

In the therapy sessions with Mrs. March, her troubled childhood
and feelings of abandonment and not being heard and loved emerged
very quickly. The grief and intolerable pain were approached over
and over again, with a guiding clinical hypothesis that when the
mother's own cries were heard she would hear her child's cries. Soon
something remarkable began to happen between the mother and
her baby:

As Mrs. March began to take the permission to remember
her feelings, to cry, and to feel... comfort and sympathy
... we saw her make approaches to her baby in the midst
of her own outpourings. She would pick up Mary and hold
her, at first distant and self-absorbed, but holding her. And
then, one day, still within the first month of treatment, Mrs.
March, in the midst of an outpouring of grief, picked up
Mary, held her very close, and crooned to her in a
heart-broken voice. And then it happened again, and
several times in the next sessions. An outpouring of old

griefs and a gathering of the baby into her arms. The
ghosts in the baby's nursery were beginning to leave. . . .
Within four months Mary became a healthy, more
responsive, often joyful baby.[27]

Later in the treatment, Mrs. March revealed the origins of much
of her suffering: Her father had exhibited himself to her when she was
a child, and she had been sexually molested by a cousin. She confronted these issues during therapy, and when her therapy ended
both she and her daughter seemed to have a promising future free of
the terrible pain that had nearly destroyed them.

This is a pattern we see often in helping: The ability to care
for oneself is made possible by the experience of caring and valida-
tion in the helping relationship. Feeling cared for and valued in the
helping relationship leads to a new sense of self and of the world—
something like "I am a lovable and worthy human being, and there
are people in the world who are sensitive to me."[28] When Mrs. March
felt the therapists' caring, she could begin to care for herself, and this
in turn allowed her attachment to her daughter to blossom. There is
a message here for us as helpers. If we can't reach in to ourselves
with love and acceptance, we can't reach out to others with caring
and compassion.

RESPECT

Mrs. March had her worth as a person restored during the course of
counseling. Another way of saying this is that her self-esteem improved dramatically. Almost everyone who seeks help faces different
kinds of threats to self-esteem. We have already seen the central role
self-esteem plays in the stress response. Self-esteem is also an important dimension within every helping relationship.[29]

Clients confirm this, saying the most important condition for
them is that they feel liked or respected.[30] There are many different
words that are roughly interchangeable for respect and self-esteem
enhancement—*warmth, positive regard, interest,* and *rapport.* Your
undivided attention and empathy enhance self-esteem because they
say to clients that "you and your feelings are worth making this effort
to understand you."

You also enhance your clients' self-esteem and communicate respect by conveying acceptance and warmth and by affirming each
client's uniqueness and capacity to solve his or her problems.[31] True
respect means that we never lose sight of the dignity of the person
we are helping. This moment of precious dialogue between a caregiver and an elderly dying man captures the essence of respect:

Man: Why do you continue to hold my hand and listen?

Caregiver: Just to get the blessing of one more of your smiles.

Man: Thank you—I am glad I still have value.

In one study reported by Rogers, an experimenter used a gal-
vanic skin response (GSR) measure to record threatened reactions of
clients in response to variations in some therapists' degrees of acceptance. Whenever the therapists' attitudes changed even slightly
in the direction of less acceptance, their clients showed a dramatic
increase in the number of abrupt GSR changes, a sign of anxious or
threatened reactions.[32]

It is difficult to trust and be open with a stranger, to share problems and overcome the distress-disclosure dilemma.[33] The mere acceptance of help can represent a threat to one's self-esteem because
it can suggest a sense of inferiority and dependence. Although these
emotional realities can interfere with helping, at the same time their
predictable presence almost guarantees the success of certain interventions early in a newly formed helping relationship.

As the helper, you can often get things off to a productive and
positive start by complimenting a new client for his or her courage
and assertiveness in seeking help. I often say, "Just asking for help is
a very positive step that you've already taken." If appropriate, you
can ask how having this problem makes the person feel about himself
or herself, and thus you can begin to look together at the self-esteem
issues that inevitably accompany unsuccessful efforts to solve life's
problems. This kind of intervention can rapidly deepen the client's
level of self-exploration.

Asking your clients to tell you about their past successes and
about positive personal qualities such as perseverance can enhance
their self-esteem. You can always point to something an individual is
doing right even when things are going poorly. I often point out how
much a particular family member cares for his or her loved ones: "This
is why coping is so difficult, because you care so much" or "It really
matters to you that you do a good job because you care so much."

There will be times when your ability to appreciate and respect
the people you help is severely strained. Not everyone is the kind of
person you feel a natural closeness to, but in these situations, where
it is difficult to side with the other person, your empathy can still inspire and guide your helping.

AUTHENTICITY: BEING YOURSELF

Learning how to be yourself is one of the greatest challenges you face
as a helper. If you don't play at roles, and you are real, honest, and

authentic in your helping relationships, you will have more success and less stress as a caregiver.

The idea that being yourself as a helper can reduce your stress may seem somewhat counterintuitive. Isn't the detached helper who stays in a safe and distant role less likely to burn out than the helper who acts more authentically and is more personally involved in caregiving? The truth is that helping is more stressful if you aren't authentic and are missing the sense of spontaneity and personal discovery that can be part of the helping experience. We have seen how distancing oneself as a helper has the paradoxical effect of increasing stress (see chapters 2 and 3). That same dynamic is at work here. Your helping is also more stressful because you are denying it the greatest single instrument of healing at your disposal—yourself.

Personal self-disclosure is a major component of being genuine. People want their helpers to be both skilled and human, professional and vulnerable, competent and caring.[34] Now you are probably thinking, "Just how open should I be? Does this mean I express my thoughts and feelings on everything the client is talking about?" No, it doesn't. I will say more about appropriate and inappropriate self-disclosure in the next chapter, but the general rule is that you don't want to shift your attention to yourself at the expense of the person you are helping.

Self-disclosures are usually helpful because they demonstrate that you are a real person involved in a real relationship with the person you are helping. I often find it useful to share how I am feeling at a particular moment. For example, I might be feeling sad because of someone's loss or angry at their victimization. I might also be feeling scared, confused, or excited. Self-disclosures create a kind of two-way intimacy that can have powerful benefits. But many kinds of self-disclosures should only be communicated after considerable trust and rapport are established.

FLEXIBILITY

Flexibility is another key attribute of the effective caregiver. This dimension was identified by Ruth Hyman and Pierre Woog, who studied a sample of helping professionals including nurses, nursing supervisors, administrators, educators, psychologists, aides, and social workers. They administered measures of eight personality variables thought to be characteristic of competent helpers and found that their data analyses yielded a single factor, which they labeled flexibility.

The flexible helper, according to the researchers, "thrives in the complex and ambiguous, is governed more by internal cues rather than rules or authority, has a searching experimental orientation, and is basically freeing rather than controlling."[35] They elaborate on the nonauthoritarian features of the flexible helper:

> Perhaps the most important characteristic of an effective helper is the ability to be freeing rather than controlling. The helper must be able to sit back and watch the helpee try a solution that may not work. Helpers must care enough for their helpees to allow them to develop their own way of doing things separate from the values of the helper. The helper cannot impose self as an authority and cannot be oriented toward rules and regulations or place too much value on order, procedures, custom, or tradition. All of these may impede openness, which implies ability to perceive reality without applying preconceived categories.[36]

When you are open to the reality of the person you assist, your empathy will be more accurate and creative, and you will help that person tell his or her—not your—story and grow in the direction he or she chooses.[37]

Being flexible also means knowing that you can't solve every problem or have an answer to every question that you encounter as a helper. Most veteran helpers know this, but this awareness doesn't lead to feelings of helplessness or to being overly anxious or defensive. Instead, they recognize that at these times they must be honest, let their intuition guide them, and, above all, communicate their intention to continue caring for the person they are helping.

The following story, shared by hospice worker Susan Johnson, illustrates the value of flexibility, empathy, and faith in yourself and in the people you care for:

> It was my third day of working at North Hospice. I was feeling totally overwhelmed, learning about bereavement assessment forms, monthly statistics, and the importance of documentation, when we admitted a new patient to our unit. She was a 27-year-old woman, comatose after an unsuccessful brain surgery. Many of her family members were present, so Jon, our chaplain, and I went to her room to introduce ourselves and offer our support. We learned that Karen, the patient, had three children. I offered whatever words of wisdom came to me, about being here to be of assistance to children, and if they had any concerns, to be sure to ask. In this new position as "Family

Support Coordinator," I had been hired not only for bereavement care, but also to begin to develop support for children. Connie, the director of our program, described the position as "evolving," and she said that what our support for children would be was yet to be discovered. So it seemed appropriate that I would offer my assistance to this family with children.

I had much to learn yet and went back to the mountain of forms and notebooks I needed to figure out for my orientation in this new job. Little time had passed before Joyce, Karen's sister, popped her head into the doorway of my office and asked if she could talk with me about Carrie, Karen's 8-year-old daughter. Carrie lived with Joyce and had more than her share of problems in her short life. Carrie had been in the hospital to see her mother the day before and had left the room crying hysterically. Joyce had questioned the child psychologist Carrie was working with about what to do and was told to talk with us at hospice, that we were the "experts" in dealing with death. Joyce was beside herself and asked if she could bring Carrie in to see me the next day. Without hesitating, I said, "Of course."

That answer came from within my heart. When my head kicked in, I wondered what in the world I was doing! This was my very first week working in hospice. I'd never been around anyone who was dying. I'd never even seen anyone in a coma before this day. And I wasn't an "expert." But I couldn't have not been there for that child. I stopped to think of what I did have. I did have some experience being with people in their pain. Five years of working as a spiritual director had given me that. I'd worked with children enough to know that they were so wise, and that *they* taught *me* what I needed to know to be able to help them. And I had my faith.

The next day, driving into the hospital, I prayed. It was a simple prayer. I asked that Carrie would tell me what she needed and that I would hear it.

When Joyce and Carrie arrived at hospice, we sat down to talk. I introduced myself and "Spinoza" (the stuffed bear with a tape recorder in his belly) to Carrie and told her we had come to help the kids. I asked her to tell me about herself and learned that she was quite anxious about school starting while she was so worried about her mom. We figured out together that it might help if Joyce talked to her teacher about Carrie's concern. I noticed her visible relief and made a mental note that my prayer was being answered so far.

I plunged ahead and asked her what she thought would happen with her mom. She told me her mom was going to die. In the conversation that followed, I learned that she didn't think her mom could hear her and that she wanted to tell her good-bye. I told her even though her mom was in a coma and couldn't see her or talk to her that she may well be able to hear her and even feel her touch. I asked her if she wanted to go see her mom now. She said she did and asked if she could carry Spinoza and if I would go with her.

It was a long walk down that hall for both of us, but we held hands. As we entered Karen's room, Carrie's grandmother very wisely suggested that all the other family members leave the room so that Carrie could have her time alone with her mom. Carrie and I approached Karen, and I asked Carrie if she would like to hold her mom's hand. She did. She told her mom what was in her heart, that she loved her, that Mom was going to go to heaven to take care of Sally (a baby who had died earlier), and she said good-bye. Then she was done. I asked Carrie if she wanted to give her mom a kiss, and she did.

As we left the room, Carrie asked if she could listen to one of Spinoza's tapes. I took her back to my office and let her choose a tape. She chose "the pink one," which just happened to be the one entitled "Hold Onto Me." Spinoza is designed for seriously ill or dying children. The series of tapes that comes with him provides little songs and stories of love, hope, and courage. The tape Carrie happened to choose was about the dying process. The little song and story offered her assurance that it would be a safe journey. Spinoza's message was comforting and reassuring. Carrie listened to the tape, and now, believing that her mother could hear, took Spinoza into her mother's room, placed him on her pillow beside her head, and played the tape for her mother to hear.

The family asked to use the tape for Karen's funeral. I was truly amazed at how simple it had been for a little girl to change from a hysterical "problem" one day to a sad but confident little girl the next day, able to say good-bye, help her mom die, and proudly make a significant contribution to her mom's funeral. Carrie was her own "expert." All I needed was to have the courage to listen to her and to be with her. It's a lesson I will always remember.

After it was all over, I sat down at my desk, still covered with the mountains of paper, and marvelled at what had just transpired. Then I cried tears of absolute awe. I knew in that instant why I was there. I was profoundly grateful for the gifts of courage and faith I'd been given, for the sake of helping Carrie.[38]

MUTUAL PARTICIPATION

The kind of empowering qualities that can make an 8-year-old girl into an "expert" are most likely to flourish in a helping relationship distinguished by mutuality. However, not all helping relationships can be characterized this way. Psychiatrist Thomas Szasz and Marc Hollender have described three basic models of helping relationships, and only one, the mutual participation relationship, has these qualities.[39] Although they concern physician-patient interactions, these models can be applied to any caregiving relationship.

According to Szasz and Hollender, in the activity-passivity relationship, the patient's contribution is small, and the physician's is paramount. The physician does something *to* the passive patient (e.g., he or she administers anesthesia or treats a severe injury). The relationship resembles that of a parent and a helpless infant.

In the guidance-cooperation relationship, the physician tells the patient what to do, and the patient essentially obeys. This type of relationship is common when the clinical problem is something like an acute infection. The patient has more opportunity and likelihood of involvement than in the activity-passivity scenario but is still expected to follow whatever orders are given. If he or she doesn't do so, strong persuasion can be brought to bear by the physician. This model has its prototype in the parent-adolescent relationship.

In the mutual participation relationship, the physician helps the patient to help himself or herself, and the patient is a participant in a partnership that makes use of the expert help of the physician. The relationship is that of one adult to another—human being to human being—and is predicated on a belief in equality. This type of relationship is most appropriate for the management of chronic illnesses and for interventions with psychosocial problems such as grief and loss, where the goals are to mobilize and support the individual.

Of course, in different circumstances each of these kinds of relationships is appropriate, but in the modern world, where complex medical decisions that must be made by patients and families, chronic illnesses, and difficult psychosocial problems are the rule, helping relationships based on equality and mutual participation are usually most effective.

DIRECTIVENESS, CONTROL, AND RESPONSIBILITY IN HELPING

Who is really responsible for change in the helping relationship? What kind of control and direction should you as a helper provide? What are your basic assumptions about these important dimensions of the helping relationship?

As we have seen, a helping relationship based on mutual participation implies a less directive and controlling style of involvement by the helper. This relinquishment of control by the helper has the paradoxical effect of restoring control to the person being helped. That new sense of control can be a powerful antidote to the loss of control that most people feel during negative and stressful life events. Loss of control is perhaps the central experience of dying and grieving persons; it is not surprising that the common purpose of most of our interventions is to restore a sense of control to the people we are helping.

It is important to clarify that there are many situations where you as the helper *do* solve the problem in the sense that you provide a medication, share some specific information, teach a skill, or massage a sore back. This kind of active assistance is necessary and vital in caregiving; sometimes it is all that is needed. But when we look at emotional difficulties, interpersonal dilemmas, treatment decisions, and other psychosocial problems, the appropriateness of the patient as problem-solver becomes more clear-cut. Here, even though you are active and may even teach skills or offer educational input, the responsibility for change remains with the client.

The ancient Chinese proverb "Give a man a fish, he has one meal; teach him to fish, he can eat for the rest of his life" is a good rationale for this nondirective approach. The helper with a directive and controlling style is always giving people answers and ideas (i.e., giving them the fish). The nondirective helper teaches people to fish by helping them find their own answers and by teaching them problem-solving skills they can use in the future. Educating people about their illnesses or disorders, training them in specific therapeutic techniques, and urging them to participate directly in the treatment, management, and prevention of their conditions are all examples of teaching people to fish.

A problem-solving intervention program for cancer patients developed by psychologists Harry Sobel and William Worden illustrates the use of a skills-training approach in the medical field. This portable, self-contained program consists of a manual, problem-solving cards, and four audiotapes. It provides cancer caregivers with a practical method for helping patients deal more effectively with typical psychosocial concerns, such as sexual problems, interpersonal isolation, and communication with health professionals. Sobel and Worden state that they chose a problem-solving, cognitive-behavioral orientation because of its "short-term structure, here-and-now focus, emphasis on psychotherapy as a learning or psycho-educational experience, and an attitude which promotes the value of patient self-control, collaboration with the clinician, and responsibility for health."[40]

Taking a nondirective approach as a helper requires a basic confidence in other human beings because without a deep belief in the people you are helping you can't remain optimistic that they will move in a positive direction. If you hold a cynical view of other people and tend to see their bad choices and life problems as reflecting fundamental flaws in human nature, a more authoritarian and directive helping style may seem warranted (i.e., you think you have to save people from themselves).

Many theorists have described a belief in a self-actualizing tendency in all humans as the basis for a more optimistic view. Here, Carl Rogers states this belief:

> The individual has within himself vast resources for
> self-understanding, for altering his self-concept, his
> attitudes, and his self-directed behavior—and . . . these
> resources can be tapped if only a definable climate of
> facilitative psychological attitudes can be provided.[41]

Besides having this inherent tendency toward growth and self-actualization, people also know more about the solutions to their problems than even they realize—certainly more than we often think they do. They know, but they don't know that they know.

Think of a time when you were on your way to the airport, and you suddenly knew—with absolute certainty—that you had forgotten something, but you weren't sure exactly what it was that you had forgotten. You would wager your life savings that you had forgotten something, yet you couldn't remember what it was.[42] At times like these, we might stop and review our packing routine and hope that we can remember the item. Checking inside to discover what we have forgotten is similar to what we all go through when we are solving a problem. We check inside, and gradually the many facets of the problem come into awareness. The actions we need to take can also become clear to us. There is often a sense of relief that comes even before we take these actions—just knowing what we need brings some comfort. Eugene Gendlin calls this inner release a "body shift."[43] We can then decide when and how to take action in the world.

To successfully facilitate this inner problem solving, we must believe in the wisdom of the total organism, the mind and the body, the conscious and the unconscious self. Goethe said, "Just trust yourself, then you will know how to live."[44] Much of our journey as helpers is learning to trust ourselves and helping others to trust themselves.

I find it helpful to think of the appropriate helping stance as one of controlled nondirection.[45] You want your efforts to be freeing and facilitating rather than manipulative, but you also want to exert significant control over the helping process. To achieve this twofold goal, you can be directive with regard to the *process* of helping but nondirective with regard to the *content* of helping. In other words, you can influence the helping interaction by structuring the conversation, by jointly defining what the problem is and how your client can begin to solve it, and by focusing and deepening his or her experiencing. But you are also nondirective in that you exert little control over what your client says or does. As much as possible, you respond to the forward-moving process and inner reactions of your client rather than having him or her respond to your ideas and frame of reference.

This controlled nondirection is reflected in the kinds of communication skills you use. By using less directive interventions, like paraphrases, reflections of feeling, and self-disclosures (see chapter 6), you can provide structure without taking the initiative and control away from your client.

If people have a sense of responsibility over the outcomes in their lives, they are more likely to succeed in their goals. Instilling this sense of responsibility and an expectation of success is a key ingredient in the helping process. Another good reason to adopt this helping philosophy is that it relieves you of the debilitating burden of the misguided belief that you are responsible for solving all the problems of the people you help.

I learned something about how to do this for the people I help from my professor and mentor, the late Sheldon Korchin. Shelly had polio as a child living in New York City. Franklin Delano Roosevelt, himself a polio victim, was governor of New York State then. On weekends, he took Shelly and other children with disabilities on river outings. The children rowed the boats, and, with Roosevelt's inspiration, they were able to expand their visions of what they could accomplish in life. I don't know what happened to the other children, but Shelly went on to lead an inspiring and dynamic life, and he became a luminary in clinical psychology. As one of my professors who taught me therapeutic skills, Shelly told me that he often said to his psychotherapy clients, "I can help you steer the boat, but you have to pull the oars." Shelly never mentioned this connection himself, but I think that as he encouraged his clients to pull the oars in their lives and to overcome their hardships, he was sharing the lesson he learned from Roosevelt: If we take responsibility for improving our lives, no disability can prevent us from achieving our dreams. I often share this metaphor with the people I help.

There is an element of paradox in this stance of controlled nondirection. We need to inspire people to take responsibility, to pull the oars in their own lives, but at the same time, we shouldn't try to tell them what to do. Lao-tzu expressed this paradox in the following saying:

> If I keep from meddling with people, they take care
>   of themselves,
> If I keep from commanding people, they behave
>   themselves,
> If I keep from preaching at people, they improve
>   themselves,
> If I keep from imposing on people, they become
>   themselves.

A similar perspective is reflected in this passage from Zen master Shunryu Suzuki's *Zen Mind, Beginner's Mind:*

> The best way to control people is to encourage them to
> be mischievous. Then they will be in control in its wider
> sense. To give your sheep or cow a large, spacious
> meadow is the way to control him. So it is with people:
> first let them do what they want, and watch them. This is
> the best policy. To ignore them is not good; that is the
> worst policy. The second worst is trying to control them.
> The best one is to watch them, just to watch them, without
> trying to control them.[46]

This orientation is part of the modern outlook that encourages us to be advocates for the people we care for and to do everything possible to involve them in their own care. The emphasis is on the "activated" patient, who, like Norman Cousins, knows about his or her disease, looks at the medical chart, and is a full participant in any treatment decisions.[47] This image is in sharp contrast with that of the "good patient" of several decades ago, who was compliant, unassertive, and did what he or she was told.

The problem is that many helpers have discovered that a more egalitarian relationship is not always easy to manage. It is often much simpler to have people just follow instructions and not ask too many questions about what you are doing and why you are doing it. The litigious atmosphere of our times can also fuel this ambivalence toward the activated patient. If you are a health care worker, what is your first reaction to "May I see my chart?" Most likely, it isn't "Wonderful, I'm glad you're so involved" but rather something more like "Oh boy, did we chart everything accurately?" or "What's she been told?"

Adopting a nondirective stance as a helper is also difficult because it requires us to relinquish some of the gratification that comes from giving our clients *our* answers to their problems and from being seen in the flattering light of advice giver. The best helpers get little recognition for much of the good that they do.

An emphasis on personal responsibility presents yet another kind of challenge to us as caregivers. Encouraging a responsible approach to the future without promoting blame for creating the problem can be a difficult task in a culture like ours, where responsibility and blame are so deeply intertwined in our everyday thought and language. This dilemma is particularly apparent in work with people with cancer. The popular press and some professionals have been presenting the view that one's attitudes and personality traits play a key role in the onset and course of cancer. When told that their thoughts and feelings probably had these kinds of negative effects, patients tend to blame themselves and think, "I caused my cancer." In other words, they assume that they are bad or wrong for having done this to themselves.[48]

As a counselor to people with cancer, I practice a kind of "deresponsibilitization," in which I deemphasize the notion of blame while simultaneously accenting personal responsibility for doing everything possible to enhance total well-being in the future.[49] I also stress that positive coping and the communication of suffering are not mutually exclusive.

One common and unfortunate consequence of the popularization of psychological theories of cancer is that people with cancer conclude that the anxiety and other emotional distress they experience must not be revealed to others. In other words, highly distressed cancer patients might be reluctant to share their suffering with helpers and family because it would reveal that they weren't coping very well and were "making themselves sick again." Ironically, the work of inhibiting the expression of these feelings adds to the stress of the illness. It is important to explain to people that the expression of these difficult feelings is a normal and healthy response to their situation. This approach gives them permission to feel their feelings—both good and bad—and to develop more positive coping strategies.

Philip Brickman and his colleagues have studied attributions of responsibility for problems and solutions and by distinguishing these have arrived at distinct models of coping and helping.[50] In what they call the moral model, people are held responsible for both problems and solutions and are believed to need only the motivation to help themselves. In the compensatory model, people are seen as not responsible for problems but as responsible for solutions, and they are believed to need power to solve these problems.

Brickman's compensatory model is highly compatible with a nondirective, mutual participation approach to helping. According to him and his colleagues, the spirit of this model is that people are deprived or suffering not as a result of their own deficiencies but because their environment has failed to provide them with the resources necessary to prevent the problem they are experiencing. A simple example of what working within the compensatory model looks like is reflected in the helper question "How can I help you?" rather than the statement "Do what I say."[51] People are not blamed for their problems, and rather than focusing on personal deficiencies, attention is given to making adequate resources available so that they can arrive at their own solutions.

The compensatory model is an encouraging approach because it avoids lowering one's self-esteem and empowers the individual to solve his or her own problems. Jerome Frank recognized the importance of this dimension in helping when he said that the central tasks of psychotherapy are to restore a sense of mastery to the demoralized person and to counter the feelings of impotence and isolation that are so prevalent in our modern world.[52] Reassurance and encouragement can reduce a client's fear and anxiety, and promote positive coping. And if patients do not get well, they can still be reassured that they won't be deprived of the necessary pain medications and won't be emotionally abandoned.[53]

Strengthening the support systems of the people you help is another key aspect of effective, empowering interventions. Most people facing major losses and other negative life events feel the need to talk about the event and their reactions to it with others. The Schachter studies examined in chapter 4 demonstrated that people tend to seek companionship when faced with an aversive experience. However, family and friends are often ambivalent about these efforts to reach out to them. They can often become upset by the suffering of their loved ones and respond by getting angry or attacking the patient (fight), avoiding the topic or the individual (flight), or not making any response. Faced with these unpleasant and unsupportive responses, and feeling rejected and increasingly self-critical, the distressed person can withdraw from others and conceal his or her suffering. The dynamics of self-concealment and avoidance lead to a further lowering of self-esteem as the person thinks, "If I have to conceal this, it must be because my reactions aren't normal."[54]

This is why it can be so important and helpful to ask distressed people how they might be keeping their suffering from others. I find it most effective to ask them first how they feel about their ability to cope and to listen carefully for critical thoughts like "I should be doing better by now" or "I expected to be a bit further along at this time." This kind of self-reproach is usually accompanied by the concealment of suffering and by social isolation. Then I assess their levels of social support. Are they part of a community? Who offers them assistance? Whom have they confided in? Whom could they confide in? How can I help create or strengthen their social support resources? How can I foster additional companionship that will make their lives easier?

In our best moments as helpers, we encourage clients to look inside for the wisdom to make healthy choices, we invite them to take responsibility for their lives without the onus of self-blame, and we support an openness to additional support from their community. To do this, we must resist our impulses to provide them with all the answers, to point out what they are doing wrong, and to single-handedly meet all their needs. These principles are the foundation for successful and empowering helping relationships.

CONCLUSION

In a thoughtful and humorous article, Quentin Rae-Grant describes the art of being a failure as a consultant.[55] His guidelines for ensuring failure as a consultant are equally applicable to other kinds of helping and are consistent with this chapter's suggestions for ensuring success, only presented in reverse form. To guarantee failure, says Rae-Grant, simply present yourself as knowing all the answers; ignore the client's ideas, desires, and goals; insist upon complete reliance on your authority as expert; and have lots of hidden agendas. Above all, he argues tongue-in-cheek, if you want to prevent success, avoid the development of a warm, trusting, and empathic relationship.

When we avoid these and other pitfalls in our helping relationships, a different scenario unfolds, one in which we can clearly see the value of our efforts:

> We continually get phone calls from people who don't know what to do. They call me as a last resort when they find they have nowhere else to turn. In many cases there is nothing we can do either—but invariably I hear "Thank you—you've helped so much—you're the first one who has listened and understood."

> I received a nurses' day card which said, "Thanks for allowing me the opportunity to grow and all that you have taught me. Thanks for being there."

> A terminal patient with paralyzed vocal chords whispered to his son in his native tongue that he wanted me to come spend time with him anytime. I had been uncomfortable with the communication problems and cultural differences, and I was not sure that I was being effective. It made me feel very good to know he valued my presence.

> I gave time and presence and a caring heart to a child who was not permitted to grieve the suicide death of her very close uncle. The transformation of this intensely sobbing child into a giggling, alive 6-year-old was profound and sacred.

This chapter has identified the qualities of helpers and helping relationships that lead to successful and rewarding outcomes like these. But what does empathy look like? What, specifically, does a helper do to convey respect or to develop an empowering helping relationship? The next chapter will attempt to demystify the art of helping and identify the specific communication skills that are the vehicles for putting our compassion to work.

6

*When I say that I enjoy hearing someone, I
mean, of course, hearing deeply. I mean that
I hear the words, the thoughts, the feeling
tones, the personal meaning, even the
meaning that is below the conscious intent
of the speaker. Sometimes too, in a message
which superficially is not very important, I
hear a deep human cry that lies buried
and unknown far below the
surface of the person.[1]*

Carl Rogers

Healing Words: Communication Skills for Helping

Our helping reflects, first of all, who we are. Our personal experiences, attitudes, and beliefs all contribute to the quality of the helping relationships we establish. The distinguishing qualities of successful helpers—sensitivity to the distress of others, flexibility, genuineness, empathy, respect—are not simply external behaviors that can be assumed at will. They are the product of a lifetime of experiences that shape us into the particular kinds of people and helpers that we are.

Your experiences, attitudes, and beliefs must be brought to life through your words and your actions to be healing (i.e., they must be communicated). The communication skills that make this possible set helping conversations apart from our everyday interactions and distinguish effective helpers from those who are less successful. These distinctive communication skills are the vehicles for expressing your caring and helping people solve their problems. If you don't have these skills, your helping actions can frustrate your helping motivations (e.g., you can be sensitive without being able to communicate this caring clearly to your clients). These skills are the focus of this chapter.

EXAMINING YOUR COMMUNICATION SKILLS

Before learning the communication skills presented in this chapter, it would be useful for you to take some time to look closely at your current communication style and habits. You can do this by audiotaping or videotaping an interaction with a friend or colleague. Tell the other person to talk about anything stressful or worrisome. Reassure him or her that no one else will hear or see the tape you make. You might even offer to give this friend the original copy of the tape after you complete your analysis of it. *Caution:* Don't conduct this interview as a role-play; only "real-plays" prepare you for the real world of helping. Save the tape and analyze it as you continue to read this chapter.

Here is a quick opportunity to look at your communication skills right now. Imagine that you have just walked into the hospital room of a young woman named Jenny, a 25-year-old cancer patient who is not responding well to her treatments. She turns to you and says:

> I'm just sick and tired of being some kind of guinea pig! All these damn drugs! My hair is falling out. I feel sick to my stomach. And what good is it gonna do? Everyone *knows* I'm not gonna get better! You don't know what it's like! You get to go home every day. I don't! I'm stuck here! You don't care, anyway! How could you? Just get out and leave me alone!

Now take a piece of paper and write down what you would say or do with Jenny if you were with her in real life.

Let's compare your response with those written by other caregivers who were presented with this vignette. One possible response might be to leave the room. Some helpers wrote that they would say, "I'll be back whenever you're ready to talk" or "Turn your light on when you want to talk." After all, this is what Jenny seems to be requesting. Still, simply to leave without responding to Jenny's implicit request for greater understanding and involvement wouldn't be very helpful to her. This distancing could also increase your stress level, as it did for this caregiver:

> When a patient is difficult to care for, belligerent, or states, "Get out of here—leave me alone"—I have sometimes done just that! I do only what I have to do for him and then tend to have limited contact with him. Later, though, I feel like I short-changed him and then I feel guilty, like I haven't done my best.

Like the nurses in the Stotland study (see chapter 2), this helper didn't know how to respond in a way that allowed her to stay in the room and maintain her caring connection with the patient. I believe that most of the U-turns made at the foot of the bed of dying patients result more from a lack of communication skills than from a lack of caring. That's why it is so important to identify and learn these skills.

Another caregiver suggested the possibility of ignoring Jenny's feelings and trying to turn her thoughts toward more pleasant topics:

> I can empathize with all you are saying and how you must
> be feeling. Let's try to think together about a very special
> day when something wonderful happened to you. Who did
> you share it with? What did you do? Was it a beautiful
> day? Try to remember and tell me!

This caregiver added that she would touch Jenny's hand as she said this. What would this response feel like if you were Jenny? Would you feel supported? Heard or not heard?

Jenny's anger could also pull you into the Helper's Pit, which could lead to responses like these:

> Jenny, I didn't make you sick. I can't help it that you are
> sick. But I care and want to help you cope the best way
> I know how.

> I know I don't know what you're going through, but I want
> to try to understand. *Can you help me?* [italics added]
> Someday I'll be facing death, too.

In this next response, the helper is detached but simultaneously demands greater involvement from Jenny:

> I am here to share your human condition. You can give me
> the privilege of doing that, or you can reject me. I think
> together, our sharing of your suffering will help us all. If
> you refuse, we both lose.

The irony here is that Jenny *is* sharing her human condition. The problem lies in the helper, who is threatened by Jenny's demand that she leave and can't communicate her caring in a way that earns her the right to stay in the room. Instead, she holds Jenny accountable for whether they "win" or "lose."

When we are threatened as helpers, we are prone to making defensive, falsely reassuring, and disrespectful responses such as:

> It's all part of your illness. Don't be so angry. It will only
> make you feel worse. You know that what we are doing
> for you is for your own good in the long run.

> You may feel awful now, but you'll eventually feel
> much better.

You must make the best of whatever time you have left. I
cannot tell you that I know how you feel—because I don't.
I will pray for you to accept.

In a similarly disrespectful kind of response, we find ourselves
saying, "I know" or "I understand":

I understand your feelings, but these treatments are
necessary for you to get well.

I know you feel that way. We shouldn't give up hope yet.

I know it isn't easy for you, but we're doing everything
possible to make it easier for you and hopefully help to
make you a little more comfortable.

These responses suggest that the helper is thinking, or is beginning
to think, that he or she knows more about Jenny than Jenny does. Few
messages are more likely to get you into trouble more quickly than
ones that begin with "I know how you feel" or "I understand." Helen
Perlman makes a strong case against the "I understand" helper
message:

There is probably no more annoying or even threatening
person than one who "understands" too quickly and too
deeply, before you have had a chance to get the words out
of your mouth, who reassures too swiftly because of his
sometimes erroneous assumption that you and he are on
the same wavelength. Such a person may often make a
quite different interpretation of what you said from what
you meant. Such a person may be quite sympathetic, bent
on making you feel better fast. But he is not empathic.[2]

Another variation on this theme is the "I know where you're going; let me take you there" stance. A more helpful alternative message is "I don't know where we're going, but I *do* know how to get
there."[3] This more accurately matches the reality of the situation,
and it also conveys your confidence in your ability to facilitate a
healthy and growth-producing relationship.

Sympathy—feeling *for* Jenny—is another useful response:

Jenny, I'm very sorry these things are happening to you.
I wish I could take all that away, but I can't.

Effective helpers can admit that they don't have any answers,
that they don't know what to do, that they don't understand—but

they also don't run away. They communicate that they care and won't abandon the person. Genuine and caring responses like the following ones can be extremely reassuring to someone in Jenny's predicament:

> I wish I had the answer for why you have to lie here
> and I get to go home at night, but I *do* care.

> I know this is tough. I don't have the answers, but I'm
> here for you.

Other helpers see their major task as problem solving:

> Jenny, you're right! I don't know how you feel, but you have
> choices. You can continue treatment and live here for as
> long as it takes, or you can stop treatment and go home
> to make each day a quality day for the rest of your life.

> You're right, I don't know what it's like. But I'd like to try
> to learn from you what I can try to do to make things
> more bearable.

These last two responses include somewhat premature problem-solving efforts, but both also include an elegant and disarming way of responding to Jenny's accusation that these helpers don't really know what it is like to be in her shoes. By saying to her, "You're right, I don't know," these responses neutralize her aggression and direct the interaction in a more constructive direction, similar to the way an aikido master disarms an opponent.[4] In the following responses, we see a kind of psychological aikido at work, plus some good empathy, personal sharing, and reassurance:

> I can hear how angry and frustrated you are. I've never
> been in your situation, but I'm sure I would feel the same
> way. I admire you for hanging in there despite how difficult
> it is.

> I don't understand everything you're feeling! But I
> understand that you're mad! I'd be mad, too! I just want
> you to know that if you need me, I'm here! Just to hold
> your hand, or yell at, or *anything!*

> I don't know what it's like to be in your situation, but
> I'm here and I'll do what I can to help.

> I know you're feeling bad, and there's no way I can
> understand it fully, but I want to be with you and hear
> what you have to say.

Each of these last four responses avoids the conflict and misunderstanding that would inevitably follow if the helpers had attempted to convince Jenny that they really know how she feels. This kind of exceptional knowledge is simply not possible, even if we have been in a similar predicament in our own lives. In *Zen and the Art of Helping,* social worker David Brandon explains why "I know how you feel" responses—even those based on similar life experiences—diminish our helping:

> "I know exactly how you feel" must be mistaken however
> good the intent of the speaker. How can it be possible
> to make any kind of accurate analogy, experiential or
> otherwise, between two persons' feelings, even about an
> apparently similar happening? When you tell me about the
> death of a friend, it is most probable that it is my pain I
> feel about the death of someone close to me. I cannot tell
> whether what moves inside my heart is similar to that
> which moves inside yours. I can share it but must be
> careful not to drown your grief and sorrow with my own.[5]

The final four caregiver responses also show that the helpers who made them are confident enough in themselves to admit that they don't really know what it is like to feel what Jenny feels and that they *do* go home at night. But they also care for Jenny and clearly communicate that caring.

Take another look at your response to Jenny. Did you stay in the room? Did you show that you heard her anger? Did you acknowledge that you don't know what it is like to be her or that you *do* get to go home? If you were Jenny, how would you react to your own response?

COMMUNICATION MICROSKILLS: TALK TOOLS FOR HELPING

Another way to look at your response to Jenny is to take a microskills approach, focusing on the specific communication skills you used, or didn't use, in the interaction. Did you respond with a question or a paraphrase of what Jenny said? Did you restate her feelings or disclose your own feelings or experiences? Did you give advice, make an interpretation, or stay silent? These possible responses can be considered communication microskills, or, as psychologist Gerald Goodman calls them, talk tools.[6] The emergence of the microskills approach to helping communication is an exciting recent development in the helping field. Pioneered by Goodman, Allen Ivey, and others, this approach looks at helping from the perspective of specific communication skills.[7]

The microskills approach to helper training is based on the detailed study of real-life helping encounters made possible by audio and video recording. These studies opened helping to public and research analysis and demystified the art of helping, making it a teachable, though complex, set of skills or competencies. Today, skills training programs teach the active ingredients of effective helping to ever-widening populations of professional, paraprofessional, and volunteer helpers.[8]

THE STAGES OF SKILL DEVELOPMENT

The word *skills* suffers from some rather ignoble associations. In our culture, skills are something you learn in the army, and training is something you do with your dog. However, skills are simply actions that are under your voluntary control, and learning them can be empowering and humanizing.[9]

Learning a new skill—whether it is empathic listening, problem solving, dancing, playing the violin, managing money, or being assertive—involves learning subskills, which are then hierarchically organized in the execution of the skill. Gerard Egan and Michael Cowan comment: "In the beginning, skills and models use the trainee, but with sufficient time for practice and application . . . the trainee begins to use the skills and models."[10]

A model of skill development that makes good psychological sense says that there are four stages in the acquisition of a skill.[11] Initially, there is a state of unconscious incompetence: We don't know what we don't know. For example, do you remember the first time you tried to drive a car with a clutch? As the car lurched forward for the fifth time, you probably had a surge of newfound admiration for the way your parents flawlessly operated this recalcitrant machine.

We are all at a stage of unconscious incompetence with many communication skills that could make us more effective as helpers. One reason for this is that our patterns of communicating have been strongly shaped by our social conditioning and are enacted automatically, with little awareness. How many questions have you asked today? How many self-disclosures have you made? Few of us are aware of the many communication microskills that we use every day. Yet these same patterns of communication significantly

affect the levels of intimacy we experience in our helping relationships and our general ability to achieve positive helping outcomes.
Because these communication patterns are largely outside our awareness, we can't map out alternate ways of responding and may feel
helpless and stuck at times.

Some prevalent communication patterns in our culture are an
overuse of questions and quick advice by listeners, an extremely
brief (1 second or less) pause between speakers, lots of verbal
crowding, and an absence of quality listening responses that sensitively restate what the other speaker has expressed. Carefully observe your own and others' conversations for the next week and see
whether you notice these or other patterns.

The problem for us as helpers is that these culturally conditioned patterns of communication are the exact reverse of the communication style demanded by the intimate encounters of the
helping relationship. For example, to be effective as a caregiver, we
must learn to ask fewer questions, give advice less quickly, allow
more time before we respond, and mirror the feelings and content
communicated by the people we are helping. When we begin to study
our everyday patterns of communication and attempt to change
them in our helping encounters, we enter the unsettling second stage
of skill development: conscious incompetence.

Conscious incompetence is a painful state in which the subskills
are not integrated and the learner is self-conscious and awkward.
This phenomenon is a generic characteristic of skill acquisition. Re-
turning to our driving example, in this stage you are fully aware of
your limitations as a driver but haven't begun to learn the skills necessary for smoothly shifting the gears.

The third stage is that of conscious competence. In this stage of
learning, you can execute the skill, but not without giving it your full
attention. To use our driving example, now you can shift, but you
can't talk with a passenger while you are doing so. With time and
practice, the component skills will require less and less conscious
attention, allowing you to devote increasing attention to higher level
strategies for achieving your goals. When we are at this stage in skill
acquisition, we can get so excited by the successful execution of the
skill in question that we lose our hold on what we are doing, and our
next response is significantly worse than our last one.

When a particular set of skills becomes automatic for you, you
have arrived at the final stage of skill acquisition: unconscious competence. The golf swing of Jack Nicklaus, the dancing of Ginger Rogers, and the therapeutic responses of Virginia Satir are all skillful
performances at this level, as is your performance behind the wheel
of your car. You already have many skills that you use competently

without thinking about what you are doing or why you are doing it; the skills are automatic, and you draw upon them as situations call for them.

With all the new communication skills you learn, the challenge is to make them your own and integrate them within your natural helping style. The goal isn't to become an obsessive imitation of the good helper and to make unauthentic, textbook responses. You need to discover what works best for you.

Remind yourself that becoming a master helper all at once simply isn't possible. Skillful performances must be broken down into their component microskills. Then the microskills have to be learned and practiced separately before they can be combined in the execution of the larger task. It is common for beginning helpers to observe an expert helper in action and immediately want to duplicate the expert's helping style. This seems possible to the neophyte only because he or she isn't aware of the many component skills that are a necessary part of the expert's performance. This state of unconscious incompetence ends abruptly when the neophyte attempts to imitate the expert, with much less effective results.

You can't learn all the skills you need all at once. But you can be encouraged by the knowledge that small, consistent changes in your communication style can lead to truly enormous changes in your helping relationships.[12]

THE IMPORTANCE OF PRACTICE

It has been said that a tourist in New York City once asked violinist Yehudi Menhuin for directions:

> Tourist: Excuse me, how do you get to Carnegie Hall?
>
> Menhuin: You practice! You practice! You practice!

No skill can be learned, refined, and truly grasped without repeated executions. This saying of Confucius expresses the idea well: "I hear and I forget. I see and I remember. I do and I understand." Yet we frequently stop practicing a skill when we can execute it successfully just once. The problem is that when that happens, the skill is still at the stage of conscious competence, and it will not be accessible to us in a wide range of situations with varying levels of complexity and demands. We can make the appropriate caring responses in an exercise with a peer, but put us in a room with a family, time pressure, and competing demands for our attention, and we will naturally revert to those behaviors most familiar to us.

This kind of skill regression can also occur when our emotional buttons are being pushed and we are feeling some pain. As we struggle to get out of the Helper's Pit, we usually attempt to regain control and find ourselves asking lots of questions, giving lots of advice, and sometimes making inappropriate self-disclosures.

In our analysis of the responses to Jenny, we began to identify some general principles for effective helping communication. I would now like to suggest some additional guidelines for successful communication in the intimate process of helping. But I need to acknowledge that writing on this topic is inherently risky. Any textbook solutions I might offer are at best mere guidelines for action in these difficult situations; at worst, they might lead to misapplications and failures. And, of course, I can only include a handful of the many skills that are necessary for effective communication. However, the following sections offer some suggestions you can experiment with.

NONVERBAL ATTENDING SKILLS

Much of helping communication is nonverbal—your posture, the tone of your voice, the look in your eyes, the touch of your hand. These nonverbal channels of communication are probably more important than verbal channels in determining what meaning others receive from our communications.[13] They play an important role in creating an experience of "being with" the person you are helping.

For empathy to develop, we must resist outside distractions and give the other person our deep, undivided attention. The way we attend to him or her plays an important role in fostering and maintaining quality attention. There is a saying that empathic listeners develop big eyes, big ears, and a small mouth. Another variation on that saying is that we have two ears and one mouth because we should listen twice as much as we speak. James Lynch's discovery of the calming effects of listening[14] suggests that this ratio of listening to talking also makes good sense in terms of the benefits to you as a helper.

The SOLVER acronym, based on a similar acronym devised by Gerard Egan, can help remind us of some key elements of our attention to the other person:[15]

> **S**quarely Face the Other Person. Even if you are only
> making a brief visit or just stopping to talk for a minute
> or two, always turn your body directly toward the other
> person. If the person is in bed, sit near him or her and get
> at the same level. If you doubt the wisdom of this, try
> having a conversation with a friend while you are lying on

the floor and your friend is standing over you. You will see how uncomfortable that listening position is and how it creates a passive-active, child-parent style of relating.

Adopt an **O**pen Posture. Don't cross your arms or legs or clasp your hands. These nonverbal behaviors signal defensiveness or unavailability, messages you don't want to communicate to the people you are assisting.

Lean Forward. This is a nonverbal behavior that clients frequently cite as an important cue in giving them the impression that their helper is genuinely interested in them and their problems. Of course, you don't want to lean forward compulsively in every moment of every helping encounter. But if you experiment with this behavior, you will find that when you *act* interested you will find yourself *being* more interested in what is happening. This happens in part because if you look interested, your client begins to respond to this felt interest and so becomes more interesting.

Verbally Follow. Don't jump from topic to topic. Try to stick to the themes and content that the client is bringing up. This is one way you can communicate respect to the other person. You are saying, "What you're sharing is important to me."

Maintain **E**ye Contact. This is an important way of saying, "I'm with you." The trick is to do it in a way that feels comfortable for you and for the other person. What this recommendation refers to is the kind of gentle and engaging eye contact we make in our everyday lives when we are in emotional contact with someone.

Be **R**elaxed. There are many distracting behaviors that we can unconsciously engage in, like fidgeting with something, playing with a pen or pencil, or rubbing our hands together. Videotape feedback is extremely helpful in identifying and changing these bad habits.

VERBAL MICROSKILLS

The verbal microskills that will be considered here include the following:[16]

- Silence

- Minimal encouragers and repetitions

- Paraphrases
- Summarizations
- Reflections of feeling
- Additive empathy responses
- Client frame of reference responses
- Reflections of meaning
- Questions
- Self-disclosures
- Confrontations
- Interpretations
- Directives or advice

Silence: The Helper's Friend

Plato gave us sage advice when he said, "Wise men speak because they have something to say; fools speak because they have to say something." We are usually busy formulating our next response while the person we are helping is still speaking to us, and so we don't hear the last—and often the most important—thing the person said. This interval—between the time the other person stops talking and you begin—is crucial in helping. Unfortunately, we are usually unaware of our own tendencies to overtalk, crowd, or hurry the other person. This crowding conversational style prevents the development of intimacy in the helping relationship and hinders self-exploration by the client.[17]

If you give yourself permission to wait 1, 2, or sometimes even 3 seconds before you respond, you will most likely be pleasantly surprised by the results. Although you might think other people will criticize you for being slow to respond to them, in fact, they won't. Because you will have an opportunity to be more fully immersed in empathy and more slowly feel your way into what your clients share with you, the accuracy, conciseness, and creativity of your responses will dramatically improve. Once your clients hear your more thoughtful and empathic responses, they will start to enjoy waiting for them. They will also discover that this small break gives them a chance to attend more fully to their inner experience, and they may jump in during this interval with another thought or feeling they have had.

Don't forget that empathy takes time! If you are rushed, your responses will remain at a superficial level. Remember that you are there to listen; take time to consider what you say. An ancient Chinese proverb tells us that we can chase butterflies all day, but only when we finally sit still will one come and alight on our shoulder.

Minimal Encouragers and Repetitions

Minimal encouragers are simple but important responses that tell the other person you are right there and interested in hearing more.[18] Silence can be considered a minimal encourager. The nonverbal attending behaviors already described—leaning forward, good eye contact, and focused attention—are also minimal encouragers. When you nod your head, say, "Tell me more," or utter "uh-huh" or "hmm," you are responding with minimal encouragers.

We engage in repetitions when we restate some exact or almost exact words of the other person. We might select just a few words from several sentences and repeat them for emphasis—for example, "nowhere to turn" or "it feels like a dream." We can also add a questioning or interrogative element to the repetition—for example, "at loose ends?" or "unglued?" Repetitions are useful because they highlight an important part of the message we are receiving and give our client an opportunity to elaborate on this theme.

Paraphrases

Paraphrases are real workhorses of helping; mastering this technique will significantly improve your helping communication. When you paraphrase, you freshly state the content of the message and represent it, often using some of the client's exact words and personalizing the response by adding the client's name or by including "you" in the response.[19] This talk tool is unfortunately often confused with parroting what someone has said, but it isn't actually that. Although the paraphrase may include some of the client's words, its main job is to summarize the essence of what the client has said—staying true to his or her ideas without repeating them exactly.[20]

When done skillfully, paraphrasing can have an extraordinary impact. Paraphrases are reflections of content that do not include feelings; if feelings are included, the response is considered a reflection of feeling, to be discussed next.

Here are some examples of paraphrases from interviews with two bereaved spouses. The first is from an interview with Anne, whose husband died 5 years ago:[21]

> Anne: I was totally unprepared to accept the fact that he wasn't alive, and it took me a long time to come to terms with the reality of the fact that he wasn't in this world in a physical way anymore. And . . .
>
> Dale: To come to grips with the finality of that.
>
> Anne: Yes, definitely. I remember initially thinking that he'd still be coming home.

You can see that, although my response didn't use Anne's exact words, my words are close to hers in meaning and mirror her initial difficulty accepting the reality of the loss.

Bill's wife died a year ago. Here he is describing his current reactions:

> Bill: I think that's what's been happening over the last year, going through the good . . . We'd been married almost 24 years. Going through all the good and the bad, and a lot of good memories.
>
> Dale: You were able to go back to some of the good memories.
>
> Bill: A lot of bad ones, too. I didn't realize they were there.
>
> Dale: The complete picture of who you were together.

My first response wasn't totally accurate, and Bill corrected me by clarifying that the memories of him and his wife together aren't all good ones. I think I highlighted the good memories in my response because that was the last thing he said, but my paraphrase obviously didn't feel exactly right, and Bill let me know. My "complete picture" response, also a paraphrase, simply restates what Bill said but adds a bit of my understanding as well. Good paraphrases require you to give of yourself; you synthesize what someone is saying and then share your best approximation of the essential message.

This kind of listening and responding is hard work, and we often think we are doing a better job at it than we actually are. When we carefully study our actual responses in real-life helping encounters, we might realize that we have repeatedly missed the essence of what someone was saying to us or that our paraphrases have significantly detracted from the meaning communicated to us. We understand how much we still have to learn.

Quality listening requires hearing the entire message being communicated by your client. The best way to develop this skill is to pay close attention to the content of his or her words and remember them as you go along. I've developed an exercise that will heighten your awareness of just how difficult accurate listening is; it will also improve your listening skills. Pair up with another person. One person will be the helper, while the other will be the helpee. The helpee will talk about a problem, and the helper will try simply to repeat verbatim what the helpee has said. The helpee will give feedback to the helper concerning any deleted words and missed meanings. The catch here is that the helper must repeat everything exactly the way the helpee has stated it.

When you try this exercise, you will quickly see how difficult this is. You will discover how many sentences or words you can hear and still repeat verbatim. You will also begin to see how much editing we do in even the simplest of verbal exchanges. Although verbatim statements aren't themselves very useful in real-life helping situations, the listening skills that underlie them are essential to our success as helpers.

Summarizations

I think of summarizations as big paraphrases. Summarization responses usually reflect the content of more than just the previous exchange. Sometimes they reflect content shared earlier in the meeting or even content shared days or weeks ago. Summarizations can also pull different contents together, identify themes, or recount what has happened up to a given point in a meeting. They are an excellent tool for making sure that you and the client share an understanding of what is going on. It is worth making a mental note to remind yourself to summarize several times in each helping encounter.

Unfortunately, we often neglect this skill because it is easier not to do the hard work of formulating clear and succinct summaries. When we leave a great deal as understood between us we risk that a great deal will be *mis*understood between us. The best way to prevent this is to pause and punctuate the encounter with a summary of what you are hearing, feeling, or seeing.

In the next interchange, a mother whose daughter died 2 years ago is discussing how she is experiencing the passage of time during her bereavement. I first make a paraphrase, then a summarization that responds to both her statements:

> Nancy: I don't know that the space of time changes in my
> mind. It sometimes it seems like it's been 10 years
> since I've seen her, and smiled at her, and held her
> in my arms, and talked to her. I miss that.

Dale: That's what you miss.

Nancy: Yes. And other times it seems like, well, she hasn't really been gone that long.

Dale: So your experience of time is not just linear—sometimes it seems like a long time, sometimes it seems like a short time.

Nancy: Yeah, right, two different ways. And, so far, the length of time has not made it any easier for me.

Reflections of Feeling

The reflection of feeling response is at the heart of empathic responding. These responses include a direct reference to the emotional part of the client's message and re-present the context of the feeling (i.e., why the person is feeling this way).

At its simplest, this response takes the following form: "You feel *(feeling word or phrase)* because of *(source or context of feeling)*." For example, a reflection of feeling response to Jenny might be "I can hear how angry and frustrated you are about your illness and what you're going through." This response identifies both her feelings (angry and frustrated) and their context (her illness and its painful effects on her).

You need to be careful, though, because sometimes we think that we are responding to feelings when we are really responding to thoughts. A useful rule of thumb is that feelings can usually be expressed in one word, whereas thoughts rarely can. Ask yourself, "How does he or she feel about that?" If you can formulate the answer in one word, chances are good that you are dealing with a feeling, not a thought. The word *feeling* itself does not guarantee that feelings are being discussed. In fact, when the phrase "feeling that . . . " occurs, feelings are rarely being referred to. For example, "I'm feeling that you are taking advantage of me" is more focused on the behavior of the other person than on my own feelings of hurt. A more direct feeling statement is "I'm feeling taken advantage of" or "I'm hurt by this."

Once you are sure you are responding to feelings, a useful initial step is to distinguish whether what you are hearing is a positive or negative emotion. Positive emotions include love, caring, concern, joy, hope, confidence, delight, and relief, among others. We are often so attentive to the suffering of the people we are caring for that we fail to hear and respond to their positive feelings. Negative emotions include depression, inadequacy, fear, confusion, hurt, anger, loneliness, guilt or shame, victimization, and others.[22]

The next step in responding to feelings is to identify the level of intensity of the feeling. The angry person can be furious (high intensity), resentful (moderate intensity), or simply put out (low intensity). The depressed person can feel hopeless (high intensity), discouraged (moderate intensity), or disappointed (low intensity). A frequent error helpers make in responding to feelings is misidentifying their level of intensity.

Finding exactly the right word is the final step. You need to find a word or phrase that the other person can understand and relate to. For instance, some people can relate to feeling *impugned,* whereas I would respond better to the word *mistreated* or *exploited.* Therefore, it is very helpful to develop a large vocabulary of feeling words and to put that vocabulary to work every day in your caregiving. An impoverished vocabulary of feelings can lead to uninspired and uninspiring responses that have little emotional impact on your clients.

Much of the work of helping is finding exactly the right word to capture the experience of the other person. We all tend to overuse certain of our favorite feeling words; words like *upset, depressed, angry, hurt,* and *happy* don't adequately reflect the many nuances and contexts of our emotions, and when they are used too often, they tend to lose their meaning and effectiveness.

Good poetry has exactly the reverse effect: Particular words or lines in poems touch some aspect of our experiencing in amazingly precise and affirming ways. In this sense, effective empathic responding is a poetic process. You are painting a picture in words, a picture that mirrors or re-presents what you have heard or seen. As in poetry, metaphors and imagery are highly appropriate. Clients can talk about things in metaphors that they could not find words for otherwise—a grieving person describes "coming out of the fog"; a stressed caregiver feels like she's "swimming in Jell-O"; a woman recovering from cancer describes her inner emotional work and healing as "interior decorating."

Here are some examples of the reflection of feeling microskill. Linda's father died just 6 months before this interview, and she is describing the upsurges of her grief. I make a repetition response that encourages her to elaborate what "it" is and then a second response that reflects the ambivalence she feels toward her emotional pain:

Linda: For me, just being with it was really hard, still is really hard, but it's getting better.

Dale: Being with the . . .

Linda: Being with the grief. It just comes. Everything's OK for a while, and then something just happens, you know.

Dale: It's a kind of ambivalent feeling about it. Part of you really wants to go with it, and embrace it, in a way, and say, "This is a remembrance," and another part is saying, "Hmm, this doesn't feel so good."

Linda: Yeah, it's still uncomfortable, and I don't know when that changes, or if that changes.

In this next exchange, Anne describes being suddenly cast into the difficult role of single parent by her husband's death and her feelings of abandonment:

Anne: I mean, like I felt that I had people dependent on me all the time, and I didn't have someone else that was sharing what I was feeling. This was a commitment that we made to have these children, and that we would both raise them, and love them, and raise them, and care about them, and I felt very abandoned, and I felt like I was now the person that was responsible for these kids all the time, there was no one else that was really behind me in what I was doing or could give me a break, and say, "You are really doing a great job." It wasn't a team effort anymore.

Dale: Before that you couldn't or didn't even realize how much relief he did provide.

Anne: Exactly.

Dale: Or how important he was to you and the children. It's funny, isn't it? It was almost invisible, although you knew he was important. And also it sounds, like, maybe, with feeling abandoned... I don't know... some anger at this—to be left alone to deal with this.

Anne: I don't think I allowed myself to really get in touch with how angry some of it made me.

My response to Anne's anger was intentionally tentative. I could hear the anger implicit in her statements and in her voice and expressions, but even though I was fairly certain of this, I didn't know if *she* was aware of it. The fact that *I* heard her anger didn't give me license to tell her what she was feeling because she was the authority on her experience. If I was correct, she might have explored that feeling more deeply. If I was wrong, or if that feeling was too uncomfortable for her to acknowledge or fully experience, she might have directed me to the areas of her experience that she could safely talk about at that time.

Tentativeness is appropriate and helpful but shouldn't be confused with a timid and diffident interviewing style. The tentativeness must be the kind that says, "Does this fit?" or "Am I on track with this?"

One way to ensure greater tentativeness in your communication style is to develop a large repertoire of what are known as empathic response leads. Beginning helpers often get into ruts by beginning each of their empathy responses in a stereotyped fashion. Such stereotyped responses as "I hear you saying . . . " or "You feel . . . " or "So . . . " repeated three or four times in a row draw attention to your technique and away from the content of your message. Using a large repertoire of different communication leads can help your client respond to what you are saying and not how you are saying it. The best way to add these to your repertoire is to memorize them and then practice them in your everyday caregiving. Here is a brief list of some of these introductory phrases:

- If I'm hearing you correctly . . .
- To me it's almost like you're saying . . .
- So, you feel . . .
- So from where you sit . . .
- As I get it, you're saying . . .
- Sort of like saying . . .
- You believe . . .
- I'm picking up that you . . .
- I wonder if you're saying . . .
- Sort of like feeling . . .
- In other words . . .
- I gather that . . .
- From where you're sitting . . .
- It's like . . .
- I'm kind of hearing you say . . .
- You think . . .

We need to continually check out the accuracy of our understanding with the person we are helping. This doesn't mean that we can never directly state what we see (e.g., "I can see that this is really painful for you").

Additive Empathy Responses

Beyond the simple reflection of feeling responses are what are called additive empathy responses, which reflect underlying or implicit feelings. These responses add something by making the client's implied feelings explicit. My response to Anne's anger in the example just given was additive because, although her anger was implicit in what she said and how she said it, she didn't explicitly communicate it.

When you are responding to implicit feelings, it is extremely important that you be somewhat tentative because you are inviting the person to explore what is going on for him or her openly and to share what might be uncharted emotional territory, and that can be frightening. Often people will approach some of their more difficult feelings in steps; for example, after a client first acknowledges and feels his frustration, then he can explore the full force of his anger.

The best advice is to approach feelings as a process and not to try to identify *the* feeling the client is experiencing. Feelings occur as part of emotional complexes containing a variety of feelings, and they change when they are exposed to the light of our awareness. Beginning helpers often make the mistake of relating to feelings as fixed, unchanging entities inside the other person. But the reality is that when clients turn their attention inward and make contact with the problem they are having, many different kinds of words and images might emerge. When responding to this emotional complexity, I often find it helpful to say, "Part of you is feeling ... but the other part feels ... " or "One part of you wants to do this, but another part is afraid."

As a helper, your task is not to tell the client what he or she is experiencing; it is to assist the client in bringing the unclear parts of his or her experience into focus.[23] If your responses as a helper are on target, your client will receive them as totally congruent with his or her experiencing, as the next thing he or she might have said or felt. He or she can then continue in this process without having to stop and negotiate with your response.

This process is analogous to a quarterback's throwing the football down the field to a receiver.[24] If the quarterback throws the ball ahead of the receiver, the pass has too much "lead" in it. The same is true with our empathic responses. We have to estimate where the client's experience is going next and throw the ball (our response) to exactly that point. If we are on target, the client catches the ball without missing a step and continues down the field. If we throw the ball behind the client, he or she must slow down or stop and back up to catch the pass. For example, if someone says, "I'm really hurt that my sister hasn't visited me," and we respond by saying, "You're feeling hurt that your sister hasn't visited you," we've thrown the ball behind her. She might think, "Yes, that's what I said, all right" and then hope that our next response is better. If we continue throwing the ball behind her, she'll become irritated and probably not want to continue the interaction.

In this situation, sensing their clients' growing irritation, many beginning helpers become threatened and decide that they need to do something dramatic to get the interaction back on track. So they throw the ball all the way down the field (a "Hail Mary" intervention) with a response something like "This feeling of abandonment is like what happened with your father, isn't it?" The client dives for the pass but fails to catch it because it is way ahead of her own experience. Seeing this, the helper then returns to responses with less lead, but the same problem recurs.

This sequence can repeat itself again and again—inadequate low-lead responses followed by even less effective high-lead responses and then more weak low-lead responses—as the client feels alternately frustrated and confused or defensive. The key to preventing this pattern is to work hard at freshly phrasing what the client is explicitly saying to you, to listen for the implied parts of his or her message, and to respond to the forward moving edge of experience that is reflected in this implicit message.

When successful, this way of responding puts the other person in touch with the complex of feelings and meanings he or she is speaking from, and the exchange continues in a pattern much like the children's game where a searcher attempts to locate a hidden object by following clues of "warmer" and "colder."

Another metaphor for this is that of climbing a ladder. Visualize yourself and your client climbing a ladder together, with each new awareness moving your client one rung up. Your additive responses should be directed to the next rung on this ladder but not beyond it.

Client Frame of Reference Responses

Another powerful microskill is what I call the client frame of reference response. This microskill is an excellent way to respond when you are really empathically attuned to what the other person is experiencing and want to communicate your understanding in the most direct way possible.

In the client frame of reference response, you speak from the point of view of the client, using the first-person. Rather than responding to Jenny with "I can hear how angry and frustrated you are about your illness and what you're going through," you would instead say, "What I'm hearing you say, Jenny, is, I'm angry and frustrated by this illness and what it's putting me through." This response mode can be used to paraphrase, summarize, or reflect feelings.

Here I make a client frame of reference response to Anne, and she responds by disclosing the feelings of hopelessness she had after her husband's death:

> Anne: I guess the thing that comes most to mind is change. I mean phenomenal changes that occurred after Chris died. Changes—for me, it was who I was, what my role was, and how I was going to survive, initially, the first 5 years . . .
>
> Dale: So, for you, it was a "Can I go on?" kind of feeling?
>
> Anne: A tremendous amount of hopelessness initially. Chris died 33 days after an acute leukemia diagnosis.

My response to Anne is a classic client frame of reference response because it includes the introductory phrase "So for you it was," which told Anne that I was reflecting what I heard *her* saying. This is important because things said in the first-person can be mistaken as self-disclosures. If I had said only, "Can I go on?" Anne might have wondered if I was saying, "Can I [Dale] go on?" To avoid this confusion, it is best always to introduce the client frame of reference response with a phrase like the following:

- I'm hearing you say, for me . . .
- It sounds like you're saying, I . . .
- So for you, it's I . . .
- The way you see it is, I . . .

But be careful. Even if you become proficient at using the client frame of reference response, resist overusing it. It is an ideal communication skill when your other listening responses have set the stage for this more powerful intervention. It is not such a good skill for *getting* on track with your client; paraphrases, questions, and simple reflections of feeling are best for that purpose. But when you are already accurately empathizing and want to respond in a way that can deepen this empathy, making a client frame of reference response is an excellent choice.

Grief's Questions and the Client Frame of Reference Response

The client frame of reference response is particularly helpful in responding to grief and loss. The person confronting grief and loss has more questions than answers and asks these—of us, of himself or herself, and of God. The questions include the following.

Why me? Why did this have to happen?

These are probably the first questions every bereaved person asks. Why did my loved one have to die? Existential questioning is common: Are we ants on the railroad track, or is there some reason for this suffering?

We attempt to get a kind of secondary control over the loss experience—to make sense of it, to find meaning in it, and to prevent it from occurring in the future. At a time when our basic assumptions about the world and ourselves can be either shattered or transformed, these efforts to restore our psychological equilibrium make eminent sense and are a critical component of coping.[25]

What is happening to me?

The grieving person feels radically different from his or her former self and wants to know what is happening to him or her. Here I respond to Bill's questioning with a client frame of reference response and with questions that check out the accuracy of my response:

Bill: I was at a retreat house this summer. It was something I found in common with some of the people there. You think you are going out of your mind. Everyone else is normal, thinking it's crazy. The feelings are so strong. They are so intense that you don't have anything to relate them to.

Dale: So, what is this process? What is this? What's happening to me? Is that it? Is that how you feel?

Bill: Is this normal, or am I just completely whacko?

How can I go on?

Feelings of hopelessness are common in people who are grieving. In the exchange with Anne, presented previously, I made a client frame of reference response—"So, for you, it was a 'Can I go on?' kind of feeling?"—that reflected her struggle to continue on with life after the loss of her husband.

What can I do?

The "problem" of grief has no easy solutions. The grieving person's course of action is unclear, and at the same time a cascade of advice pours in. Friends advise the individual to go on, have another child, remarry, or find meaning in the experience. The problem is that there is often a painful discrepancy between these expectations and the inner experience of the grieving person.

Who will help me?

The grieving person asks, "Who will be there for me?" "Whom can I count on?" There are often many surprises—some pleasant, some unpleasant, as the grieving person seeks out support from family and friends.

What do I need?

A fog of ambiguity can envelop the grieving person, making it difficult for the person to tell us how we can be of assistance. The grieving person often just does not know what we could possibly do that would be helpful.

Will this ever end?

The grieving person asks, "How long will this last?" "When will I feel better?" This question becomes more urgent when the individual feels just as awful, or even worse, months or years into the bereavement. For many people, it is particularly upsetting when they feel no better at 13 months than they did at 11 months because they expected things to change for the better at the 1-year mark. Other people think they should be finished grieving at 3 months or 6 months, or they are frightened when they experience waves of grief that are triggered by certain events. I call these upsurges "grief attacks" and explain that they are normal and to be expected.

Who am I now?

Our identities consist of the images of self that important people in our lives reflect back to us, and when we lose the mirror that uniquely defines us, we have lost that part of ourselves. Here Linda grapples with the change in her identity—the redefinition of self—that is part of grief:

I think, after the initial shock of it all, it's just been hard to figure out who I am now. I'm a daughter without a father. And that was the first thought that came to me after I settled a little bit. Who am I, now that I don't have my dad? The other thing that I remember feeling, and still feel now, is that my life hasn't changed dramatically. I mean, I still do the same things, but, I feel, really feel different, and I wonder why, and will I feel the same again? And, I know, I obviously am not the same, I no longer have a father. And just that, dealing with it when it comes up, is sort of difficult for me.

How will my life be?

The final task of grief is to become an active agent for one's own well-being, to reinvest in life, and to love again.[26] All grieving people have some uncertainty about this new future that lies ahead and how they will find their way around in it.

The client frame of reference response can work remarkably well when you are responding to these profoundly existential reactions. The structure of this response fits perfectly with the process of the grieving person, and it feels quite natural to say, "So for you it feels like, I'm different now," or "I get a sense that you're saying, I don't know who is really going to be there for me, and I'm a little afraid to ask." We can't give easy answers to these questions. But if we hear them and help the grieving person live the questioning process, the answers may someday appear, in a way described by Rilke in this beautiful passage:

> Have patience with everything unresolved in your heart
> and . . . try to love the questions themselves as if they
> were locked rooms or books written in a very foreign
> language. Don't search for the answers, which could not
> be given to you now, because you would not be able to live
> them. Live the questions now. Perhaps then, someday far
> in the future, you will gradually, without even noticing it,
> live your way into the answer.[27]

Reflections of Meaning

As the preceding discussion of the client frame of reference response illustrates, we are often responding not just to thoughts and feelings but also to the underlying, deeper meanings that tie these thoughts and feelings together. Here we enter into the realm of values, beliefs, and the sense people make of events in their lives.[28] These basic theories (schemata) about the world can be severely threatened by negative or unexpected life events such as loss, life-threatening illness, or pain. Assumptions of personal invulnerability, of a meaningful and benevolent universe, and of one's own self-worth no longer seem adequate to explain what is happening, leading to a search for a new set of personal beliefs that can make these traumatic events more comprehensible.[29]

Responding to meanings is similar to responding to feelings. The reflection of meaning response can take many forms, but it is in essence an elaboration of a basic "You mean" message, just as reflections of feeling have "You feel" as their core message. You can respond to meaning and this search for it with a variety of microskills. For example, you might ask a question: "What does that mean to you?" or "What sense are you making of this?" You could also use a paraphrase to reflect meaning: "It looks like the world sometimes just isn't fair" or "It sounds like you value the closeness you've had during this time."

Many assumptions and beliefs that people have about life and themselves are implicit and are only brought to awareness when they are threatened by events that contradict them. As a helper, you need to make a determined effort to listen carefully to people as they struggle with these often confusing and uncertain experiences. As with grief's questions, there are no easy answers you or anyone else can provide. But if you recognize this search for meaning and can find words that offer comfort and understanding in this time of crisis, the people you help will be more likely ultimately to find positive meanings in these painful events.

Questions

Questions—the kinds we ask as helpers—are the most overused and misused of all the helping microskills. We know that beginning helpers use more questions than experienced helpers.[30] One of my favorite exercises for my graduate counseling students is the No Questions Asked exercise. I instruct them to refrain from asking any questions for several 15-minute conversations. At first, they are either speechless because they can't imagine how anyone could converse without asking questions or they are confident that this won't be a difficult assignment for them. All finally do succeed in this task, but not without great difficulty and many valuable learning experiences along the way. I encourage you to try this exercise sometime in the next week and see what you discover about your own use of questions.

A discovery my students frequently report after doing the No Questions Asked exercise is that the absence of question asking dramatically affects their interactions. There is usually one person in the class who reports a communication breakthrough of some kind. For example, many students who are parents say that they had the most intimate and revealing conversation with a teenage son or daughter that they have ever had. No small effect for simply deleting the use of one microskill!

Others report refreshing changes in their interactions and describe a new awareness of the liberating effects of not asking questions, not just for the person with whom they were talking but also for themselves as listeners. They felt they responded more sensitively and accurately to the content and feelings of their conversational partner because they had more time to think about what they heard and formulate their responses.

We usually think of questions as the best way to get people talking or gather information. We fail to see what most helping theorists do—namely, that questions are ineffective in helping someone explore thoughts and feelings and that they often fail to gather the most helpful information. Asking questions creates the expectation that we will do something useful with all the information we have collected. One of our key goals as helpers can be conceptualized as helping people get a better understanding of their situation; questions tend to increase *our* understanding, not theirs. The other person must respond to us rather than our having to respond to him or her.

In everyday conversations, questions can serve the function of keeping the conversation away from intimate topics and feelings, which is probably appropriate most of the time. However, in the intimate communication of the helping encounter, these effects are undesirable and undermine our efforts. A rapid-fire series of closed questions is appropriate for an IRS audit or a courtroom interview, but in an intimate, egalitarian relationship this communication style can be highly counterproductive. The advice of most helping experts is to ask very few questions and, if you do ask a question, to ask only one.

There is a dramatic difference, too, in the effects of different kinds of questions. The two basic types of questions are closed questions and open questions. Closed questions can usually be answered with a yes or no and typically begin with *are, is, can, do,* or *have.* For example:

- Are you feeling nauseated today?
- Is your sister going to visit?
- Can you understand what she's going through?

- Do you want to go there again?

- Have you had anything to drink this morning?

Closed questions can also be of the multiple choice variety: "Whom do you want to see most—your father, your mother, or your sister?" or "Is the pain sharp, throbbing, or dull?" Closed questions are highly directive because they drastically limit the range of responses that can be made to them.

Open questions begin with *how, what, could,* or *why* and are less directive than closed questions because they permit a greater range of responses. If you visualize the helping conversation as a funnel, open questions expand the conversation into the large section of the funnel, and closed questions squeeze it into the funnel's narrow opening. This is why open questions are effective at the beginning of a conversation to "open things up" and why we often rely on closed questions to help us end or leave interactions (e.g., "Is there anything else I can do for you today?"—"No."—"Then I'll see you tomorrow.").

Different kinds of open questions have considerably different effects. *How* questions are best for eliciting feelings and exploring psychological reactions: "How do you feel about that?" or "How is that for you?" *What* questions are better for eliciting less affective content: "What's been happening in the past week?" or "What do you think about that?" *Why* questions should be used sparingly because they are usually not easily answered and tend to provoke defensiveness. For example, "Why are you doing that?" might be a simple request for information, but it could easily be interpreted as including a veiled opinion about what the other person should or should not be doing.

There is another type of open question, the indirect open question, that I find useful because it diversifies your communication style and because it is particularly effective in inviting the client to take an active role in the conversation. The indirect question requests information in a first-person statement rather than in question form:[31]

- I'd like to know more about how your chemotherapy has been going.

- I'm wondering how your husband is responding to all this.

- I'm curious about your plans for taking care of yourself.

- It wasn't clear to me what you meant earlier when you said . . .

- I need some information about any childhood illnesses you might have had.

This way of responding can keep you from getting into a flurry of questions when you don't understand what the other person has said and need something clarified. When this occurs, it is good to say something like, "I missed what you were saying about how . . . "

One way to decrease your use of questions is to transform your questions into statements. We often observe or hear something and then ask an obvious question about it. For example, we might see someone in physical discomfort and ask, "Are you feeling more uncomfortable today?" We could instead say, "It looks like you're feeling less comfortable today." This makes for a more direct and engaging style of interacting and puts less pressure on the client to respond to what he or she might perceive as a demand.

An important step in getting more control over your use of questions is to study yourself to see what your current questioning pattern looks like. If more than 10 to 20% of your responses are questions, particularly closed ones, you can enjoy quick success by beginning to experiment with other ways of communicating. Of course, you will have to go through a painful period of conscious incompetence and conscious competence en route to a new helping style less encumbered by question asking, but it will be well worth it. As your use of questions decreases, other microskills will take their place. These other microskills will soon become more natural to you, and you will begin to use them at higher and higher skill levels.

Self-Disclosures

Most people think that self-disclosures are the most natural and spontaneous of all communications. The reality is that this communication microskill is usually either overused or underused—and unskillfully delivered. Few helpers have developed the skill of self-disclosure—they remain limited to a few basic ways of disclosing themselves as helpers. Usually, they offer a "me-too disclosure" that says, "I've experienced something like that myself."[32] This can be a helpful response if it isn't overused, but there are other kinds of self-disclosure that can also be effective.

One important rule of helping is that when there is a problem in the helping relationship we need to address that problem right away; it must become our number one priority. But how do we do this? Gerald Goodman coined a phrase that I've always found helpful in these circumstances: "When in trouble, disclose on the double."[33]

For example, we saw self-disclosures used in many of the more effective responses to Jenny: "I don't know how you feel," "I've never been in your situation, but I'm sure I would feel the same way," and "I wish I had the answer for why you have to lie here and I get to go home at night, but I *do* care."

If you are having a difficult interaction with someone, it is usually best to talk about the problem—to acknowledge the "elephant in the room" so that it stops interfering with your relationship. This kind of immediacy is best achieved by self-disclosure—by making a statement like "I think we're having a difficult time agreeing on how to do this" and then adding something like "I really want to be helpful to you. Let's try to find some ways we can begin to work together to achieve the goals that really matter to you." You might choose different words, but the principle is to nondefensively acknowledge that there is a problem, then disclose your caring and your desire to make things work better. Few people can resist the disarming and supportive qualities of genuine self-disclosures at moments like these.

We often resist self-disclosing as helpers because this behavior doesn't match that of our internalized ideal helper. Would Florence Nightingale admit she made a mistake or say that she didn't know what to do? My argument is that nothing inspires confidence as much as a nondefensive, truthful approach. However, once you have either disclosed personal content to convey empathy or acknowledged an error or the fact that you *do* get to go home at night, it is critically important that you keep your focus on the person you are caring for and that you acknowledge that you are going to continue working to help solve his or her problems. Nothing inspires less confidence than a personally distressed helper.

Using self-disclosure in situations like these is a high-level skill that some helpers acquire naturally and others never do. When you are considering self-disclosing, always ask yourself, "For whom am I doing this?" The answer should always be "For my client." If not, don't self-disclose.

Confrontations

Confrontation responses are not what most people first think they are. Confrontation in this context does not mean attacking or in any way lowering the self-esteem of the other person. The most critical and defining feature of a confrontational response is that it points to a discrepancy in what the client is saying, thinking, feeling, or doing.

Because of this, confrontations can often be worded as follows: "On the one hand, you said, felt, or did this one thing, but on the other hand, you said, felt, or did this other thing." For example, someone might say, "I am all alone; there's no one to turn to." A confrontation response might be "On the one hand, you feel all alone, but you've told me that you do have some friends who have come through in the past, and I wonder if they might do it again." A somewhat gentler confrontation would be "You've told me that you have some friends, but even though you have them, you still feel alone."

The trick with confrontation responses is to deliver them in a way that doesn't lower the person's self-esteem by denying the emotional truth of his or her statements. Also, because confrontation responses are more action-oriented responses and sometimes bring attention to touchy topics like self-deception and patterns of avoidance, they shouldn't be used until a supportive relationship is firmly established.

Interpretations

Interpretations are responses in which the helper offers an idea that the client hasn't already thought of and that might not even be implicit in what the client has shared to that point—there is an element of "news" involved. For example, a female client might be having a recurring problem in all her relationships but not be aware of this pattern. You might present your observation of this pattern with an interpretation: "You know, Jane, I see some of the same patterns in your relationship with your mother that are in your relationships with Karen and Joan. In each relationship, you're always the one who gets stuck in the caretaking role, and you're not really getting *your* needs met."

It is sometimes difficult to distinguish interpretations from empathy responses that address the client's implicit message because both responses go beyond what is explicitly stated. The best way to make this distinction is to keep in mind that empathically responding to what is implicit means that, if you are successful, the client will not have to stop and think about the correctness of your response— if it is on target, the client will continue without skipping a beat. An interpretation, on the other hand, always makes the client stop and think because interpretations introduce a new idea.

These kinds of responses are, I think, best reserved for the more uncovering and insight-oriented work of psychotherapy. But an occasional interpretation, if offered tentatively and in a way that doesn't lower the person's self-esteem or put that individual on the defensive, can be thought provoking and helpful in any caregiving situation.

Directives or Advice

We work with people in situations that are highly stressful. That inevitably pushes some deep and frightening emotional buttons in us. When that happens, we and our clients are vulnerable and eager to solve the problem to ease our shared discomfort. Unfortunately, there are usually no simple solutions, only questions—questions about what we are doing and how we might help in better ways.

For example, we might ask, "How can I help Joan's family deal with their struggle around holding on versus letting go of her?" In a different situation we might wonder, "Am I the only one around here who feels all this pain about Jimmy's dying? How can I get his family to tell him how they really feel? Or don't they feel anything?" Faced with a young, terminally ill mother who is trying to keep the truth of her condition from her children, we might think, "How can I get through to Sally? She has to make plans so her kids are taken care of. I feel like I have to get her to talk about just how sick she is."

Such questions are inevitable and necessary to the work we do. And we sometimes feel almost desperate to find answers to them. This urgency makes us susceptible to the quick advice that we often receive from others when we raise questions about our situation. Trouble is, this advice doesn't usually solve our problems, because, as H. L. Mencken once said, "There's always an easy solution to every human problem—neat, plausible, and wrong."[34] Even when solutions are simple, carrying them out can be difficult. So the advice may leave us feeling unsatisfied, misunderstood, discounted, or even angry and resentful.

Sometimes people *do* want and need our advice. Problems about money or wills may best be handled with advice. Concerns about health, exercise, diet, and even certain feelings might benefit from an educational and advice-giving style.

The problem is that some people don't know any other way to say what they feel without asking for advice. For the most part, they want to unburden themselves—just as we do. They want to be heard. Listening carefully and empathically to someone without trying to solve his or her problem is an important form of skilled communication. But knowing this is not always enough to prevent us from jumping in with our answers, solutions, and explanations.

In those situations where advice is called for, I've found that an effective way to offer it is through a kind of self-disclosure. If you have been in a similar situation, you can share what worked for you: "This might not work for you, but what I found helpful for me was to . . . " The introductory phrase "This might not work for you" softens the advice and makes the other person more likely to explore this option. When someone is facing a problem I have previously helped dozens of other people grapple with, I sometimes summarize three or four of the solutions my former clients arrived at for this situation and then let the person consider which one (if any) of the alternative responses seems best.

RECOMMENDATIONS FOR LISTENING AND HELPING

Here are some general recommendations for listening and helping that build on the microskills model already explored in this chapter.

Develop a Wide Range of Helping Responses

One way to fulfill yourself as a helper is to increase your repertoire of helping skills. To do this, you will need to practice the different microskills presented in this chapter and experiment by using them in real helping situations.

If you have moved to the stage of unconscious competence with a wide range of microskills, you will avoid skill ruts and mechanical repetitions in your responses. Repeating "Sounds like you're feeling . . . " "Sounds like you're feeling . . . " "Sounds like you're feeling . . . " begins to sound like you're feeling bored, and it will surely bore or annoy the person you are helping. By using a variety of response leads, a diverse vocabulary of feelings, and a wide range of microskills, you will be a much more interesting and effective helping companion.

If you increase your skill repertoire, you will be able to generate many different helpful responses in any given situation. Remember, there is no single "correct" response; there are only effective and ineffective ones. As your skill repertoire increases, you will feel more confident; this in turn will enhance your creativity and instill more confidence in the people you care for. As these new skills become second nature to you, you will be able to, as Eugene Kennedy and Sara Charles put it, "respond to the person instead of trying to make a good response."[35]

A good skill-building exercise to help you vary your responses is to delete the word *feeling* from your helping vocabulary for a week. Take the following response to Jenny: "I can hear that you're feeling angry because of the treatments and their side-effects." Omit the word *feeling*, and it becomes "I can hear that you're angry because of the treatments and their side-effects." That word unnecessarily draws attention to the style of your intervention and adds little to the impact of your message.

Another approach would be to put the feeling word at the end of the sentence, where it usually has a greater impact: "I can hear that the treatments and their side effects are really making you angry."

Use Different Skills at Different Stages in Helping

Most theorists divide helping into three general stages.[36] These three stages are exploring, understanding, and acting.[37] The helper has different tasks in each of these three stages.[38] In the exploring stage, the primary goal is to establish trust and rapport, communicate respect, explore the problem, and begin developing empathy and understanding. In this stage, sensitive listening is critical.

In the second stage, understanding, you can begin to facilitate a deeper exploration of the problem and start to help your client establish workable goals. Goals are, after all, the flip side of problems. For example, if a client is lonely, his or her goal might be to become better connected socially. In this stage, helper self-disclosure and additive empathy responses become more appropriate and useful because they foster the trust and insight necessary to examine inner barriers to change.

In the third stage, acting, you can make sure that your client's goals are clearly defined and that he or she is supported in taking first steps toward the fulfillment of those goals. Here, advice and confrontation begin to play a larger role because the issue now is how the person can take his or her new awareness and act differently in the world.

In any given helping relationship, several different problems can be worked on simultaneously, and each can be in a different stage of the helping process. You might just be beginning to hear the outlines of one problem while you are well along in your progress on another.

Use the Least Amount of Authority and Control Necessary

In a nonauthoritarian helping relationship based on mutual participation, the helper is encouraging but not controlling and exerts the least amount of authority and control necessary to achieve the desired results.[39] Success or failure in this task is closely linked to the helper's use of microskills. Take a second look at the list of microskills presented earlier in this chapter. Can you identify the quality or characteristic that increases as you move from the top of the list to the bottom? The quality is control or directiveness. Silence exerts almost no control or directiveness on the client, questions exert considerably more, confrontations exert yet more, and so forth.

Authoritarian helpers use more closed questions, give more advice, make more interpretations, allow for fewer silences, and generally dominate the helping encounter. The nondirective, flexible helper is highly active (a nondirective style must not be confused with passivity), but the content of the interview—and the solutions to problems—comes from the client. Advice, confrontations, interpretations, closed questions, and other more directive responses are not prohibited and can often be used to good effect, but they should be used sparingly and with awareness of their intended and unintended outcomes.

In helping interactions, the goal is to keep the conversational ball in the client's court as much as possible. This has an empowering effect, giving our client the time and psychological space to explore his or her feelings and ideas and ourselves an opportunity to really observe the other person and to deepen our empathy. Because of our overuse of questions, everyday conversation has a ping-pong quality. We ask a closed question, the other person answers with a single word, then the conversational ball is instantly back in our court. We then respond with another closed question, and the pattern continues.

Less directive interventions, like silence, minimal encouragers, paraphrases, reflections of feeling, and client frame of reference responses tend to keep the ball in the client's court. The use of these microskills leads to more moments when as a helper I *can* respond, but the conversational rules don't demand that I do so. If I ask, "Did your sister visit yesterday?" and the client says, "Yes," the ball is back in my court, and I can either respond to this new information or ask another question. But I must do something. If I had said, "I noticed that your sister didn't visit yesterday," and the client responded with "No, she didn't," there might be a pause, during which either of us could speak next.

You should try to keep the ball in the client's court as much as possible. Making a checking-out response such as "Is that it?" will often elicit an acknowledgment, but then the client can also go on to bring up something related or perhaps something different that is currently significant.

One way to describe this general interviewing style is to say that you are helping people to tell their stories.[40] Theologian Henri Nouwen put it this way:

> The counselor is the student who wants to learn. The counselee is the teacher who wants to teach his story. Just as a teacher learns his own material best because he has to prepare himself and order his ideas for presentation to his students, so the counselee learns his own story by telling it in an ordered way to his counselor who wants to hear it. The counselor is the host who patiently and carefully listens to the story of the stranger. The counselee is the guest who rediscovers his own self by telling his story to the one who offered him a place to stay. And in the telling of the story, the stranger befriends not only his host but also his own history.[41]

Suspend Your Judgments

Our perceptions and our evaluations are often dangerously intertwined. To be an effective helper, we need to allow the helpee's statements to sink in without trying to make decisions (e.g., "Is this right or wrong, responsible or irresponsible?"). It is always tempting to overlay our values on the experiences and actions of the people we help. But each of these judgments erodes the sense of we-ness we have with the other person. As much as you can, listen with an open mind and an open heart to the other's message, without making any decisions about it.

Listen for Themes

A technique I find helpful is to listen for themes. These themes can often help you organize and understand the different content that is shared with you. They might be things like "Nothing is going to work out," "Life is the pits," "I'm the kind of person who can't say no," or "I don't understand."

I note or "red flag" these themes and keep them in my mind as the conversation continues. I might explicitly describe or summarize the theme if it seems helpful, or I might instead simply add it to my understanding of the client and our current interaction. Most helping conversations or dialogues, no matter how chaotic or disparate the content seems, are of a piece, and your challenge is to make sense of how it all fits together.

One organizing theme that we should always pay attention to relates to important things being said about a client or family member's self-image, goals, disappointments, emotions, or other highly personal concerns. When this happens, your sole task is to concentrate on understanding the individual's inner world.

An important goal for you as a helper is to facilitate the self-exploration of the person you are helping. Your client will be facing the distress-disclosure dilemma, and your task is somehow to facilitate his or her self-disclosure while maintaining or enhancing his or her self-esteem.

It is important not to have "opening the other person up" as a goal you doggedly pursue and feel disappointed about if you don't reach. As Kennedy and Charles note, a client doesn't come to you to get "opened up."[42] However, if you provide an environment of acceptance, warmth, and respect, this will happen, but it will happen naturally, and the client will be able to take responsibility for having moved forward.

Meet the Request That Is Being Made

As helpers, we should always try to empathize with the people we are caring for. However, it isn't always important for us to communicate this empathy to them. According to psychologist George Gazda and his colleagues, people seeking help make at least three different kinds of requests of their helpers: requests for action, requests for information, and requests for understanding and involvement.[43]

Requests for action include statements like "The light's in my eyes" or "My pain is acting up. Can I have some of that pain medication my doctor recommended?" Requests for information might include "Are you going to be working tomorrow?" or "Can this prescription be filled at the pharmacy?" Requests for understanding and involvement are communications in which the client is asking for a relationship—not action or advice—and in which the major message is an emotional one. Some examples would be "I feel really helpless, just watching her get worse and not being able to do anything about it" or "Being alone is what gets to me. No one seems to care. I feel pretty abandoned by all those people I thought were my friends." Identifying effective responses to these kinds of requests is a central goal of this chapter.

There can also be more than one request in a single statement: "I'm worried about the way things are heading (*a request for understanding and involvement*). Are the staff really telling me everything about my illness (*a request for information*)?"

It is extremely important for us to know when each of these different types of requests is being made and to respond accordingly. For example, Jenny, the cancer patient we responded to earlier in this chapter, was clearly making a request for understanding and involvement when she expressed such strong feelings. But we could easily have responded to a request for action by leaving the room or to a request for information by telling her that we would go find out more about her current medical condition and treatments.

When a client says, "The light is in my eyes," the appropriate response is to pull down the shade, not "You're really upset about that light in your eyes." There is an old maxim that says, "Don't scratch where it doesn't itch." It is a myth, for example, that when working with grief, loss, and life-threatening illness, helpers should always or exclusively attend to deep existential and inner emotional concerns. In fact, clients' concerns about work or finances or physical pain are often most pressing. And problem solving, taking care of their daily concerns, or giving them a little information would probably be the best way to help in these areas. On the other hand, because it is often much easier and more comfortable to deal with our clients' surface issues and obvious requests for action and information, many times we miss their more subtle requests for understanding and involvement.

Frequently, clients and their families are unclear about what they want or need from us. Often they mix two different kinds of requests. If you hear more than one kind of request in your client's communication, ideally you should try to address both requests. However, demands on our time or limits to the situation often permit us to address only one; unfortunately, because requests for information and action are most likely to get our attention, requests for understanding and caring are often missed or ignored.

On the other hand, I've known some clients who needed understanding but couldn't really receive it because it was too threatening. They felt more comfortable constantly complaining or asking for more physical comfort or information. This is probably what is happening when a call light goes on repeatedly. Usually that person needs more than just information or action. What they really need is a caring and understanding person. If they could let us into their feelings, we could help—but only if we make ourselves available.

Avoid Trivializing Distress

Underresponding or overresponding to distress is an even larger issue, particularly for caregivers working with people facing grief and life-threatening illness. As caregivers working in these contexts, we can easily make one of two kinds of mistakes.

One error is that we can dismiss or trivialize the real suffering of clients, family members, and coworkers. This occurs when we underestimate or fail to respond adequately to the actual distress someone is experiencing and instead emphasize the positive side of things. We can refuse to acknowledge suffering by blocking communication about it:

> I find myself trying to make everything *all right!* The
> patient is dying. She reveals her concern that her husband
> doesn't even care. Though I feel the same distancing of the
> spouse to his dying wife, I gloss it over. I *refuse* to let her
> talk about it. I make excuses for the husband. I cut off
> healing self-disclosure. The last 2 weeks of this patient's
> life were spent in uncontrollable pain.

Another helper confessed how only the insistence of her patient overcame her tendency to minimize the communication of difficult feelings:

> Attempting to comfort a dying patient, absolutely
> breathless from lung involvement, I was trying to get her
> to be quiet and relax so she would be more comfortable.
> My mistake. Her reply: "I have so much to say and no time
> left to say it, so I need you to be uncomfortable and
> listen."

We can encourage people to be "super copers" or urge them to see their illness or grief as a challenge, not as a threat. As discussed in chapter 5, this stance can lead people to conceal their suffering because they see it as a symptom of their failure to cope.

Psychologist Richard Lazarus gives several reasons for this trivialization of distress in our society. First, in our culture suffering is seen as a waste of time.[44] Death is a problem, and grief is inconvenient. We hear authorities say that we should grieve in an effective and timely fashion and that grieving can be a "hero's journey."

Second, the enormous popularity of the stress management principle of converting our threats into challenges has led to the misapplication of this simple wisdom to grief and grieving. For everyday stressors that are neither clearly positive or negative, this strategy can work, as Kobasa's research on stress hardiness has shown (see chapter 3). However, the benefits of this kind of attitudinal shift should not be romanticized as being applicable to all stressors because many tragic stressors have little or no redeeming value. The idea of having a good attitude can have many unintended consequences for the management of suffering. Many cancer patients have told me that they resent being told "Cancer is a challenge," "Have a good attitude," or "Hope dispels fear" because they are left not knowing what to do with their negative feelings. One patient said to me, "I don't *want* to be a hero! I don't want to be challenged by this! I just want to be healthy again!" Likewise, the person who has lost his leg in a car accident might feel something like this: "Don't tell me I am physically challenged and show me a film of someone with one leg climbing El Capitan! Instead, first hear my distress, my pain. Then, when I'm ready to move forward, look to me for my hope and strength and support this strength that comes from within *me*."

Third, these efforts often have the well-meaning intention of trying to encourage hope and promote a positive outlook. As a caregiver, you have to be an ambassador of hope who can help clients and family members overcome their pessimism, despair, demoralization, and helplessness. However, we must not offer false hope; real hope comes from our genuine interest and concern and from an accurate response to the feelings of the people we care for.[45]

Finally, we trivialize distress in others because we often have an unconscious desire to avoid suffering. This is a very difficult motivation to identify in ourselves because we like to think of ourselves as being open to the suffering of others. In fact, that is an important part of our helper self-concept. Yet the natural human inclination to avoid distress (see chapters 2 and 3) can prompt us to focus only on the positive and to unconsciously discourage the disclosure of suffering by clients and family members.

Thus, our motivations for trivializing distress can range from the altruistic ("It's better to think positive") to the self-serving, as when we avoid the discomfort of exposing ourselves to this distress. In effect, we are saying to the victims of a tragedy that they don't have a right to their painful feelings and that continued distress represents a failure of coping or even a spiritual failure. This leads to greater self-concealment and lowered self-esteem in the people we are helping. They feel that no one understands them, and their fears that disclosing their suffering will lead to a loss of support are confirmed.

The trivialization of distress in grieving persons can also be fueled by misconceptions concerning grief and loss. In a paper on the myths of coping with loss, psychologists Camille Wortman and Roxane Silver point out that certain common beliefs about grief are not supported by empirical data.[46] One unsupported myth is the notion that people always reach a state of resolution of their grief and that they recover in a relatively short period. Consistent with this belief, many authors write that "Grief is a process; recovery is a choice." Terms like *resolution, recovery, reestablishment,* and *reorganization* all suggest a return to normalcy.

However, Wortman and Silver cite research showing that suffering related to grief can continue for many years and that it is common for there never to be any real resolution. Thus, the stage is set for a collision between social expectations and the inner reality of the bereaved person. This discrepancy can lead to lowered self-esteem ("I shouldn't be having these feelings. I'm not coping very well") and to concealing distress from others.

Some other psychonoxious forms that this failure to empathize can take include cliches that offer no real comfort and discourage further disclosure of one's distress: "They're better off now," "Be brave," "Time heals everything," or "Don't cry—you'll only make yourself worse." These platitudes are well-intentioned yet fail to offer the empathy and compassion that the grieving person so deeply needs.

Don't Scratch Where It Doesn't Itch

The other kind of error we make is to overrespond to our clients' distress. With life-threatening illnesses, this occurs when we adopt the attitude that everyone in this situation requires counseling and that we must be psychothanatologists probing the depths of the psyche for existential anguish. It is important to remember that we most often work with normal people who are confronting abnormally stressful life events and that many of them do just fine without any additional psychosocial interventions.

In the case of grief, Wortman and Silver also note that another myth about coping with loss is that intense emotional suffering is a universal phenomenon. In fact, they point out, the experience of distress or depression is not inevitable, and its absence is not indicative of pathology (e.g., "disordered," "delayed," or "complicated" grief). Thus, when we work tirelessly to uncover the hidden distress of our clients, we may indeed be scratching where it doesn't itch.

To avoid underresponding or overresponding to distress and to avoid other mistakes we can make as helpers, we need to listen more closely to the people we care for. They will tell us what is true for them—by their reactions, by the hopes and fears they express, and by the actions they take or don't take. If we pay close attention to these cues, we can respond to their painful feelings and encourage genuine hope in a way that respects the whole individual and his or her emotional world.

CONCLUSION

Good communication skills are the tools by which we exercise caring and compassion. We are naturally more helpful than unhelpful, but to express our helpful natures to the fullest, we need continually to learn new skills that support helping and to delete others that detract from it.

Two caveats must be added to this discussion of skillful performance. First, no matter how skillful you are, any of your responses that is not grounded in a caring attitude and genuine concern for the person you are helping is likely to be unhelpful, despite how technically correct or dazzling it may be. Technique can never replace the genuine intention to help.

Second, no matter how skillful you become, you will continue to make errors. What helper has never asked too many questions, given too much advice, talked too much, feigned understanding, uttered a cliche, said the wrong thing, been impatient or defensive? If this person exists, I know I have never met him or her; it certainly isn't me. You might make fewer errors as you become more skilled, but you will always make them.

There is a saying that an error doesn't become a mistake until you refuse to correct it. This might be the best piece of advice. The greatest mistake you can make as a helper is believing that you don't make any mistakes. Your tribulations as a helper can be turned into personal and professional growth if you accept that you *do* make mistakes and that you are willing to listen to feedback and take the necessary self-corrective actions.

When our helping journey includes being a member of a helping team or leading a support group, opportunities for personal and professional growth—and embarrassment—are even greater. To be successful in these challenging contexts, we must learn yet other skills and add these to the caring connections and healing words that remain our basic helping tools.

PART THREE

Creating Caring Systems

7

If they don't have scars, they haven't worked on a team.[1]

Balfour Mount

In medieval times, alchemy was a symbol for transformation of what is most common (lead) into what is most precious (gold). So, too, do learning teams practice a special form of alchemy, the transformation of potentially divisive conflict and defensiveness into learning.[2]

Peter Senge

The Caring Team

Working on a team can be both frustrating and fulfilling. As a team member, your success as a helper is interwoven with your teammates' success. If the team fails in its tasks, you will also fail. If the team doesn't safeguard and encourage you and your caring, your idealism and morale can be threatened, paving the way for disillusionment and burnout. But if your team invites you to grow and to learn and supports your doing what you really care about, your team caregiving experiences can be among the most rewarding of all those on your helping journey.

This chapter concerns interdisciplinary helping teams—what they are and what makes them succeed or fail. Many basic concepts applied earlier to caregiving in one-on-one contexts also apply to this larger caregiving system. For example, models of self-esteem regulation, approach and avoidance as responses to distress, and the principles of effective helping communication are immediately applicable to the team context. The vignettes and examples I will use mainly come from the hospice and oncology fields, but the basic ideas developed here can be extended to all helping teams, groups, and organizations.

TEAM MISSION AND GOALS

Why do we have teams? The answer is simple: Caregiving teams are a response to complex human problems that demand the focused attention of experts from more than one discipline. An individual caregiver can't meet all the needs of a person who is terminally ill, or of a person coping with chronic illness or severe disabilities. The expertise of several disciplines is required to understand and care for people facing these kinds of difficult life circumstances. In the interdisciplinary team, for example, caregivers from a variety of disciplines work together to achieve goals that none could accomplish alone.

199

Acting in concert, team members can convert a collective commitment to a worthy purpose into specific caring acts that fulfill this shared mission. One essential team task is to reach agreement on the basic purpose or mission of the team and on the best way of getting there. If you are currently a member of a caregiving team, how would you define the mission—the shared purpose or "why" of the work—as the members of your team experience it? Is your team's mission closely aligned with your own purpose in helping? What does the team allow you to achieve that you couldn't accomplish alone?

There is a big difference between the objectives and guidelines that are given to a team by the larger organization to which it belongs and the kind of personal ownership that results from the team members' discussing and arriving at what they believe the team's mission is.[3] Has the team you are on owned its mission statement, or is the statement just a set of guidelines that has been handed down to you?

The team must also have a clear sense of the goals that it is working toward, a vision of what it will actually do to fulfill its mission. Setting clear performance goals and priorities is something teams often bypass, but it is well worth taking the time to do so. This shared vision is like a compass that can keep the team moving on course toward its goals in difficult times.

THE INTERDISCIPLINARY TEAM

In the health care field, the traditional biomedical model is being replaced by a biopsychosocial model that recognizes the complexity of the forces that affect illness, health, and healing. This model says that *bio*logical, *psycho*logical, and *social* elements must all be considered when we attempt to understand and treat any health problem (i.e., the whole person in his or her social context is the appropriate focus of our interventions).[4]

The development of interdisciplinary teams has paralleled that of the biopsychosocial model. Interdisciplinary clinical teams draw upon the expertise of specialists in each of these separate domains—biological/medical, psychological, and social—to diagnose and treat the whole person and the context of the illness because these are inseparable from the disease or problem in living that the person seeking help brings to us.

The interdisciplinary health team can include physicians, nurses, social workers, physical therapists, clinical nurse practitioners, chaplains, psychologists, music and art therapists, volunteer caregivers, and other specialists. The hospice team, a good example of a comprehensive interdisciplinary approach, extends the biopsychosocial model to include the spiritual needs of dying persons.

The interdisciplinary team represents one point or level in a developmental sequence of team development, from unidisciplinary (where there is no team at all); to multidisciplinary (where independent disciplines function largely unaffected by one another); to interdisciplinary (where the interaction of the team is necessary to produce the final product); and, finally, to transdisciplinary (where team members train one another and there is a phenomenon of "role release" in which roles and responsibilities are shared).[5] Working together in a truly interdisciplinary or transdisciplinary fashion is an ideal state that most caregiving teams aspire to but not all achieve.

Interdependent collaboration—the key to successful interdisciplinary teamwork—is often undermined by the failure of team members to understand the unique contributions and expertise of their colleagues from other disciplines. Most professional training includes little attention to other disciplines and to what members of these other disciplines can contribute as caregivers. This lack of understanding and appreciation can be responsible for a variety of communication problems and conflicts. One is a kind of role competition commonly known as "turfdom":

> The major conflict in our hospice is a turf issue: Who is best able to deal with emotional/counseling issues with patients—the RN case manager or the MSW? The MSW wants nurses to deal *only* with physical problems and leave counseling to the MSW.

A related phenomenon is what I call the one-person multidisciplinary team—the caregiver who refuses to collaborate and attempts to do it all alone. This stance probably originates in feelings like these:

> I often feel that no one cares as much as I do about the patients and their individual needs. Consequently, I feel ultimately responsible for the care the patients do or don't receive.

The resulting situation can look something like this:

> A nurse complains about carrying the whole load of a patient and family's care. The other team members complain that the nurse refuses to call any of them into the care even when the care plan is developed to incorporate them. The nurse "controls" the case and is exhausted by it.

Working collaboratively in a highly interdependent mode is intrinsically difficult. Every caregiver team faces the challenges of blending cooperation and competition, working together and working separately. For the individual caregiver, meeting these challenges entails tremendous personal vulnerability.

TEAMWORK INVOLVES PERSONAL VULNERABILITY

When you are a member of a multidisciplinary or interdisciplinary team, your work is constantly exposed to the critiques of others. You don't have the comfort of working in a unidisciplinary context, where it is possible that no one will see what you do or how well you do it. The close scrutiny of other team members really forces you to look at your own behavior and your ability to receive feedback or give it.

For example, I feel much more comfortable doing counseling in my private office, where no one can observe me, than I do intervening in a health care situation as a team member. In the team setting, if I fail to communicate effectively with a patient but other team members are successful, all my credentials and degrees won't protect me from the judgments of my fellow team members. One social worker shared similar feelings:

> I am a social worker, and I am supposed to be the expert
> on our hospice team on psychosocial issues. However,
> during the course of everyday hospice practice, I see the
> nurse or volunteer providing this type of support as well
> or better than myself. Even though I am the one with the
> master's, education, and experience, at times the work
> seems easier and more natural for others.

Being a team member means looking at yourself—your needs for power and control, your difficulties with sharing or collaborating, and a host of other personal issues related to team functioning.[6] This forced self-awareness can be painful, but it can also be an opportunity for personal growth if you approach yourself and the members of your team with an attitude of openness, flexibility, and respect.

Just as happens in your significant personal relationships and in your individual helping, working as part of a caregiving team will bring you face to face with both your strengths and your weaknesses. This usually leads to some combination of personal growth and personal distress; there is no pain-free way to be a team member, as Balfour Mount's quotation at the beginning of this chapter suggests.

However, sometimes our experiences as team members woefully lack this redeeming element of personal growth. If the team atmosphere is dominated by put-downs, gossip, power plays, and other negative behaviors, the personal growth of team members and the team's effectiveness will be severely limited.

CONFLICT IN THE TEAM

Interpersonal conflicts and other communication problems present the greatest challenges for most caregiving teams. Remember that the issue of communication problems with fellow team members is often the number one stressor reported by caregivers (see chapter 3). These conflicts and communication problems can lead to the development of dysfunctional alliances or subsystems within the team. The structures of these team subsystems reflect the basic interpersonal dynamics associated with the conflict or communication problem.

Donald Bailey, an interdisciplinary team theorist and researcher, has outlined a number of possible dysfunctional team subsystems.[7] Each of the subsystems Bailey identifies diverges from an ideal model of team functioning in which, he proposes, the leader acts as a member of the team, team members have comparable power and influence, and conflicts and other disagreements revolve around substantive issues, not personality conflicts. The following statements illustrate each of the dysfunctional subsystems Bailey identifies.

Factions within the team

Disagreements/conflicts are handled in 2s or 3s and avoided in a full-team discussion. Nursing area is the largest and tends to segment off at times.

As our hospice grows, old-time staff members have difficulty accepting changes. They view change as preventing them from delivering "good care." Old-time staff view hospice as being too businesslike. [They think there is] too much concern over cost containment, and they feel this concern reduces quality of care.

Conflict between two team members

A personality conflict and power struggle between our medical director and executive director makes almost every discussion an issue of control.

A dominant leader

We have a dominant team leader who controls all meetings but skirts direct discussion or solutions to problems.

Our hospice director feels "It's my hospice."

A dominant team member

A member of the psychosocial staff has comments on all patients and all aspects of their care. She interjects at all times during the meeting and at other times. She is the ultimate expert in everything and enjoys arguments.

At the weekly team meeting, one nurse constantly runs on and on about peripheral details and many examples of patient/family behavior. Even though one of us may try and "rein her in," nothing changes from one week to another.

An isolated team member

A patient care nurse is consistently delinquent in turning in paperwork. Her body language in team conference [reflects her] feelings because she is always sitting alone at another table. How can we turn her around?

One person who is in conflict with the rest of the team

The conflict is between the only male (a nurse) and three female nurses, one female MSW, and a female counselor. The male nurse functions as a one-man team, rarely seeks assistance from others or team, is not a collaborator, and if he's corrected or spoken to about a situation, he goes back to the others and confronts each person about "who told on him."

One nurse on the team clearly shows very poor clinical judgment, and when she asks for advice she always responds with "Yes, but that won't work." No problem is ever solvable as far as she is concerned. The nursing supervisor refuses to intervene. Direct intervention by other nurses has not helped. Other nurses no longer trust her nursing judgments.

I am a hospice director. Although recognized at the local, state, and national levels, my own staff mistrusts me greatly. The direct care staff has gone "over my head" repeatedly. When I encourage them to share concerns with me, they are silent, but behind my back, they are very verbal. I do not like using "us and them," and I feel strongly that we are all part of the same team. But some of the staff have been with hospice since the beginning of the program and feel an unhealthy degree of ownership. They are unwilling to change anything. For example, all direct care staff are involved with every patient.

There's a continuous conflict between the doctor (medical director) and the hospice nurses. Whenever a nurse makes a suggestion, it is "cut-down" and "taken apart" by him. This causes the team to withdraw and become split and nonproductive.

Conflicts within the team sometimes stem from sharp differences of opinion about what to do in extraordinarily complex and difficult caregiving situations. There are no simple answers to the ethical, legal, and psychosocial problems that modern caregiving teams often confront, and team members can have widely diverging views as to the best course of action to pursue.

Here are some examples of caregiving situations that challenge the team in these ways:

A 39-year-old patient with advanced cancer asks the RN about her prognosis. The RN states it is 3 to 4 weeks, which the MD has told the RN and which the RN understands was communicated to the patient. The patient becomes upset. The husband is enraged. He directs criticism towards the RN and the hospice. The hospice coordinator and other staff are critical of the RN's blunt disclosure. A team conflict ensues.

Our hospice takes a variety of students, who accompany regular team members. Recently, a nursing student who himself has AIDS was assigned to a patient. He would be doing home patient care. What are the rights of our patient to know the student's diagnosis and of the student to confidentiality?

A young physician became a quadriplegic during body surfing. He was healthy physically but went into a major depression and was in a nursing home. He refused medication for bedsores (ulcers) and was slowly allowing himself to die of infection. It was taking a long time. This issue rocked the family, team, nursing home staff, and community. A court upheld his right to refuse medications. It caused major conflict and upsets within the team.

The team suspects that a patient and/or family members are abusing pain meds. The primary physician has pulled back from the situation. The patient needs more medication. The nurse has been hesitant to reveal the problem. A patient is in pain. The physician is unwilling to prescribe more or different medication. What should I do?

It is difficult to imagine that any team could deal with these complex, painful, and trying situations without gaining a few of the scars Balfour Mount described. However, if a team can openly deal with disagreements among its members, deeply reflect on what its mission is, and reach agreement on how its members are going to fulfill that mission, times like these can lead to tremendous personal growth for team members and a strengthening of the team itself. Sometimes the team can even be surprised by how well it handled what seemed like an impossible situation.

However, a less appealing alternative is too often the case. Ethical dilemmas that tear at the soul, unresolved conflicts among team members, exponential growth and organizational restructuring, the departure or serious illness of a team member—all these can disrupt and threaten the helping team and leave it uncertain as to whether it can really cope with the new demands it must face.

Confronted with these threats, teams can opt to avoid difficult and uncomfortable feelings and engage in various defensive maneuvers that can be crippling to the team's growth and well-being. By doing so, the team can avoid the pain of looking at the core problems it is having. But it will suffer the consequences of that avoidance later. Essentially, this is a group variation on the neurotic paradox discussed in chapter 3. In other words, the short-term gains (anxiety reduction) of avoidance behavior outweigh the long-term pain associated with it, leading to what is ultimately self-defeating behavior.

Unhealthy Agreement, Team Secrets, and Defensive Routines

Many team and organizational experts emphasize that patterns of avoidance are among the most destructive and dysfunctional of all team dynamics. In *Groupthink,* psychologist Irving Janis documents how teams can make bad decisions even though some or all team members have serious misgivings about the wisdom of these decisions.[8] The team can ignore these misgivings and dissenting opinions as it works hard to be in a state of agreement, and then it takes the easy way out by accepting the first solution that rises to the surface. The guiding principle is that we are nice people, and nice people agree with one another. The problem is that important ideas and contributions can get lost along the way.

Pointing to similar phenomena, team expert William Dyer describes how a kind of unhealthy agreement can become a self-defeating pattern in organizations.[9] When this kind of unhealthy agreement pattern exists, team members feel frustrated and powerless trying to deal with a specific problem, and they tend to blame one another for the problem. They also tend to discuss these issues in small subgroups of friends and trusted confidants, but they don't directly communicate their ideas in team meetings. Therefore, in public situations, they try to figure out what other team members' positions are without sharing their own. Ultimately, they often feel that they should have said something at a certain point, but they don't do so. This pattern of collective avoidance and unhealthy agreement continues until the problem precipitates a major crisis.

I think of this kind of a team as having a team secret analogous to the secrets we have as individuals. Even though all the team members might be able to identify the problem or conflict, it is never discussed openly by the entire group. Because no one can talk about the problem, the team's decisions lack feedback and commitment from team members and thus usually fail.

Low trust levels go hand in hand with this failure to deal openly with team conflicts. When team members don't trust one another's intentions, they feel threatened and perceive the risks of sharing information and addressing the conflict as outweighing the benefits. Ideally, team members should always feel safe enough to talk about not feeling safe. But the problem is that once you begin talking about the "elephant in the room" it is hard to selectively deny the particular aspects you *don't* feel safe talking about. If even a small piece of the truth is discussed, the rest inexorably follows, so denial is often carefully maintained.

In *The Open Organization: The Impact of Secrecy and Disclosure on People and Organizations,* Fritz Steele makes a strong case for openness:

Unless there is the opportunity and ability to disclose
information about what is actually happening in the
system, including both behaviors and feelings, then it
is very difficult for that system's members to be masters
of their own fate and for the system to be self-correcting.
In this sense, the importance of disclosure is not only in
doing the day-to-day work which requires information
flow (that kind of disclosure happens fairly regularly),
but also in examining *how* things are being done, so
that maintenance can be done on the system to keep
it healthy.[10]

Steele also notes that we often blame the sharing of information about a problem, as if it had created rather than simply signaled the problem. When information is not being shared openly, the team encounters more rumors and gossip, it doesn't learn and self-correct, and then there are more elephants in the room that can't be discussed. In other words, what the team doesn't know *can* hurt it.

In *The Fifth Discipline*, organizational expert Peter Senge describes the forces preventing productive dialogue in working teams. "Chief among these," says Senge, are "*defensive routines,* habitual ways of interacting that protect us and others from threat or embarrassment, but which also prevent us from learning."[11] Examples of defensive routines include "smoothing over" differences or having big theoretical debates that go nowhere. To retain their power, these defensive routines must, according to Senge, remain "undiscussable."[12]

Antidotes to Avoidance and Defensiveness

For Senge, the antidote to defensive patterns of behavior is a commitment to telling the truth about the team's current reality (i.e., a commitment to self-disclosure and to a quality of reflectiveness and openness that fosters a deeper understanding of what other team members are thinking and feeling). If these conditions are absent, though the individuals on the team may all be highly intelligent, the team itself will have a subpar IQ.

But I need to stress that openness in the organization or team doesn't just mean speaking out and airing every thought or feeling you have. It is a more demanding stance, a kind of "reflective openness," as Senge describes it, in which we can challenge our own and others' thinking, "suspend our certainty," and share our feelings and ideas with a receptiveness to having them changed.[13] This parallels what I suspect is true for the individual regarding his or her personal secrets: Confiding can have positive health effects, but telling the whole world your secrets probably has none.

The successful management of conflict requires what author Alfie Kohn calls a "cooperative framework for dealing with disagreement" so that competition and win/lose dynamics don't interfere with the healthy exchange of differing views by team members.[14] When a cooperative context exists, Kohn notes, conflicts can become what Roger and David Johnson have termed "friendly excursions into disequilibrium."[15] Senge also emphasizes that no team can avoid all conflicts and defensive maneuvers, but a healthy team is the one that learns from them.

In chapter 3, I emphasized that it is rare to experience significant and lasting personal growth without feeling any pain or suffering as an essential part of that growth. This idea applies to teams as well. Conflicts and defensive operations can make or break a team, but effective teams can recognize these phenomena, learn from them, and then continue to work toward the team members' shared goals.

Dealing With Conflicts in the Team

Openly dealing with conflicts and sharing potentially threatening information are tough assignments for any team. However, we can begin to develop a more workable approach to these tasks by first accepting that conflict is a natural—and often desirable—team experience, as Howard Margolis and Joseph Fiorelli indicate:

> To view disagreement or conflict as unnatural is a mistake which disrupts effective team functioning. Realization that the expression of dissimilar opinions is more often a natural expression of differing world views by sincere, dedicated professionals is essential for combating the all too common proposition that "If they disagree with me, they're bad, stupid, or both." Accepting conflict or disagreement as a stimulus that can provide opportunities for achieving a more complete and comprehensive understanding of the problem and more alternatives to the solution enhances the probability of choosing a superior solution.[16]

When we see conflicts and disagreements as the inevitable concomitants of working so closely with others, we are more likely to approach these issues nondefensively, to feel less need to blame others, and to encourage a joint effort to solve the problem.

The examples of team conflicts presented earlier are good illustrations of the downstream consequences of not dealing effectively with conflict and disagreements over a long period of time. In the everyday work of the team, the small conflicts that can develop over time into major problems like these often begin with a simple failure to communicate clearly about what team members expect of one another.

In the productive and healthy team, members have a clear understanding of what their own and others' job responsibilities are (i.e., there is a state of role clarity). Role ambiguity, in contrast, exists when team members don't know what they should be doing, aren't clear about what other team members expect of them, or aren't clear about their own expectations of others.[17]

Role conflicts are another related problem. Here there are inconsistencies in the expectations of team members. Team members can have expectations for themselves that are inconsistent with the expectations other team members have of them. Two or more team members can make conflicting demands of a colleague, or there can be a kind of role overload in which there is simply not enough time for certain members to meet all the expectations of the other team members.[18]

When not discussed and openly negotiated, role conflicts, role ambiguity, and differing views of what the team is trying to do can all lead to team strife and escalating patterns of conflict among members that eventually come to be seen as "personality clashes." When we consider how these different kinds of conflicts are mismanaged or not managed at all, a common theme emerges. These conflicts tend to become personalized (i.e., they become expressed as different variations on the "they're bad, stupid, or both" phenomenon Margolis and Fiorelli note).

This tendency to personalize conflicts is reinforced by our natural inclination to explain behavior by making attributions about the other person rather than the situation the person is in. This is another instance of the fundamental attribution error discussed in chapter 2. Rather than seeing ourselves as struggling with a problem that is common to many teams or viewing the problem as a consequence of team members' failure to do the hard work of getting clear about their goals and expectations, we tend to see ourselves as struggling against people who are "bad, stupid, or both." The result is that the ensuing patterns of behavior become self-reinforcing and tend to escalate over time.

The personalization of conflict also means that the potential recipients of feedback are less open to that feedback because it is likely to be delivered as an unwelcome message about some perceived flaw within themselves. We all want feedback—and yet we don't want it. We want to know how we are doing in the tasks of achieving our goals, but we don't want to know that others don't like what we are doing.

It is instructive to think about similar situations in your personal life. What is your first reaction when someone tells you they don't like what you are doing or asks you to change your behavior and do something differently, whether it is closing the tube of toothpaste, wearing different clothes, or behaving differently at the dinner table? For most people, there is a natural tendency to resist this kind of feedback and the corresponding behavior change. This is because we want to feel good about what we are doing, and accepting that we need to change our behavior implies that we are wrong in some way.

This is the point at which the request to change can be potentially threatening to our self-esteem and therefore potentially stressful. In our personal lives and on caregiving teams, we need to find ways to give and receive feedback and to change our behavior accordingly. The obstacle is that there usually isn't an easy and pain-free (i.e., self-esteem maintaining or enhancing) way to ask someone else to change his or her behavior, particularly when the other person is not experiencing any distress associated with that behavior. In fact, it is usually the case that the other person is fairly attached to this particular behavior and it is meeting various needs for that person, thus making it even more likely that he or she will resist changing.

In the ideal situation, our feedback to one another would be frequent and timely (not 6 months after the troubling event), nonjudgmental (not threatening to the self-esteem of the other person), and concrete (focusing on specific, observable behaviors).[19] When these conditions are met, feedback and conflict resolution are much more likely to be effective.

Conflicts as Unmet Expectations: A Practical Model for Conflict Resolution

People are particularly motivated to give feedback to someone when his or her behavior doesn't match their expectations. This simple fact is the basis for a powerful model of conflict and conflict resolution that discourages the personalization of these kinds of problems within the team. This model defines conflicts simply as unmet expectations.[20]

When we experience a conflict with other people, they are either doing something we didn't expect them to do or they are not doing something we did expect them to do. Virtually all conflicts will fall within this model.

Unmet expectations are a major source of team stress; they underlie many interpersonal communication problems that team members typically cite as among the most stressful aspects of their work. When you are experiencing unmet expectations concerning another person's behavior, the first step toward conflict resolution is to let the other person know about these unmet expectations. Of course, I'm talking about unmet expectations that are worthy of such attention—namely, conflicts that cause you stress, interfere with the optimal performance of your caregiving duties, and so forth. There are more unmet expectations in our lives than we could—or should—ever address.

One fascinating phenomenon I've encountered as a team and organizational consultant is that when I ask people to think of the most troublesome unmet expectation they have regarding someone in their workplace, a majority of them admit that they haven't told the other person about it. Their explanations include statements like these: "She'll never change," "I've given him enough hints to sink a ship—if he wanted the feedback, he'd have figured it out by now," "She'd be devastated," or "I want to continue working here and don't want to make him my enemy."

Each of these reasons seems to have some validity. There *are* risks involved when you approach another person to ask for a change in his or her behavior. However, the consequences of the alternative course of action are more definite: If the other person is never directly told about your unmet expectation, there is no chance that the behavior will change, and the problem is likely to get worse.

A paradoxical finding is that, although most people say that they would like feedback on their *own* behavior if someone had a problem with it, these same people insist that the other person would not respond in a similarly positive and welcoming fashion. In these situations, we often believe that the other person couldn't possibly have the same psychological maturity, win-win attitude, empathy, or goodwill that we see in ourselves, and so it is difficult to imagine the person cooperating with our requests for behavior change.

There is a kind of self-deception operating here that also contributes to the perpetuation of conflicts within teams. Although few of us really believe we are perfect, when we are having problems on the team, too often our first thoughts when we arrive at work in the morning are something like this: "If only this other person or these other people would get it together, things would be much better around here." If all 10 members of a 10-person team feel this way, the results are predictable. In contrast, if everyone approached the team with the attitude "What can I do differently that would make things work better for other members of the team?" many conflicts would rapidly disappear.

Even if we recognize that others might be amenable to changing their behavior and that we might need to change our own behavior as well, dealing with these issues is usually uncomfortable for everyone. The good news is that there can be many more positive outcomes than our fears would suggest are possible. These positive outcomes are even more likely if structures and norms exist that support the ongoing negotiation of roles and expectations in the team. Successful conflict resolution is more likely if there is a group norm that all team members should routinely discuss unmet expectations with other team members as part of continual team development.

Let's look at some skills that can make these exchanges of information safe enough for teams to embrace and practice openly. We will discover how you can ask others to change their behaviors in a way that doesn't lower their self-esteem and evoke angry and defensive responses.

A key first step is to see the problem as existing in the relationship or in the fit between you and the other person, rather than in you or the other person. This more systems oriented perspective will help you avoid blaming yourself or the other person and distorting the reality of the situation. It is better to adopt the expectation that successful resolution of the conflict will involve change on both your parts.

During the first few seconds in which you are presenting an unmet expectation to the other person, the outcome of the encounter is rapidly being decided. The encounter is likely to go in one of two possible directions: mutual discovery or combative defensiveness. Think about the encounters of this nature you have had in your personal and work lives. When the outcome was positive, you and the other person were probably able to listen to each other and understand the impact of the behavior in question without getting locked into a competitive, angry, and defensive state. You weren't thinking, "How can I protect myself?" or "What can I do to get my own way?"

How can we increase the likelihood of mutual exploration, empathy, and cooperation? One way to do this is to express our unmet expectations as "I-statements" or "I-messages." This is the same talk tool that many self-help books recommend for parents, managers, and just about anyone who must solicit changes in the behavior of other people. When you present your conflict via an I-message, the key is to begin by stating it as a problem *you* have and not as a problem the other person has. This way of stating things is effective for two reasons: First, it *is* in fact your problem—the other person might be perfectly happy with his or her behavior; second, by stating it this way, you increase the likelihood that the other person will empathize with your position and not immediately adopt a defensive stance.

The next parts of the message should include a description of the behavior that is troubling you, how it affects you (include your feelings), and why. Help the other person understand and empathize with your point of view. The emotional issues in the conflict must be approached and resolved before the content issues are handled, and both of you really have to understand what this conflict looks like from the other side.

The more strictly behavioral (as opposed to personal) your description of the troublesome behavior, the better. If your comments contain even an implicit evaluation of the general abilities or worth of the other person (e.g., "I guess you just don't care" or "You have an attitude problem") the possibility of a defensive or hostile response is much greater.

Here are some examples of I-messages: "Jean, I'm having some difficulty because when I don't get the paperwork from you in time to do my own notes when they're due, I get lots of complaints from everyone else." Or "Ron, I'm really struggling with something. When you don't let me know what happened on your shift, I'm left in the dark, and I'm afraid that I could make a serious mistake because of this. What can we do about it?"

Though I might not be stating these messages exactly the way you would, it is the form that is important, not the content. Own the problem. Be specific about what in the other person's behavior is causing problems for you. Describe how it is affecting you, including your feelings. Then submit the problem for joint consideration rather than make a unilateral demand for behavior change.

Think of your conflict resolution intervention as a confrontation response (see chapter 6). In other words, you are pointing to a discrepancy between something specific in the other person's behavior and your expectations of that person's behavior. There should be no aggressive element in your message. However, what frequently occurs is that we wait such a long time before bringing up a subject that by the time we do discuss it, our anger has built up and quickly comes to the surface if our comments meet with any resistance. This is why all the members of the team should give one another feedback frequently as an essential part of team maintenance. When these communication channels break down, the team suffers and the problems become increasingly more difficult to address in a productive manner.

Here are some additional principles that can make conflict resolution or role negotiation interactions more successful:

- Don't confront anyone in a group setting, and never encourage ganging up on one person so that they will "get the point."

- Be supportive. Go one better than the Golden Rule and treat others *better* than you want them to treat you.

- Find ways to share information without lowering the self-esteem of the other person. How would *you* like to hear the message you are about to convey?

- Imagine what the other person needs from you and offer it, and the other person will be more likely to give you what you need.

- Make frequent negotiations of role expectations among all team members a part of the normal ongoing life of the team. This prevents the buildup of tensions that lead to the crises and emotional eruptions that characterize the dysfunctional team.

- Write out your agreement. "I'd like you to do more of _____ (or) less of _____. Also write out how it will help you, give an example of how you would like the other person's behavior to change, and include the behavior changes you are willing to make in exchange. The idea here is quid pro quo—something for something. If you want me to wear different clothes to work, you'd better be willing to change an equally important and central aspect of your own behavior. Many people find that a written contract, with a date for checking in on how the agreement has worked, leads to better results.

- Be sure the other person really wants to experiment with this new way of talking about working together before you initiate any conflict resolution sessions. Explain this model in some detail. You might even ask the other person to read this chapter before beginning.

STRATEGIES FOR TEAM DEVELOPMENT

What can you do to make your caregiving team healthier and more productive? We have already discussed one approach to conflict resolution that you can use as a guide for approaching other team members when unmet expectations are an issue. Here are some other general guidelines for improving your team, including some specifics for making staff/helper support groups work more effectively.

Encourage Shared Leadership

Team development expert Irwin Rubin and his colleagues stress that to effectively achieve the team's goals, leadership functions must be shared throughout the team. Just as no single person can achieve the basic task or mission of the team, no single person can make the decisions, monitor and coordinate team progress, and lead the team in every situation. Instead, team members must assume shared leadership responsibilities.[21] These leadership functions can be divided into two categories: those that focus on *what* (content/task) the group is doing and those that are concerned with *how* (process) the group is working.

Task-oriented leadership functions include initiating problem solving or building work agendas, giving and seeking information and opinions, clarifying and elaborating on the various inputs of group members, summarizing where the group is and where it needs to go, and checking to see if people are clear on the goals and decisions of the team.

Process-oriented leadership functions include ensuring that everyone's contributions are considered, encouraging the participation of group members, harmonizing different points of view, and finding creative solutions to problems the group tackles. When these leadership functions are shared, an ethos of participation and empowerment and a greater sense of commitment to the team's goals can develop.

Enhance Team Members' Self-Esteem

Making team members feel good about themselves is another important leadership function that team members can share. To a large extent, leadership involves just that—making people feel good about themselves, enhancing their self-esteem. The praise, awards, and recognition dispensed within the team are part of this core leadership function. Burnout is much less likely when team members feel they and their work are truly valued and valuable. This is particularly important in the human services, where self-doubts, helper secrets, and self-blame can lower one's self-esteem. High self-esteem is an excellent buffer against stress and inhibitor of burnout. We all need occasional affirmation of the good things we do and of our importance to the team effort.

How much do you feel your work is recognized and rewarded by your team? Although you can't change everyone else's behavior toward you directly, you can recognize and reward the work of your teammates. These positive actions will earn the goodwill of your colleagues, making them more likely to reciprocate in kind in the future. The moral is, if the world feels cold, light a small fire, and it will spread. The positive effects of being more generous with your praise and thank-yous are more immediate, however. As discussed in chapter 1, caring for others is good for you as the caregiver; offering caring expressions to your teammates will benefit you by improving your own mood and self-esteem.

How can we increase these kind of affirming behaviors among teammates? Too often, months or even years go by without team members sitting down and sharing their appreciation of one another. Some people might say that to be genuine, positive feedback and thank-yous must be spontaneous, unplanned, and "from the heart." But I believe that a structure is necessary in order to build these "spontaneous and heartfelt" communications into our busy helping worlds.

For example, I encourage caregiver teams to do a brief round of acknowledgments and thank-yous at least once every 3 months. The feedback should be specific, acknowledging things that you have seen the other person do that struck you as a positive contribution to either the team effort or your own work. For example, you might acknowledge a creative intervention, someone's sense of humor, or anything else about the person that inspires or supports you. Don't spend more than a minute or two on each person, but be sure that everyone is included. You might think that doing this regularly would lead to all the positive comments being saved for "appreciations day" and that the number of spontaneous expressions of appreciation between these sessions would decrease. But the reverse is actually true. Giving acknowledgments is a good habit that can be strengthened by occasionally giving it the team's exclusive focus.

Build Caring Relationships

Your relationships with other team members will be most rewarding and productive if they are endowed with the same qualities of openness, trust, respect, and authenticity that you are striving for in your helping relationships. When teammates are in the Helper's Pit or in the midst of a personal crisis, it is natural to share our best helping selves with them:

> I was being there—present, listening, feeling, receiving—
> for one of my staff, a social worker, who was going through
> a significant experience of a personal grief/loss/health
> crisis. As we sat together, sharing tea and a poppy seed
> muffin, she said, "I'm really not so different from the
> people we take care of." Then she hugged me, and
> we cried.

An important kind of empathy to have for other team members, particularly members of other disciplines, is a clear understanding (both intellectually and emotionally) of what it is like to do their job. Here is an exercise you can try with your team: Have all your team members write what they think each other team member does and how they think each person feels about doing it on identical sheets of paper, then read these sheets anonymously.

What do you think this exercise would reveal? One discovery might be that most team members have surprisingly incomplete and erroneous pictures of what the other team members do and how they feel about doing it. If you try this exercise, be sure that the team members are given an opportunity to correct any inaccurate perceptions and to provide a more complete picture of what it is actually like to do their jobs. The group can also discuss how some of their ongoing communication problems might be related to the incomplete views they have of one another's roles and work experiences. You can devote some time to renegotiating what team members expect of each other as well.

This exercise is a quick technique for overcoming the interdisciplinary myopia that affects us all. You can also achieve this in one-on-one settings by arranging extra meetings with individual teammates for sharing these perceptions.

When there is empathy among team members and when there is an atmosphere of goodwill, trust deepens and expands, leading to greater openness, fewer negative interactions, and the sustained personal growth of team members. Fear has exactly the opposite effect on these qualities of team life. If every team had a "fear detector" and used it, the possibilities for team development would be enormous. Of course, not all our fears need to be discussed in the group context, but when an atmosphere of fear replaces one of goodwill, the negative effects on the team are pervasive. Then the team needs to be aware that this is occurring so the members can address the problem.

One fear-engendering behavior teams can engage in is spreading rumors and gossip. A rumor is a statement or opinion circulated among team members that has no known source. Rumors are hazardous to teams because innocent statements can, as they are passed from person to person and changed along the way, become explosive "news" items with serious implications for particular team members.

Gossip—rumors linked to a specific individual—is even more hazardous to the team. We all know this, but it is often difficult to politely resist participating in gossip. If all team members agree that gossip is unacceptable, and if each team member makes an effort to politely refuse to listen to gossip about teammates, the norm of no gossip will quickly develop.

An appropriate response to gossip is to say, in effect, that although you appreciate that the other person just wants to keep you informed about what is happening, you don't think you need to know about this piece of information. Then shift the conversation to another topic.[22] Each person must find his or her own way to say no to gossip.

If you think that it is impossible to avoid participating in gossip, given your network of friendships within the team, then you might need to examine whether that network is really healthy for you and the team. The dilemma with gossip is that people don't think they are doing anything wrong when they indulge in it and therefore see no need to change their behavior. We often partake in gossip because we don't want to alienate the person who is sharing it with us and consequently have him or her also talking about us behind our backs. But another part of us knows that a better response is to let the person know we are simply not interested.

Empower One Another

Empowerment has become somewhat of a cliche, but even so it retains its relevance for all our caregiving efforts. In essence, our human presence, support, and communication skills empower the people we care for—they gain a greater sense of control over the difficult situations they face so they are able to live in more fulfilling ways.

This should also be our goal in our relationships with our fellow caregivers. The helper's journey is not that of the isolated individual working wonders on a mountaintop. It is more like being part of a team of climbers who are working together interdependently to get to the top of the mountain. In the end, each member is able to achieve something he or she could not alone.

High-functioning groups are exciting to participate in because the group often generates solutions to problems that all team members recognize as better than those any a single team member could have arrived at. This is the kind of empowerment that comes from participating in a team. Team members can also empower one another by teaching skills and sharing their knowledge. This kind of transdisciplinary team functioning gives the team added flexibility and confidence, and reduces disciplinary myopia and feelings of "This is *my* turf."

Establish Caregiver Support Groups

Creating a support group where problems, concerns, and feelings are communicated openly is an excellent means of preventing burnout, reducing turnover, and improving team morale.[23] A support group is a place where you talk with people who appreciate the difficulties and the joys of your shared work and who understand your motivations for doing it. "The secrets of life," as Emerson wrote, "are not shown except to sympathy and likeness."[24]

In helper support groups, as in personal support groups, members share a common concern (i.e., stress at work) and there is an emphasis upon peer help. Members meet to learn together and to support one another in their work as helpers. These groups provide a unique opportunity for interpersonal learning and for receiving assistance in coping with work stressors, dealing with issues of professional identity, and team building.

An important kind of learning that occurs in group members during these regularly scheduled meetings is a shift from believing that "I'm the only one having a difficult time with this" to knowing that "We're all in the same boat" (i.e., that everyone has a difficult time with these stressful situations). Sharing common concerns in an egalitarian atmosphere can lead to a kind of instant empathy and a sense of we-ness among group members, and unrealistic self-expectations can be tempered and corrected. Difficult feelings and helper secrets can be shared and worked through. Once this occurs, the bias toward self-blame can be corrected, and one's energies can be directed toward developing better coping and problem-solving skills and strategies.[25]

Many different kinds of support and learning can occur in an effective support group. These include direct assistance, feedback, sharing and modeling of problem-solving strategies, ventilation of feelings, and encouragement. Each of the six different forms of social support described in chapter 3—listening, technical appreciation, technical challenge, emotional support, emotional challenge, and shared social reality—are usually exchanged among group members. These different support needs can also be met through unstructured interactions among team members.

Some characteristics that distinguish successful from less successful groups have been identified. Studying both personal and professional (i.e., caregiver) support groups, British psychologists Keith Nichols and John Jenkinson defined six core interactions that characterize successful support groups: (a) focusing on issues of personal significance, (b) confronting difficult issues—getting beyond superficiality, (c) making feeling-based reflective self-disclosures, (d) using the responses of other group members to increase self-awareness, (e) aiding other members with the previous tasks, and (f) learning to give and receive support.[26] Groups vary widely in the frequency and intensity of these core interactions and needn't be high on all of them to offer worthwhile help to their members.

It is important to realize what these groups are *not* as well as what they are. Most important, they are not psychotherapy sessions. In therapy groups, a professional therapist leads the group as it focuses on intrapsychic issues with the goal of personality change in the individual group members. Support groups can be self-led or can have a facilitator or consultant who is ideally not a member of the team. This person can be a mental health professional, but needn't be. In the support group, the focus is on problem solving and strengthening relationships among group members, with the goal of increasing team members' effectiveness and well-being.

Although personal problems do come up and are appropriate topics in a professional support group because they affect our work with the team, serious personal problems should be taken to a counselor rather than to the group. It is also important to note that staff support groups are not a palliative treatment for organizational problems (e.g., a lack of space, personnel, equipment, or quality leadership) and will only further demoralize caregivers if they are used in this way.[27]

Support groups can also fail for a variety of other reasons. Breaches of confidentiality, presence of a dominant facilitator, and failure to establish and maintain trust and a caring atmosphere in the group are just a few of the many problems groups can and do have. Michael Boreing and Leta Adler have identified 10 behaviors that are counterproductive to group goals: silence or withdrawal, anger, intellectualizing, dominating the conversation, undermining the facilitator or group, nonattendance, scapegoating, interrogating, rescuing, and forming coalitions.[28] Training materials now exist that can help staff support groups avoid some of these predictable problems; they can also be profitably reviewed by newly forming or existing caregiver (or personal, i.e., for patients/clients) support groups.[29, 30, 31, 32, 33, 34]

Here are some useful guidelines for successful support group functioning that come from the training literature and from my experiences with caregiver support groups:

For the group as a whole, decide:

- How big will it be? (5 to 12 members is optimal)
- When, where, how frequently, and how long should meetings be?
- Will it be open or closed?
- Will it be facilitated or self-led?

- Will there be an educational component?

For group members:

- Remember that each member is the authority on his or her own experience.
- First make contact with other group members, then address specific needs.
- Let others know what your ideas are.
- Don't do all the talking.
- Help other members participate by encouraging them.
- Listen carefully to other members.
- Don't ask too many questions or give quick advice.
- Disclose your own experiences, especially those that convey empathy for the experiences of other group members.

For facilitators:

- Use the open-ended communication skills from chapter 6 to exercise the least amount of authority necessary to promote beneficial interaction in the group.[35]
- Don't dominate, sermonize, evaluate, teach, or moralize.[36]
- Do promote cohesion, develop a safe climate, reinforce productive behaviors, and give information when appropriate.[37]
- Avoid carrying on a conversation with each member in turn. Instead, encourage members to speak directly to one another.
- Encourage the expression of feelings, exploration of problems, and sharing of coping strategies.
- Focus the group on topics pertinent to the main concerns of the group.
- Mediate when the friction gets too great.
- Establish rules of confidentiality.
- Manage the logistics (e.g., scheduling, physical setting, notices, refreshments) for the group.

Most experts agree that staff support groups should be held in addition to staff meetings and other ad hoc support efforts within the team.[38] However, these same guidelines can also be used for the brief planned or ad hoc segments of team meetings devoted to staff support. The guidelines can also be applied to personal support groups (e.g., bereavement groups or cancer support groups) that might be part of the team's caregiving efforts.[39]

Although group members have needs for both security and structure, these must be provided without the facilitator's taking an overly directive role and becoming an authority figure for the group. Structure and security can instead be provided through the group's use of designed exercises or formats that can increase the participants' feelings of safety and prevent some problems that groups, especially unstructured ones, experience.

For example, occasionally dividing the time into equal segments for each group member will ensure that everyone will participate and prevent the monopolization of the group's time by one or more members. Another format that can quickly and safely promote intimacy among group members involves beginning meetings with each member's sharing for just a few seconds how he or she is feeling at the moment. In the *Common Concern* support group training program, this technique is called "Moodcheck."[40] My helper secrets exercise can also be used to facilitate the anonymous sharing and discussion of troubling or stressful caregiving experiences (see chapter 4).

Another key to success is to have the support group study itself or evaluate how it is doing on an ongoing basis. A brief discussion (5 minutes) at the end of each session to focus on the best things and the worst things about the session can be useful. Howard Kirschenbaum and Barbara Glaser recommend that the group periodically give each member a few minutes to answer these questions: "What is one thing you appreciate about our support group?" "How do you see your own participation in the group?" and "How do you feel about the role you've played?"[41]

Study the Team's Process

To be effective, the caregiving team, like the caregiver support group, needs to study itself. To paraphrase Irwin Rubin, football teams practice for 40 hours each week and play for only 2. The typical caregiving team, in contrast, plays for 40-plus hours each week and doesn't have any time to practice (i.e., to discuss how the team can work together more effectively and to work through any problems that may exist).[42]

This self-study requires that the team look at its own process by asking about *how* they are talking and acting with one another, rather than studying *what* they are talking about. Process questions the team can ask might include the following:

- Who talks and for how long?

- How are decisions made?

- Are differing points of view encouraged or discouraged?

- How safe do members feel talking about a particular issue?

- Are there any "elephants in the room" that everyone is aware of but no one addresses openly in the meetings?

The content of the team's interactions is important, but if the team fails to look at how it is interacting, it will inevitably lose control of that process and of its helping outcomes. An atmosphere of respect, trust, and openness will encourage this kind of process awareness and self-study and will promote sensitivity to the changing needs of the individuals in the group. A process orientation is proactive because it detects team problems in their earliest stages and leads to adjustments that ensure the continued productivity and well-being of the team and its members.[43]

Proactive, process-oriented teams regularly assess how they are doing. The most essential task in this area is to stop and collectively take note of any team problems. Rubin and his colleagues emphasize that there is one leadership role that belongs to every team member—the "stopper."[44] A person acting in the stopper role says, in essence, "Something doesn't feel right here; let's look at our process."

The team must listen to its members when they are having concerns like these:

- Things aren't getting done, and I always have to check to make sure they do.

- I don't feel safe enough to say what I'm thinking.

- It seems as though everyone is giving the work only half the attention it needs.

- Our meetings and conferences are boring, lack energy, and are dominated by a few people.

- There is a lot of complaining behind the scenes.

- We often seem to be working at cross-purposes.

- Things are getting done, but I'm being pushed to
  the breaking point.[45]

Rubin and his colleagues offer this list of concerns as warnings that signal a need for team development.[46] The problems reflected by these concerns increase stress for the team as a whole because they threaten the members' self-esteem and prevent them from achieving the team's goals.

Questionnaires that assess different aspects of team functioning can also be useful. Many good instruments exist for this purpose.[47] One extremely brief questionnaire can serve as an example of what the team needs to look at. Respond to each of the following items as they apply to your team, using this scale: (a) strongly disagree, (b) disagree, (c) neutral, (d) agree, and (e) strongly agree.

- There is a high degree of trust and openness
  in the group.

- The team is effective at achieving its tasks.

- I get all the information I need to do my work
  and make effective decisions.

- Good work is recognized and rewarded in this group.

- Assignments (who does what) are clearly defined.

- Differences and conflicts are recognized and worked
  through.[48]

Questionnaires like this can be an excellent starting point for team discussions. Responses from team members can be gathered anonymously, collated, and then reviewed by the entire team in a team-building session.

When I have used this scale in surveys and team development sessions with caregiving teams, I have found that members of teams functioning well believe that their teams are effective at achieving their tasks. They also generally get all the information they need to do their work and to make effective decisions and believe that task assignments are clear to all group members. However, even these teams often report problems with trust and openness, as well as difficulties recognizing and working through conflicts. These two dimensions of team functioning are, of course, highly correlated—if there is no trust, conflicts aren't acknowledged, and if there are too many conflicts, trust plummets. Highly distressed teams, suffering from severe communication breakdowns and organizational upheavals, score poorly on all six dimensions of the questionnaire.

In a survey of hospice teams, I asked respondents to indicate whether or not their team regularly evaluated its effectiveness.[49] I found that 75% of the participants answered no and 25% answered yes. Those that said yes reported that they used a variety of strategies for evaluating team effectiveness, including questionnaire studies, anonymous feedback, off-site retreats, videotaping the team conference and then reviewing it, and devoting time at the beginning of the team conference once a month to evaluation and development.

A videotape (or audiotape) review of group meetings can be a powerful technique for self-study if the review is effectively structured and facilitated. However, when no electronic recording is possible, immediate recall of the interaction can also be used.

A helpful model for reviewing group interactions like these is the Interpersonal Process Recall Method (IPR) developed by psychologist Norman Kagan.[50] IPR is a simple, novel, and easily learned technique for reviewing videotaped interactions in a nonthreatening and nonjudgmental manner. The IPR training program is quite extensive, but the central feature of the process involves choosing someone to facilitate review by the rest of the group. It is best if the facilitator is not a member of the team doing the review. This facilitator encourages individual group members to stop the tape at any point during the review when they become aware of any feelings, thoughts, and other reactions they had during the videotaped session. The facilitator then helps that individual explore his or her thoughts, feelings, and reactions, using the videotape to stimulate recall of these experiences. It might take 90 minutes to review a 20-minute videotape, but the time is usually well spent. As the team reviews its behavior, many of the invisible patterns that form the core of the team's process become apparent.

In the survey of hospice teams just mentioned, I asked members to indicate whether most interventions to improve team functioning were made before or after problems developed in their team. An overwhelming majority (87%) of respondents marked "after"; the remaining 13% indicated "before." These preliminary data suggest that most hospice teams take a downstream, or reactive, approach to the management of team problems (i.e., something is done *after* a problem develops). Only 13% take an upstream, preventive stance. How does your team deal with its problems? Is its approach reactive or proactive?

The proactive team also renews itself through regular team-building experiences. Strategies for self-renewal I have seen teams use include having an outside facilitator work with them; arranging retreats; holding brainstorming sessions; or having a planning day, a happy hour, an informal retreat or social occasion, a day at the pool, or a community activity day.

To summarize, in the productive and healthy caregiving team, we find that the following are true:

- Team goals and team roles are clearly understood.
- The team is intelligent—it learns.
- There is an atmosphere of goodwill and trust.
- Conflicts are addressed and worked through.
- Secrecy and gossip are kept to a minimum.
- Leadership functions are shared.
- Technical and emotional support and challenge are frequently exchanged.
- The team studies itself.
- The team accomplishes its goals, and team members grow and learn through their work together.

CONCLUSION

The high-functioning team—like the high-functioning caregiver—has a sense of confidence that it can cope with the demands confronting it and that it is making a uniquely valuable contribution to the world. High team self-efficacy and the team's collective self-esteem are powerful deterrents to stress and set the stage for the team's continued success and well-being. This kind of team enables members to fulfill their personal missions as helpers while they pursue the team's shared goals.

The openness and feedback of the high-functioning team are as essential to its adaptiveness and ability to learn as they are to the individual caregiver. They are also essential for the larger social systems within which our caring is enacted. The high-functioning individual caregiver and the high-functioning team can be healthy and self-regulating, yet their success and well-being ultimately depend on the health of the larger social systems of which they are a part.

8

How extraordinary is the situation of us mortals! Each of us is here for a brief sojourn; for what purpose he knows not, though he sometimes thinks he senses it. But without going deeper than our daily life, it is plain that we exist for our fellow men—in the first place for those upon whose smiles and welfare all our happiness depends, and next for all those unknown to us personally but to whose destinies we are bound by the tie of sympathy.[1]

Albert Einstein

Upon meeting a new patient, an elderly woman, small and frail, I was preparing to explain how I could assist her. Before I could begin my presentation, she lifted her hand slightly and then spoke clearly, "So, you are to be my warrior."

Anonymous helper

The Collective Caregiver: Toward a Caring Society

Up to this point, we have traced your helping journey from your earliest sense of a mission to your current work on the front lines of caregiving. Our focus has shifted steadily outward, beginning with your innermost experiences of helping and eventually moving to the interpersonal and group contexts of caregiving. At each step of this journey, you have faced different challenges: studying yourself, being open to your own and others' suffering, learning new skills, and being part of a team. This final chapter will identify caring challenges we face as a nation and as a world community and will explore some first steps we can take to meet them.

To help us think about these collective challenges, for a moment imagine our entire nation as a single caregiver entity—what I'll call our "collective caregiver" or our "nation-as-caregiver." This collective caregiver faces the same psychological dilemmas that we experience in the smaller world of our individual helping journeys: stress, balancing demands with resources, burnout, and the potential hazards of avoidance.

One of our collective caregiver's prominent features is that, according to most observers, she is already showing significant signs of burnout, including demoralization and a diminished sense of connection to others. (I am using the feminine pronoun to denote our collective caregiver because the majority of individual caregivers are in fact women.) In *Learned Optimism*, psychologist and research scientist Martin Seligman argues that we are a nation demoralized by our recent history.[2] The Vietnam conflict, Watergate, and the assassinations of John and Robert Kennedy, Martin Luther King, and Malcolm X have all weakened our belief in our nation. The increase in poverty, homelessness, and lawlessness; changes in the way the American family is structured; and the fragility of some of our most closely held values have also contributed to our collective loss of something to hope for and believe in.

Partly in response to these losses, we turned inward, away from our social connectedness. We cultivated an individualistic ethic and an exclusive commitment to the self. In *Habits of the Heart,* Robert Bellah and his colleagues point to this same theme, noting how, for many of us, competitive striving and individualism have overshadowed a social life and commitments to others.[3]

This strong self-orientation, combined with a growing demoralization and cynicism, has, according to Seligman, led to a sense of helplessness and depression. The individualistic stance we have adopted doesn't appear to offer a solid psychological foundation; it leaves us vulnerable to depression and without the health-protective influence afforded by greater social connectedness.[4]

Our self-oriented stance, Seligman insists, also has deprived us of the meaning embodied in a commitment to a higher purpose, which by its very nature can only be found in something outside ourselves. He calls this the "meaninglessness that rampant individualism nurtures."[5] We are threatened with the loss of our commitment to the common good and of our sense of purpose as a people.

Demoralized and lacking a strong sense of purpose, our collective caregiver is also beleaguered by a deepening cynicism. Nearly half of us view selfishness and fakery at the core of human nature.[6] This stance toward our fellow humans can rapidly become a self-fulfilling prophecy. Like the New Yorkers who didn't return a single wallet on the day Robert Kennedy was assassinated (see chapter 1),[7] we take a step back from our shared humanity and think, "Why help someone who would never help me?"

Other societal trends further cripple our collective caregiver. Her empathy is being eroded by cultural forces that promote aggression and striving for power over others. In every sector of our society—in sports, politics, and economics, as well as in our schools—competition is emphasized at the expense of cooperation and helping.[8] Eight out of 10 television programs contain violence; 9 out of 10 weekend children's hour-long programs do.[9] Between the ages of 5 and 15, the average child witnesses the violent destruction of more than 13,400 characters on television, as well as the depiction of hundreds of violent assaults and rapes.[10] Thus, our collective caregiver must overcome many forces in our culture that discourage a caring orientation toward others.

She must also wrestle with tremendous stressors in the external world, where the demands she faces often far exceed the resources made available to her. Suzanne Gordon says that low pay, poor working conditions, and limited opportunities for advancement have brought about an exodus from nursing, teaching, child care, and other helping professions—creating what she calls a crisis in caring.[11] Caregivers must often choose between acquiring material and status rewards and pursuing their caring goals.

Our collective caregiver is also asked to do more with less, year after year. This imbalance between demands and resources appears to be getting worse, not better. The demands from the enormous problems she faces—the AIDS epidemic, homelessness, pollution, violence, and sickness and suffering generally—seem to be increasing exponentially, whereas the funding and human resources allocated to address them are falling further and further behind.

The issues and dynamics of our individual helping journeys are of course closely tied to those of our collective caregiver. Keeping balance in our lives and keeping the flame of caring burning brightly within us is a difficult task even in a highly supportive context; doing this in a society that doesn't truly value the kind of work we do is doubly difficult. How can we as individuals and as a society begin to reverse some of the forces that oppose and threaten caring and helping?

A COMMITMENT TO THE COMMON GOOD

To succeed on this collective helping journey, we first need to recommit ourselves to the common or public good. The best antidote to a self-oriented stance is to do good for others. By choosing to make caring a significant part of your life's work, you are already a force for positive change. Each time you help someone or contribute to your caregiving team or organization, you are advancing the common good and reaffirming your commitment to it. And, as every volunteer or professional helper knows, doing good for others may be the best way to sustain a sense of meaning and purpose in our own lives.

How has helping others given your life meaning? Imagine writing your autobiography. What is your life story, and how has helping others been a part of that story? If you devoted a chapter to your experiences as a helper, what would you title that chapter, and what would the chapter be about? You would probably think of the people you have felt closest to and about those who have taught you the most about life, relationships, love, and courage. You would recall both painful and happy moments. How does helping others contribute to your sense of purpose and significance in life? Take a few minutes and jot down the first ideas and memories that come to mind and then save what you have written as a reminder of what your commitment to caring has meant to you.

STRENGTHENING THE ALTRUISM–EMPATHY–HELPING CONNECTION

Our commitment to the common good will find its fullest expression in a society and world where empathy and compassion are nurtured, valued, and expressed. In *The Brighter Side of Human Nature,* author Alfie Kohn argues that we already have the power to move our society in these directions and that this power comes from inside us:

> Our obligation is . . . to work together to make structural
> changes that will facilitate caring. . . . No imported solution
> will dissolve our problems of dehumanization and
> egocentricity, coldness and cruelty. No magical redemption
> from outside of human life will let us break through. The
> work that has to be done is our work, but we are better
> equipped for it than we have been led to believe. To move
> ourselves beyond selfishness, we already have what is
> required. We already *are* what is required. We are human
> and we have each other.[12]

The kinds of structural changes that will lead to a more caring, other-oriented society must ultimately modify the fundamentally egocentric patterns of socialization and cultural influence that shape our development. First, we need to put greater emphasis on cooperation and prosocial behavior in our media, in our families, and in our schools. For example, researchers have found that exposure to prosocial television shows such as "Mr. Rogers' Neighborhood" increases cooperation, nurturing behavior, and empathy in preschoolers.[13] Childrearing techniques such as drawing your child's attention to others' feelings, explaining why people feel the way they do, or giving approval when the child is considerate encourage the development of empathy.[14]

Second, instead of devaluing caring, we need to realign our cultural values and reward structures so that caregiving is reinforced and strengthened. This could be reflected in higher salaries for caregivers and increased economic support and recognition for all volunteer and nonprofit human service organizations by our national, state, and local governments.

Third, as Marc Pilisuk and Susan Parks argue, we need a national policy that offers financial help and supplemental services to the growing number of family members being turned into caregivers by current demographic and health care changes.[15] These are just a few of the broader changes we need to make to ensure a caring future.

Making the changes that will reinforce and strengthen caring in our society and transforming this caring into helping action are formidable tasks. To achieve these goals, we will need to rehabilitate existing delivery systems and bring forth the very best in ourselves. This is underscored in a presentation of a national strategy for responding to the HIV epidemic, in which Admiral James Watkins of the Presidential Commission on the Human Immunodeficiency Virus made this call to action:

> The HIV epidemic is much more than a medical crisis or
> a public health threat. Although it is a grave tragedy, it is
> also a profound challenge. We can use the HIV epidemic as
> an opportunity to deal with many problems our society
> faces and move toward solving them. We can begin to
> eliminate the flaws in our health care system, resulting in
> a better life for all Americans. We can begin to eliminate
> discrimination against persons with HIV infection, as well
> as persons with other disabilities and illnesses, and
> embrace them as part of the mainstream of American life.
> We can begin to turn the goodness that is out there, just
> waiting to be harnessed, into an unbeatable army against
> a viral enemy that has captured early ground.[16]

"Harnessing the good that is out there" will require more than changing our health care system; it will require creating healthy caring systems in which the altruism–empathy–helping connection can flourish.

How can we create these healthy caring systems? Systems theorists agree that a key feature of all healthy living systems (whether they be cells, individuals, caregiving teams, or nations) is a free flow of information. Without an extensive exchange of information, systems cannot maintain their health and move toward their goals.[17] We have seen numerous examples of how information relevant to the individual or common good can be obstructed in caring systems:

- Fear, cynicism, and other states of personal distress keep us from responding to the suffering of others (chapters 1 and 2).

- Avoiding threatening experiences undermines our personal growth and self-esteem (chapter 3).

- A caregiver hides difficult experiences from coworkers (chapter 4).

- An interdisciplinary team avoids discussing a major conflict (chapter 7).

- Our nation fails to recognize and respond adequately to the AIDS crisis.[18]

In each of these cases, from a systems point of view, healthy self-regulation via the altruism–empathy–helping connection is disrupted by a breakdown in the exchange of critical health-related information. Also, in each of these situations, acts of avoidance are immediately reinforced by a reduction of anxiety. For example, the caregiver momentarily feels less anxious if he or she doesn't disclose problems, and team members are relieved to get through another meeting without having to deal with an uncomfortable issue. But these short-term gains are followed by long-term pain: The caregiver eventually leaves the job and the field, the interdisciplinary team has a crisis, and the AIDS epidemic decimates a generation. These dynamics parallel those of the neurotic paradox discussed in chapter 3 and explain why systems can sometimes behave in self-defeating ways.

Two guiding principles for creating healthy caring systems emerge from the present discussion: First, we must maximize the flow of health-related information. Second, in caring, as in politics and economics, we must resist the seduction of attaining short-term relief at the expense of achieving our long-term goals.

However, as we have seen throughout this book, the specific information exchange most crucial to the success of caring systems—empathy for the distress of others—is often tenuous or nonexistent. Myriad psychological factors can lead us to avoid or misjudge the suffering of the people we care for. With the best of intentions, we can trivialize their suffering or distance ourselves when their pain activates one of our own interpersonal allergies. We can also blame and stigmatize the victim, as we have seen so dramatically in our society's responses to persons with AIDS.[19] In each instance, a failure to empathize derails the altruism–empathy–helping connection.

Even if we are highly motivated and free of any of these empathy-reducing influences, we can easily fail to perceive accurately the extent of suffering in the people we care for. A recent study sheds some light on this. In an investigation of caregivers' ratings of pain, it was found that at higher levels of experienced pain, patients' ratings and those of caregivers (nurses and physicians) were not correlated.[20] The researchers saw their findings as a strong argument for the routine use of pain assessment tools for improved patient-caregiver communication. If we conducted a similar study looking at how well our assessment and treatment of suffering (understood as psychological distress) corresponded to the actual experiences of the people we care for, might not similar findings result? The importance of continuing to develop and enhance our empathic skills cannot be overstated.

The phenomenon of self-concealment further complicates our efforts to respond accurately and sensitively to suffering. Much personal distress is hidden from *everyone,* even from available and caring helpers. Our coworkers feel burned out but are reluctant to share this. A terminally ill patient is angry about dying but doesn't reveal this fact because he feels he owes his helpers a peaceful death. Unhappy teenagers secretly form suicide pacts. Family members and lovers/partners of people with AIDS become hidden grievers when faced with the responses of a society that stigmatizes nontraditional relationships and life-styles.[21]

It is a moot point which came first, the fear and shame that leads to self-concealment or a society that cannot face its own pain with compassion. What is clear is that to open the lines of communication necessary to helping and healing, we need to cultivate respect, trust, and openness in all our relationships—at home, at work, at school, in the community, and at the local, national, and international levels.

The suffering of people outside of our country is also largely hidden from us. Major crises receive extensive media coverage, then quickly recede from the front pages of our newspapers and our awareness. In one sense, we are relieved by this. Constant exposure to the enormity of suffering in the world can overwhelm us if we open our hearts to it. So our collective empathy is momentarily captured by crises that will soon be over (e.g., two whales trapped under an ice floe or a toddler trapped in an abandoned well). We can't take in the suffering of thousands of children dying of starvation or ponder for too long the long-term consequences of pollution and overpopulation. These are too immense to sustain our attention, and we feel that we must respond to the myriad details of our personal lives.

In the ideal future, our world society, responding with empathy and a firm caring ethic, will react swiftly and effectively to world suffering unencumbered by political, economic, religious, and social barriers. However, for many of the major problems and kinds of suffering in the world, the people with the most pain have the least power to help themselves, and the people with the most power to help them have the least pain. Those in power might have altruistic intentions, but often they lack the human experience that would galvanize their compassion into specific caring acts. For example, maybe no one in their families or circle of friends has AIDS or is unemployed, hungry, or mentally ill.

The distress of the people who have little political and economic power usually doesn't reach the people who have the power to do something about it. Occasionally someone acting from great personal pain can, as did Candy Lightner, founder of Mothers Against Drunk Driving, accrue through monumental efforts enough influence to help others who share a similar plight. One person *can* make a difference. But the dominant power-pain relation too often prevails, and the resulting breakdown of the altruism–empathy–helping connection leads to suffering that, however widespread, remains voiceless.

Remember the "altruistic" monkeys and rats, described in chapter 1, who sacrificed their rewards to decrease the electric shock of their peers? Animals who had themselves been shocked or who had a special connection (e.g., who had been cagemates) with the other animal were most likely to desist from shocking.[22] We are like the monkeys and rats in these studies. We share the almost universal tendency to become aroused in the presence of a distressed member of our own species and to act in ways to reduce that distress. And we are much more likely to use our power in the service of the other if we understand that individual's pain and feel a sense of connection.

Kenneth Clark discusses how empathy balances egocentricity and power gratification with concern for the needs of others:

> The inability of human beings with power to understand
> the legitimate needs and aspirations of other human
> beings—the inability of human beings to understand that
> their fellow human beings share their anxieties, their
> frailties, their posturing, their desire to make the most
> out of the limited interval of conscious and evaluative
> life—this lack of simple expanded empathy is in the eyes
> of this observer the basis of social tensions, conflicts,
> violence, terrorism, and war. One can hope that a
> disciplined and value-oriented social science will have
> sufficient time not only to study and understand the nature
> and determinants of empathy but also to develop the
> ability to increase the number of human beings who are
> functionally empathic. If this is done, there will be a future
> for humanity. The survival of the human species now
> appears to depend upon a universal increase in functional
> empathy. Trained human intelligence must now dedicate
> itself to the attainment of this goal.[23]

Skeptics might say that this vision is Polyannaish. Our self-centeredness and greed, they would argue, and the self-interested intransigence of our institutions will not permit such a future. But I believe there is no other way to move toward a positive future for all of humanity, a future in which we actually address the difficult problems confronting us.

Psychologists Michael Lynn and Andrew Oldenquist reinforce this view that an increase in "functional empathy" holds the key to a healthier future. They point out that many of the world's problems—like overpopulation, pollution, and the depletion of nonrenewable resources—represent social dilemmas, each embodying a conflict between our short-term and long-term interests. The three defining features of social dilemmas are that (a) there is a common or public good to be attained through collective effort; (b) attaining this public good is costly to the individual, though not as costly as the failure to attain it; and (c) the actions of a single individual are not sufficient to determine success or failure in this task. They make the case that the solutions to these kinds of dilemmas must ultimately come from three sources: altruistic motives linked to empathy, a stronger sense of community, and moral motives advocating cooperative, unselfish behavior.[24]

Craig Schindler and Gary Lapid, in *The Great Turning,* and Roger Walsh, in *Staying Alive,* echo these ideas and emphasize the kinds of win-win solutions we need to work toward in our international conflicts.[25] Their approach to conflict is predicated on respect for ourselves, for others, and for our planet—reverence for life in all its myriad forms. In *The Philosophy of Civilization,* Albert Schweitzer argued that if we lose our reverence for any part of life, we lose it for all of life.[26]

When we are able to create a shared vision of caring and all the parts of our social organism communicate openly, then our social system will be able to function with purpose. It will be able to self-regulate to achieve the goals of both concern for self and concern for others—just as individual caregivers who maintain balance in their lives and who have real empathy without falling into the Helper's Pit fulfill both egoistic and altruistic needs.

To extend our empathy and caring beyond the people and experiences we intimately know requires a profound shift in consciousness, the kind Albert Einstein describes here:

A human being is part of the whole called by us universe,
a part limited in time and space. He experiences himself,
his thoughts and feelings as something separated from the
rest, a kind of optical delusion of his consciousness. This
delusion is a kind of prison for us, restricting us to our

personal desires and to affection for a few persons nearest to us. Our task must be to free ourselves from this prison by widening our circle of compassion to embrace all living creatures and the whole of nature in its beauty.[27]

In the realm of caregiving, this kind of expanded empathy begins with an acceptance of our own vulnerability and losses and can grow to include compassion for the pain of all human beings. There are no shortcuts, no pain-free ways to do this. We must look into ourselves and beyond ourselves and learn to trust our common humanity. If we can do this, then our empathy will become a strong force in the world.

CONCLUSION

In my attempt to address the challenge of caring, I may have painted too dire a picture of the state of caring in our world today. It is as if I opened Pandora's box but have only allowed the Furies to escape and haven't given Hope her proper due. The three vignettes that follow remind us of the power of caring and caring actions.

In 1984, NBC broadcast a 5-minute BBC report on the massive famine in Ethiopia. The film showed the plight of the starving millions, many of them children, in graphic detail. *Newsweek* reported what happened immediately afterwards:

> No one anticipated the public response. In the 36 hours after the film was first aired, more than 10,000 people called Save the Children to offer their help. An elderly woman living on social security asked if they would accept a contribution in coins. A new father made a donation in the name of his baby son. At the end of the week the U. S. government committed $45 million for food aid—and at Save the Children headquarters, the phones continued to ring.[28]

The office staff of a Midwestern hospice told this story:

> As office staff we have little physical contact with patients, but that doesn't mean that we don't feel their pain and have a need to intervene. We received a bill one day—from a pharmacy—for a very independent patient. A young, poor, dying man with a young family. The bill was sent to us by mistake. We knew that it would be given to the family—who couldn't pay—so we opened our purses

and paid the bill. We did this three different times for three different families, until we realized that this could be the end of our finances. No one knew we were doing this, but once you start something, it's hard to end it. So we presented a proposal to David, our director, to recommend to the board, and, to make a long story short, they accepted our proposal, and now we have a special "indigent fund" so that all our people can have pain medicine without feeling that they are taking food away from their children.

A third vignette comes from the Holocaust. The Holocaust taught us about both sides of being human—our worst and our best possibilities. In sharp juxtaposition to the Nazis, there were the members of the resistance and the rescuers of the Jews. In *The Courage to Care,* Carol Rittner and Sondra Myers recount the story of Hermann Graebe, a German engineer who saved the lives of more than 300 Jews in Europe by employing them in his construction company. Graebe's involuntary witnessing of a massacre in Dubno was a critical event leading to his involvement as a rescuer. Here he describes this decisive moment, what I think is one of the saddest—and most hopeful—in human history:

> One of the most terrible things I remember seeing . . . was a father, perhaps in his fifties, with his boy, about as old as my son Friedel, was at that time—maybe ten years old—beside him. They were naked, completely naked, waiting for their turn to go into the pit. The boy was crying, and the father was stroking his head. The older man pointed to the sky and talked quietly to the young boy. They went on speaking like that for a while—I could not hear what they said because they were too far away from me—and then it was their turn. There were other members of the family there too—the man's wife and an older woman, a white-haired lady who was maybe the grandmother. She was holding and cradling a child, and singing to it softly. Then a soldier screamed for them to go down into the pit. . . . The boy cried and the father talked to him and stroked him. How do you explain that? And how do you see such a thing without being stirred into action against whatever or whoever caused it to happen?[29]

You, like me, were probably moved by Graebe's words. The feelings of sadness, loss, or anger you had as you read those words are your personal feelings, but they are also more than that. They are rooted in the connection among us all—in a human response—that holds the only hope for our collective future.

This takes us back to the first chapter of this book, where you reflected on your purpose in helping, on why you are doing what you are doing. Remember George Bernard Shaw's exuberant "This is the true joy in life, the being used for a purpose recognized by yourself as a mighty one"? Compassion is at the core of being human. This is the inner light, the "splendid torch" you have in your hands and can pass on to future generations. With this torch, you bring light when it is dark and warmth when it is cold. And when you reach the end of your journey, you will know that you have given to others the greatest gift you can give: your caring.

A Self-Diagnosis Instrument for Burnout

A SELF-DIAGNOSIS INSTRUMENT FOR BURNOUT

You can compute your burnout score by completing the following questionnaire. How often do you have any of the following experiences? Please use the scale:

1	2	3	4	5	6	7
Never	Once in a great while	Rarely	Sometimes	Often	Usually	Always

_____ 1. Being tired.
_____ 2. Feeling depressed.
_____ 3. Having a good day.
_____ 4. Being physically exhausted.
_____ 5. Being emotionally exhausted.
_____ 6. Being happy.
_____ 7. Being "wiped out."
_____ 8. "Can't take anymore."
_____ 9. Being unhappy.
_____ 10. Feeling run-down.
_____ 11. Feeling trapped.
_____ 12. Feeling worthless.
_____ 13. Being weary.
_____ 14. Being troubled.
_____ 15. Feeling disillusioned and resentful.
_____ 16. Being weak and susceptible to illness.
_____ 17. Feeling hopeless.
_____ 18. Feeling rejected.
_____ 19. Feeling optimistic.
_____ 20. Feeling energetic.
_____ 21. Feeling anxious.

Computation of score:

Add the values you wrote next to the following items:
1, 2, 4, 5, 7, 8, 9, 10, 11, 12, 13, 14, 15, 16, 17, 18, 21 (A) _____ .

Add the values you wrote next to the following items:
3, 6, 19, 20 (B) _____ , subtract B from 32 (C) _____ .

Add A and C (D) _____ .

Divide D by 21 _____ . This is your burnout score—see page 36 for interpretation.

Note. Reprinted with the permission of The Free Press, a Division of Macmillan, Inc., from *Career Burnout: Causes and Cures* (p. 219) by Ayala Pines and Elliot Aronson. Copyright © by Ayala Pines and Elliot Aronson.

Notes

Chapter 1. The Helper in Us All

1. Shaw, G. B. (1963). *Complete plays with prefaces* (Vol. 3, pp. 510–511). New York: Dodd, Mead. (Original work published 1903)

2. Quoted in Doan, E. C. (1989). *Speaker's sourcebook II* (p. 236). Grand Rapids, MI: Zondervan.

3. Nightingale, F. (1979). *Cassandra: An essay.* Old Westbury, NY: Feminist Press.

4. Egan, G. (1985). *Change agent skills in helping and human service settings.* Pacific Grove, CA: Brooks/Cole.

5. Allen, N., & Rushton, J. P. (1983). Personality characteristics of community mental health volunteers: A review. *Journal of Voluntary Action Research, 12,* 36–49.

6. Gallup Organization. (1986). *Americans volunteer 1985.* Princeton, NJ: Author.

7. Larson, D. G. (1991). [Helping motivations of hospice volunteers]. Unpublished raw data.

8. Rushton, J. P. (1980). *Altruism, socialization, and society.* New York: Prentice Hall.

9. Brammer, L. (1973). *The helping relationship: Process and skills.* Englewood Cliffs, NJ: Prentice Hall.

10. Rushton, J. P. (1984). The altruistic personality: Evidence from laboratory, naturalistic, and self-report perspectives. In E. Staub, D. Bar-Tal, J. Karylowski, & J. Reykowski (Eds.), *Development and maintenance of prosocial behavior* (pp. 271–290). New York: Plenum.

11. Items taken from measures used by Davis and by Mehrabian and Epstein: Davis, M. H. (1983). Measuring individual differences in empathy: Evidence for a multidimensional approach. *Journal of Personality and Social Psychology, 44,* 113–126; Mehrabian, A., & Epstein, N. (1972). A measure of emotional empathy. *Journal of Personality, 40,* 525–543.

12. Kanter, D. L., & Mirvis, P. H. (1989). *The cynical Americans.* San Francisco: Jossey-Bass.

13. Kohn, A. (1990). *The brighter side of human nature: Altruism and empathy in everyday life.* New York: Basic.

14. Hoffman, M. L. (1977). Empathy, its development and prosocial implications. In C. B. Keasey (Ed.), *Nebraska Symposium on Motivation* (Vol. 25, pp. 169–218). Lincoln: University of Nebraska Press.

15. Zahn-Waxler, C., & Radke-Yarrow, M. (1982). The development of altruism: Alternative research strategies. In N. Eisenberg (Ed.), *The development of prosocial behavior* (p. 126). New York: Academic.

16. Hallet, J. P. (1967). *Congo kitabu* (p. 381). New York: Fawcett World Library.

17. Masserman, J. H., Wechkin, S., & Terris, W. (1964). Altruistic behavior in rhesus monkeys. *American Journal of Psychiatry, 121,* 584–585.

18. Church, R. M. (1959). Emotional reaction of rats to the pain of others. *Journal of Comparative and Physiological Psychology, 52,* 132–134.

19. Hoffman, M. L. (1981). Is altruism part of human nature? *Journal of Personality and Social Psychology, 40,* 121–137.

20. Gallup Organization. (1986). *Americans volunteer 1985.* Princeton, NJ: Author; Independent Secton. (1988). *Giving and volunteering in the United States: Findings from a national survey.* Washington, DC: Author.

21. Omoto, A. M., & Snyder, M. (1990). Basic research in action: Volunteerism and society's response to AIDS. *Personality and Social Psychology Bulletin, 16,* 152–165.

22. Jacobs, M. K., & Goodman, G. (1989). Psychology and self-help groups: Predictions on a partnership. *American Psychologist, 44,* 536–545.

23. Dunn, A., Hudson, B., Katz, J., & Wilkinson, T. (1990, September 26). Small heroics. *Los Angeles Times,* p. A1.

24. Wispe, L. (Ed.). (1978). *Altruism, sympathy, and helping.* New York: Academic.

25. Hornstein, H. A. (1976). *Cruelty and kindness.* Englewood Cliffs, NJ: Prentice Hall.

26. Gaertner, S. L., & Dovidio, J. F. (1977). The subtlety of white racism, arousal, and helping behavior. *Journal of Personality and Social Psychology, 35,* 691–707.

27. See note 19.

28. Coke, J. S., Batson, C. D., & McDavis, K. (1978). Empathic mediation of helping: A two-stage model. *Journal of Personality and Social Psychology, 36,* 752–766.

29. See note 14.

30. Hoffman, M. L. (1982). Development of prosocial motivation: Empathy and guilt. In N. Eisenberg (Ed.), *The development of prosocial behavior* (pp. 281–313). New York: Academic.

31. Hornstein, H. A. (1976). *Cruelty and kindness.* Englewood Cliffs, NJ: Prentice Hall.

32. See note 31.

33. Hornstein, H. A. (1976). *Cruelty and kindness*. Englewood Cliffs, NJ: Prentice Hall; Hornstein, H. A., LaKind, E., Frankel, G., & Manne, S. (1975). Effects of knowledge about remote social events on prosocial behavior, social conception, and mood. *Journal of Personality and Social Psychology, 32,* 1038–1046.

34. Darley, J., & Batson, C. (1973). "From Jerusalem to Jericho": A study of situational and dispositional variables in helping behavior. *Journal of Personality and Social Psychology, 27,* 100–108.

35. Oliner, S. P., & Oliner, P. M. (1988). *The altruistic personality: Rescuers of Jews in Nazi Europe* (p. 249). New York: Free Press.

36. Oliner, S. P., & Oliner, P. M. (1988). *The altruistic personality: Rescuers of Jews in Nazi Europe* (p. 251). New York: Free Press.

37. Maslow, A. H. (1976). *The farther reaches of human nature*. New York: Penguin.

38. Kohlberg, L. (1981). *The philosophy of moral development: Moral stages and the idea of justice*. San Francisco: Harper & Row.

39. Isen, A. M., & Levin, P. F. (1972). Effect of feeling good on helping: Cookies and kindness. *Journal of Personality and Social Psychology, 21,* 384–388.

40. Isen, A. M., Clark, M., & Schwartz, M. F. (1976). Duration of the effect of good mood on helping: "Footprints on the sands of time." *Journal of Personality and Social Psychology, 34,* 385–393.

41. See note 40.

42. Berkowitz, L., & Connor, W. H. (1966). Success, failure, and social responsibility. *Journal of Personality and Social Psychology, 4,* 664–669.

43. See note 42.

44. See note 28.

45. Rosenhan, D. L., Salovey, P., & Hargis, K. (1981). The joys of helping: Focus of attention mediates the impact of positive affect on altruism. *Journal of Personality and Social Psychology, 40,* 899–905.

46. See Baumann, D. J., Cialdini, R. B., & Kenrick, D. T. (1981). Altruism as hedonism: Helping and self-gratification as equivalent responses. *Journal of Personality and Social Psychology, 40,* 1039–1046; Weiss, R. F., Buchanan, W., Alstatt, L., & Lombardo, J. P. (1971). Altruism is rewarding. *Science, 26,* 1262–1263.

47. Cohen, S., & Syme, S. L. (Eds.). (1985). *Social support and health*. Orlando, FL: Academic.

48. House, J. S., Robbins, C., & Metzner, H. L. (1982). The association of social relationships and activities with mortality: Prospective evidence from the Tecumseh Community Health Study. *American Journal of Epidemiology, 116,* 123–140.

49. Lynch, J. J. (1977). *The broken heart: The medical consequences of loneliness.* New York: Basic.

50. Smith, T. W. (1992). Hostility and health: Current status of a psycho-somatic hypothesis. *Health Psychology, 11,* 139–150.

51. Lynch, J. J. (1985). *The language of the heart: The body's response to human dialogue* (p. 181). New York: Basic.

52. Friedman, M., & Rosenman, R. (1974). *Type A behavior and your heart.* New York: Knopf.

53. Williams, R. (1989). *The trusting heart: Great news about Type A behavior* (p. 131). New York: Times Books.

54. Luks, A. (1988, October). Helper's high. *Psychology Today,* pp. 39, 42.

55. Luks, A., & Payne, P. *The healing power of doing good: The health and spiritual benefits of helping others.* New York: Fawcett Columbine.

56. Bach, G. R., & Torbet, L. (1982). *A time for caring* (p. 6). New York: Delacorte.

57. Schweitzer, A. (1963). Memoirs of childhood and youth (C. T. Campion, Trans., p. 111). New York: Macmillan.

58. Riessman, F. (1965). The "helper" therapy principle. *Social Work, 10,* 27–32.

59. McClelland, D. C., & Kirshnit, C. (1988). The effect of motivational arousal through films on salivary immunoglobulin A. *Psychology and Health, 2,* 31–52.

60. Ornstein, R., & Sobel, D. (1987). *The healing brain.* New York: Simon and Schuster.

Chapter 2. The Challenge of Caring: Emotional Involvement in Helping

1. Pines, A. M., & Aronson, E. (1988). *Career burnout: Causes and cures.* New York: Free Press.

2. See note 1.

3. Maslach, C. (1982). *Burnout: The cost of caring.* Englewood Cliffs, NJ: Prentice Hall.

4. Heifetz, L. J., & Bersani, H. A. (1983). Disrupting the cybernetics of personal growth: Toward a unified theory of burnout in the human services. In B. A. Farber (Ed.), *Stress and burnout in the human service professions* (pp. 46–62). New York: Pergamon.

5. Stotland, E., Mathews, K. E., Sherman, S. E., Hansson, R. O., & Richard-son, B. Z. (1978). *Empathy, fantasy, and helping.* Newbury Park, CA: Sage.

6. The following are excellent books on caregiver stress: Farber, B. A. (Ed.). (1983). *Stress and burnout.* New York: Pergamon; Maslach, C.

(1982). *Burnout: The cost of caring.* Englewood Cliffs, NJ: Prentice Hall; Pines, A. M., & Aronson, E. (1988). *Career burnout: Causes and cures.* New York: Free Press; Vachon, M. L. (1987). *Occupational stress in the care of the critically ill, the dying, and the bereaved.* Bristol, PA: Hemisphere.

7. Pines, A. M., & Aronson, E. (1988). *Career burnout: Causes and cures* (p. 219). New York: Free Press.

8. Lief, H. I., & Fox, R. C. (1963). Training for "detached concern" in medical students. In H. I. Lief, V. F. Lief, & N. R. Lief (Eds.)., *The psychological basis of medical practice* (pp. 12–35). New York: Harper and Row.

9. Hoffman, M. L. (1977). Empathy, its development and prosocial implications. In C. B. Keasey (Ed.), *Nebraska Symposium on Motivation* (Vol. 25, pp. 169–218), Lincoln: University of Nebraska Press.

10. Batson, C. D., Fultz, J., & Schoenrade, P. A. (1987). Distress and empathy: Two qualitatively distinct vicarious emotions with different motivational consequences. *Journal of Personality, 55,* 19–39.

11. Eisenberg, N. (1987). The relation of empathy to prosocial and related behaviors. *Psychological Bulletin, 101,* 91–119; Thompson, W., Cowan, C., & Rosenhan, D. (1980). Focus of attention mediates the impact of negative affect on altruism. *Journal of Personality and Social Psychology, 38,* 291–300.

12. Hoffman, M. L. (1982). Development of prosocial motivation: Empathy and guilt. In N. Eisenberg (Ed.), *The development of prosocial behavior* (p. 294). New York: Academic.

13. Kagan, N. (1984). Interpersonal Process Recall: Basic methods and recent research. In D. G. Larson (Ed.), *Teaching psychological skills: Models for giving psychology away* (pp. 229–244). Pacific Grove, CA: Brooks/Cole.

14. Amenta, M. M. (1984). Death anxiety, purpose in life and duration of service in hospice volunteers. *Psychological Reports, 54,* 979–984.

15. Brockopp, D. Y., King, D. B., & Hamilton, J. E. (1991). The dying patient: A comparative study of nurse caregiver characteristics. *Death Studies, 15,* 245–258.

16. Kagan discusses fear of hurting, fear of being hurt, and fear of being engulfed as interpersonal allergies in Kagan, N. (1984). Interpersonal Process Recall: Basic methods and recent research. In D. G. Larson (Ed.), *Teaching psychological skills: Models for giving psychology away* (pp. 231–232). Pacific Grove, CA: Brooks/Cole.

17. Combs, A. W., & Avila, D. L. (1985). *Helping relationships: Basic concepts for the helping professions* (3rd ed., p. 7). Boston: Allyn & Bacon.

18. Kennedy, E., & Charles, S. C. (1990). *On becoming a counselor: A basic guide for nonprofessional counselors* (p. 26). New York: Continuum.

19. Rogers, C. R. (1957). The necessary and sufficient conditions of therapeutic personality change. *Journal of Consulting Psychology, 21,* p. 99.

20. Hoffman, M. L. (1981). The development of empathy. In J. P. Rushton & R. M. Sorrentino (Eds.), *Altruism and helping behavior: Social, personality, and developmental perspectives* (pp. 41–63). Hillsdale, NJ: Erlbaum.

21. Eisenberg, N. (1986). *Altruistic emotion, cognition, and behavior.* Hillsdale, NJ: Erlbaum.

22. Batson, C. D., & Coke, J. S. (1981). Empathy: A source of altruistic motivation for helping? In J. P. Rushton & R. M. Sorrentino (Eds.), *Altruism and helping behavior: Social, personality, and developmental perspectives* (pp. 167–187). Hillsdale, NJ: Erlbaum; Batson, C. D., Dyck, J. L., Brandt, J. R., Batson, J. G., Powell, A. L., McMaster, M. R., & Griffitt, C. (1988). Five studies testing two new egoistic alternatives to the empathy-altruism hypothesis. *Journal of Personality and Social Psychology, 55,* 52–77; Coke, J. S., Batson, C. D., & McDavis, K. (1978). Empathic mediation of helping: A two-stage model. *Journal of Personality and Social Psychology, 36,* 752–766.

23. Coke, J. S., Batson, C. D., & McDavis, K. (1978). Empathic mediation of helping: A two-stage model. *Journal of Personality and Social Psychology, 36,* 752–766.

24. Batson, C. D., & Coke, J. S. (1981). Empathy: A source of altruistic motivation for helping? In J. P. Rushton & R. M. Sorrentino (Eds.), *Altruism and helping behavior: Social, personality, and developmental perspectives* (pp. 167–187). Hillsdale, NJ: Erlbaum.

25. Wills, T. A. (1991). Similarity and self-esteem in downward comparison. In J. Suls & T. A. Wills (Eds.), *Social comparison: Contemporary theory and research* (pp. 51–78). Hillsdale, NJ: Erlbaum.

26. Rosenhan, D. L., Salovey, P., & Hargis, K. (1981). The joys of helping: Focus of attention mediates the impact of positive affect on altruism. *Journal of Personality and Social Psychology, 40,* 899–905.

27. Harris, M. B., Benson, S. M., & Hall, C. (1975). The effects of confession on altruism. *Journal of Social Psychology, 96,* 187–192.

28. Staub, E. (1970). A child in distress: The effects of focusing responsibility on children on their attempts to help. *Developmental Psychology, 2,* 152–153.

29. Clary, E. G., & Snyder, M. (1991). A functional analysis of altruism and prosocial behavior: The case of volunteerism. In M. S. Clark (Ed.), *Prosocial behavior* (p. 125). Newbury Park, CA: Sage.

30. This section has been adapted from Larson, D. G. (1991, Summer). The codependent caregiver: A dangerous myth? *HOSPICE,* pp. 17–19.

31. Gomberg, E. S. On terms used and abused: The concept of "codependency." *Drugs and Society, 3,* 113–132.

32. Fausel, D. F. (1988). Helping the helper heal: Co-dependency in helping professionals. *Journal of Independent Social Work, 3,* 35–45; Mellody, P. (1989). *Facing codependence.* San Francisco: Harper and Row.

33. Lazarus, R. S. (1990). Stress, coping, and illness. In H. Friedman (Ed.), *Personality and disease* (p. 116). New York: Wiley.

34. Seligman, M. E., Abramson, L. Y., Semmel, A., & von Baeyer, C. (1979). Depressive attributional style. *Journal of Abnormal Psychology, 88,* 242–247.

35. Maslach, C., & Jackson, S. E. (1982). Burnout in health professions: A social psychological analysis. In G. Sanders & J. Suls (Eds.), *Social psychology of health and illness* (pp. 227–251). Hillsdale, NJ: Erlbaum.

36. Pines, A. M., & Aronson, E. (1988). *Career burnout: Causes and cures* (p. 5). New York: Free Press.

37. Maslach, C., & Jackson, S. E. (1982). Burnout in health professions: A social psychological analysis. In G. Sanders & J. Suls (Eds.), *Social psychology of health and illness* (pp. 231–232). Hillsdale, NJ: Erlbaum.

38. Ross, L. (1977). The intuitive psychologist and his shortcomings: Distortions in the attribution process. In L. Berkowitz (Ed.), *Advances in experimental social psychology* (Vol. 10, pp. 173–220). New York: Academic.

39. Humes, A. (1989). *Seven Days, 2*(41), 26.

40. Patterson, C. H. (1985). *The therapeutic relationship: Foundations for an eclectic psychotherapy* (p. 91). Pacific Grove, CA: Brooks/Cole.

Chapter 3. Finding the Balance: Managing the Stress of Caregiving

1. Pines, A. M., & Aronson, E. (1988). *Career burnout: Causes and cures* (p. 35). New York: Free Press.

2. Branden, N. (1987). *How to raise your self-esteem.* New York: Bantam.

3. Claus, K. E., & Bailey, J. T. (Eds.). (1980). *Living with stress and promoting well-being: A handbook for nurses.* St. Louis: C. V. Mosby.

4. Vachon, M. L. (1987). *Occupational stress in the care of the critically ill, the dying, and the bereaved.* Bristol, PA: Hemisphere.

5. Vachon, M. L. (1986). Myths and realities in palliative/hospice care. *The Hospice Journal, 2,* p. 71.

6. See note 3.

7. Ellis, A. (1962). *Reason and emotion in psychotherapy.* New York: Lyle Stuart.

8. Maslach, C., & Jackson, S. E. (1982). Burnout in health professions: A social psychological analysis. In G. Sanders & J. Suls (Eds.), *Social psychology of health and illness* (pp. 227–251). Hillsdale, NJ: Erlbaum.

9. Lazarus, R. S., & Folkman, S. (1984). *Stress, appraisal, and coping* (p. 19). New York: Springer.

10. See note 3.

11. Cantor, R. C. (1978). *And a time to live: Toward emotional well-being during the crisis of cancer.* New York: Harper Colophon.

12. Thoits, P. A. (1983). Dimensions of life events that influence psychological distress: An evaluation and synthesis of the literature. In H. B. Kaplan (Ed.), *Psychosocial stress: Trends in theory and research* (pp. 33–103). New York: Academic.

13. Lazarus, R. S. (1990). Stress, coping, and illness. In H. Friedman (Ed.), *Personality and disease* (pp. 97–120). New York: Wiley.

14. Smith, C. A., & Lazarus, R. S. (1990). Emotion and adaptation. In L. A. Pervin (Ed.), *Handbook of personality: Theory and research* (pp. 609–637). New York: Guilford.

15. Lazarus, R. S., & Folkman, S. (1984). *Stress, appraisal, and coping.* New York: Springer.

16. Bandura, A. (1977). Self-efficacy: Toward a unifying theory of behavioral change. *Psychological Review, 84,* 191–215.

17. Rice, P. L. (1987). *Stress and health: Principles and practice for coping and wellness.* Pacific Grove, CA: Brooks/Cole.

18. Csikszentmihalyi, M. (1990). *Flow: The psychology of optimal experience.* New York: Harper and Row.

19. Lazarus, R. S., & Folkman, S. (1980). *Stress, appraisal, and coping.* New York: Springer.

20. Hobfoll, S. E. (1989). Conservation of resources: A new attempt at conceptualizing stress. *American Psychologist, 44,* 513–524.

21. Tausig, M. (1982). Measuring life events. *Journal of Health and Social Behavior, 23,* 52–64.

22. Hobfoll, S. E. (1988). The ecology of stress (p. 518). Bristol, PA: Hemisphere.

23. Roth, S., & Cohen, L. J. (1986). Approach, avoidance, and coping with stress. *American Psychologist, 41,* 813–819.

24. Bednar, R. L., Wells, M. G., & Peterson, S. R. (1989). *Self-esteem: Paradoxes and innovations in clinical practice* (p. 74). Washington, DC: American Psychological Association.

25. Bednar, R. L., Wells, M. G., & Peterson, S. R. (1989). *Self-esteem: Paradoxes and innovations in clinical practice.* Washington, DC: American Psychological Association.

26. Senge, P. M. (1990). *The fifth discipline: The art and practice of the learning organization.* New York: Doubleday.

27. Solomon, R. L., & Wynne, L. C. (1953). Traumatic avoidance learning: Acquisition in normal dogs. *Psychological Monographs, 67,* 1–19.

28. Mowrer, O. H. (1948). Learning theory and the neurotic paradox. *American Journal of Orthopsychiatry, 18,* 571–610.

29. Goleman, D. (1985). *Vital lies, simple truths: The psychology of self-deception.* New York: Simon and Schuster.

30. Becker, E. (1973). *The denial of death.* New York: Free Press.

31. Yalom, I. D. (1980). *Existential psychotherapy.* New York: Basic.

32. Yalom, I. D. (1980). *Existential psychotherapy* (p. 147). New York: Basic.

33. Yalom, I. D. (1980). *Existential psychotherapy* (p. 40). New York: Basic.

34. Solomon, S., Greenberg, J., & Pyszczynski, T. (1991). Terror management theory of self-esteem. In C. R. Snyder & D. R. Forsyth (Eds.), *Handbook of social and clinical psychology: The health perspective* (pp. 21–40). New York: Pergamon.

35. Solomon, S., Greenberg, J., & Pyszczynski, T. (1991). Terror management theory of self-esteem. In C. R. Snyder & D. R. Forsyth (Eds.), *Handbook of social and clinical psychology: The health perspective* (p. 23). New York: Pergamon.

36. Kierkegaard, S. (1941). *The sickness unto death* (p. 29). Princeton, NJ: Princeton University Press.

37. Pennebaker, J. W., Kiecolt-Glaser, J. K., & Glaser, R. (1988). Disclosure of traumas and immune function: Health implications for psychotherapy. *Journal of Consulting and Clinical Psychology, 56,* 239–245.

38. See note 37.

39. See note 13.

40. Lazarus, R. S. (1990). Stress, coping, and illness. In H. Friedman (Ed.), *Personality and disease* (p. 101). New York: Wiley.

41. See note 15.

42. Weissman, A. D. (1986). *The coping capacity: On the nature of being mortal.* New York: Human Sciences.

43. Folkman, S., & Lazarus, R. S. (1988). Coping as a mediator of emotion. *Journal of Personality and Social Psychology, 54,* 466–475; Kleinke, C. L. (1991). *Coping with life challenges.* Pacific Grove, CA: Brooks/Cole; McCrae, R. R., & Costa, P. T. (1986). Personality, coping, and coping effectiveness in an adult sample. *Journal of Personality, 54,* 385–405.

44. Riordan, R. J., & Saltzer, S. K. (1992). Burnout prevention among health care providers working with the terminally ill: A literature review. *Omega, 25,* 17–24.

45. Hutchison, S. (1986). Chemically dependent nurses: The trajectory toward self-annihilation. *Nursing Research, 35,* 196–201.

46. Quoted in Fox, R. W. (1985). *Reinhold Niebuhr: A biography* (p. 290). New York: Pantheon.

47. Collins, D. L., Baum, A., & Singer, J. E. (1983). Coping with chronic stress at Three Mile Island: Psychological and biochemical evidence. *Health Psychology, 2,* 149–166.

48. Hobfoll, S. E. (1988). *The ecology of stress.* Bristol, PA: Hemisphere.

49. Pines, A. M., & Aronson, E. (1988). *Career burnout: Causes and cures.* New York: Free Press.

50. Kobasa, S. C. (1979). Stressful life events, personality, and health: An inquiry into hardiness. *Journal of Personality and Social Psychology, 37,* 1–11; Kobasa, S. C. (1982). *The hardy personality: Toward a social psychology of stress and health.* In G. S. Sanders & J. Suls (Eds.), *Social psychology of health and illness* (pp. 3–32). Hillsdale, NJ: Erlbaum; Kobasa, S. C., Maddi, S. R., & Kahn, S. (1982). Hardiness and health: A prospective study. *Journal of Personality and Social Psychology, 42,* 168–177.

51. Antonovsky, A. (1987). *Unraveling the mystery of health: How people manage stress and stay well.* San Francisco: Jossey-Bass; Scheier, M. F., & Carver, C. S. (1985). Optimism, coping, and health: Assessment and implications of generalized outcome expectancies. *Health Psychology, 4,* 219–247.

52. Lefcourt, H. M., & Davidson-Katz, K. (1991). The role of humor and the self. In C. R. Snyder & D. R. Forsyth (Eds.), *Handbook of social and clinical psychology: The health perspective* (pp. 41–56). New York: Pergamon.

53. Rice, P. L. (1987). *Stress and health: Principles and practice for coping and wellness* (pp. 353–354). Pacific Grove, CA: Brooks/Cole.

54. Blair, S., Kohl, H., Paffenbarger, R., Clark, D., Cooper, K., & Gibbons, L. (1989). Physical fitness and all-cause mortality: Prospective study of healthy men and women. *Journal of the American Medical Association, 262,* 2395–2401.

55. Benson, H. (1975). *The relaxation response.* New York: Avon.

56. For a useful, skill-oriented approach to this process, see Gendlin, E. T. (1981). *Focusing* (2nd ed.). New York: Bantam.

57. Rosen, T. J., Terry, N. S., & Leventhal, H. (1982). The role of esteem and coping in response to a threat communication. *Journal of Research in Personality, 16,* 90–107.

58. Williamson, G. M., & Clark, M. S. (1989). Providing help and desired relationship types as determinants of changes in moods and self-evaluations. *Journal of Personality and Social Psychology, 56,* 722–734.

59. Yasko, J. M. (1983). Variables which predict burnout experienced by oncology clinical nurse specialists. *Cancer Nursing, 6,* 109–116.

60. Pines, A. M., & Aronson, E. (1988). *Career burnout: Causes and cures.* New York: Free Press; Richman, J. M. (1990). Groupwork in a hospice setting. *Social Work With Groups, 12,* 171–184.

61. Selye, H. (1978, March). On the real benefits of eustress. *Psychology Today,* p. 70.

Chapter 4. Secrets: Concealment and Confiding in Helping

1. Quoted in Platt, S. (Ed.). (1989). *Respectfully quoted: A dictionary of quotations requested from the Congressional Research Committee* (p. 314). Washington, DC: Library of Congress.

2. Quoted in Maslow, A. (1971). *The farther reaches of human nature* (p. 187). New York: Viking.

3. Tournier, P. (1965). *Secrets.* Atlanta: John Knox Press.

4. Quoted in Evans, B. (Ed.). (1968). *Dictionary of quotations* (p. 613). New York: Delacorte.

5. Schachter, S. (1959). *The psychology of affiliation.* Palo Alto, CA: Stanford University Press.

6. Fish, B., & Karabenick, S. (1978). The effect of observation on emotional arousal and affiliation. *Journal of Experimental Social Psychology, 14,* 256–265; Sarnoff, L., & Zimbardo, P. G. (1961). Anxiety, fear, and social affiliation. *Journal of Abnormal and Social Psychology, 62,* 597–605.

7. Rawlins, W. K. (1983). Openness as problematic in ongoing friendships: Two conversational dilemmas. *Communication Monographs, 50,* 1–13.

8. Coates, D., & Winston, T. (1987). The dilemma of distress disclosure. In V. J. Derlega & J. H. Berg (Eds.), *Self-disclosure: Theory, research, and therapy* (pp. 229–255). New York: Plenum.

9. Coates, D., & Winston, T. (1987). The dilemma of distress disclosure. In V. J. Derlega & J. H. Berg (Eds.), *Self-disclosure: Theory, research, and therapy* (p. 230). New York: Plenum.

10. Peters-Golden, H. (1982). Breast cancer: Varied perceptions of social support in the illness experience. *Social Science and Medicine, 16,* 483–491.

11. See note 8.

12. Luft, J. (1969). *Of human interaction* (p. 13). Palo Alto, CA: National Press Books.

13. Binder, R. (1981). Why women don't report sexual assault. *Journal of Clinical Psychiatry, 42,* 437–438; Burgess, A. W., & Holmstrom, L. L. (1974). Rape trauma syndrome. *American Journal of Psychiatry, 131,*

981–986; Evans, N. (1976). Mourning as a family secret. *Journal of the American Academy of Child Psychiatry, 15,* 502–509; Karpel, M. A. (1980). Family secrets. *Family Process, 19,* 295–306; Russell, D. E. (1986). *The secret trauma: Incest in the lives of girls and women.* New York: Basic; Saffer, J. B., Sansone, P., & Gentry, J. (1979). The awesome burden upon the child who must keep a family secret. *Child Psychiatry and Human Development, 10,* 35–40; Stark, E. (1984, May). The unspeakable family secret. *Psychology Today,* pp. 38–46.

14. Larson, D. G., & Chastain, R. L. (1990). Self-concealment: Conceptualization, measurement, and health implications. *Journal of Social and Clinical Psychology, 9,* 439–455.

15. See note 14.

16. James, W. (1985). *The varieties of religious experience* (pp. 364–365). Cambridge, MA: Harvard University Press.

17. Ellenberger, H. F. (1970). *The discovery of the unconscious: The history and evolution of dynamic psychiatry.* New York: Basic.

18. Meares, R. (1976). The secret. *Psychiatry, 39,* 258–265.

19. Jung, C. G. (1954). *The practice of psychotherapy: Essays on the psychology of the transference and other subjects* (R. F. C. Hull, Trans., p. 55). Princeton, NJ: Princeton University Press.

20. Fromm, E. (1955). *The sane society.* New York: Rinehart.

21. Mowrer, O. H. (1961). *The crisis in psychiatry and religion.* Princeton, NJ: Van Nostrand Reinhold.

22. Jourard, S. M. (1971). *The transparent self* (rev. ed., pp. 32–33). New York: Van Nostrand Reinhold.

23. Pennebaker, J. W. (1990). *Opening up: The healing power of confiding in others.* New York: William Morrow.

24. Pennebaker, J. W. (1985). Traumatic experience and psychosomatic disease: Exploring the roles of behavioural inhibition, obsession, and confiding. *Canadian Psychology, 26,* p. 82.

25. Pennebaker, J. W., & O'Heeron, R. C. (1984). Confiding in others and illness rate among spouses of suicide and accidental death victims. *Journal of Abnormal Psychology, 93,* 473–476.

26. Larson, D. G. (1986). *Health and self-disclosure survey.* Unpublished manuscript, Santa Clara University, Health Psychology Program.

27. Brown, G. W., Bhrolchain, M. H., & Harris, T. (1975). Social class and psychiatric disturbance among women in an urban population. *Sociology, 9,* 225–254.

28. Miller, P., & Ingham, J. G. (1976). Friends, confidants, and symptoms. *Social Psychiatry, 11,* 51–68.

29. Eliot, T. S. (1959). *The elder statesman* (p. 102). New York: Farrar, Straus & Giroux.

30. Glaser, B., & Strauss, A. (1968). *Time for dying.* Chicago: Aldine; Parry, J. K. (1988). The significance of open communication in working with terminally ill patients. *The Hospice Journal, 3,* 33–49.

31. Herek, G. M., & Glunt, E. K. (1988). An epidemic of stigma: Public reactions to AIDS. *American Psychologist, 43,* 886–891.

32. Bok, S. (1983). *Secrets: On the ethics of concealment and revelation* (p. 41). New York: Vintage.

33. Larson, D. G. (1985). Helper secrets: Invisible stressors in hospice work. *American Journal of Hospice Care, 2,* 35–40; Larson, D. G. (1987). Helper secrets: Internal stressors in nursing. *Journal of Psychosocial Nursing and Mental Health Services, 25,* 20–27.

34. Miller, D. T., & McFarland, C. (1991). When social comparison goes awry: The case of pluralistic ignorance. In J. Suls & T. A. Wills (Eds.), *Social comparison: Contemporary theory and research* (pp. 287–316). Hillsdale, NJ: Erlbaum; Pines, A. M., Aronson, E., & Kafry, D. (1981). *Burnout: From tedium to personal growth.* New York: The Free Press.

35. Larson, D. G. (1987). Helper secrets: Internal stressors in nursing. *Journal of Psychosocial Nursing, 25,* 20–27.

36. Kolotkin, R. A. (1981). Preventing burn-out and reducing stress in terminal care: The role of assertive training. In H. J. Sobel (Ed.), *Behavior therapy in terminal care: A humanistic approach* (pp. 229–252). Cambridge, MA: Ballinger.

37. Norton, R., Feldman, C., & Tafoya, D. (1974). Risk parameters across types of secrets. *Journal of Counseling Psychology, 21,* 450–454.

38. Farber, B. A., & Heifetz, L. J. (1981). The satisfactions and stresses of psychotherapeutic work: A factor analytic study. *Professional Psychology, 12,* 621–630.

39. Maslach, C. (1982). *Burnout: The cost of caring* (p. 62). Englewood Cliffs, NJ: Prentice Hall.

40. Saunders, C. (1990). Euthanasia: The hospice alternative. In N. M. de S. Cameron (Ed.), *Death without dignity: Euthanasia in perspective* (pp. 204–205). Edinburgh: Rutherford House.

41. Muldary, T. W. (1983). *Burnout and health professionals.* Garden Grove, CA: Capistrano.

42. Steiner, C. M. (1974). *Scripts people live* (p. 223). New York: Bantam.

43. Krestan, J., & Bepko, C. (1990). Codependency: The social reconstruction of female experience. *Smith College Studies in Social Work, 60,* 216–232.

44. Lipp, M. (1980). *The wounded healer.* New York: Harper and Row.

45. Helper secrets exercise adapted from an exercise in Goodman, G. (1979). *SASHAtapes: Self-led automated series on help-intended alternatives.* New York: BMA Audiotapes/Guilford.

46. Goodman, G., & Esterly, G. (1988). *The talk book: The intimate science of communicating in close relationships.* New York: Ballantine.

47. See note 23.

48. Maslach, C. (1982). *Burnout: The cost of caring.* Englewood Cliffs, NJ: Prentice Hall.

49. Schindler, C., & Lapid, G. (1989). *The great turning* (pp. 91–92). Santa Fe, NM: Bear and Company.

50. The We Can Weekend program is a good example of an upstream, proactive intervention offering social support, information, coping skill training, resource sharing, and mutual support to cancer patients and their families. See Johnson, J. L., & Norby, P. A. (1981). We Can Weekend: A program for cancer families. *Cancer Nursing, 4,* 23–28.

Chapter 5. The Helping Relationship

1. Osler, W. (1904). The master-word in medicine. In *Aequanimitas with other addresses to medical students, nurses, and practitioners of medicine* (p. 369). Philadelphia: Blakiston.

2. Perlman, H. H. (1979). *Relationship: The heart of helping people* (p. 19). University of Chicago Press.

3. Durlak, J. A. (1979). Comparative effectiveness of paraprofessional and professional helpers. *Psychological Bulletin, 86,* 80–92.

4. Smith, M. L., Glass, G. V., & Miller, T. I. (1980). *The benefits of psychotherapy.* Baltimore: Johns Hopkins University Press.

5. Wills, T. A. (Ed.). (1982). *Basic processes in helping relationships* (p. 2). New York: Academic.

6. Wills, T. A. (1982). Nonspecific factors in helping relationships. In T. A. Wills (Ed.), *Basic processes in helping relationships* (pp. 381–404). New York: Academic.

7. Kennedy, E., & Charles, S. C. (1990). *On becoming a counselor: A basic guide for nonprofessional counselors* (p. 18). New York: Continuum.

8. Kennell, J., Klaus, M., McGrath, S., Robertson, S., & Hinkley, C. (1991). Continuous emotional support during labor in a US hospital. *Journal of the American Medical Association, 265,* 2197–2201.

9. Kennell, J., Klaus, M., McGrath, S., Robertson, S., & Hinkley, C. (1991). Continuous emotional support during labor in a US hospital. *Journal of the American Medical Association, 265,* p. 2201.

10. DiMatteo, M. R. (1991). *The psychology of health, illness, and medical care.* Pacific Grove, CA: Brooks/Cole.

11. Katz, R. L. (1963). *Empathy: Its nature and uses.* New York: Free Press of Glencoe.

12. Bergin, A. E., & Strupp, H. H. (1972). *Changing frontiers in the science of psychotherapy.* Chicago: Aldine-Atherton.

13. Rogers, C. R. (1975). Empathic: An unappreciated way of being. *The Counseling Psychologist, 5,* p. 4.

14. Fromm-Reichmann, F. (1959). *Psychoanalysis and psychotherapy: Selected papers of Frieda Fromm-Reichmann* (p. 65). University of Chicago Press.

15. Reik, T. (1972). *Listening with the third ear.* New York: Arena.

16. Katz, R. L. (1963). *Empathy: Its nature and uses* (p. 156). New York: Free Press of Glencoe.

17. See note 11.

18. Greenberg, L. S., & Safran, J. D. (1987). *Emotion in psychotherapy* (p. 193). New York: Guilford.

19. Clark, M., Powell, M. C., Ouellette, R., & Milberg, S. (1987). Recipient's mood, relationship type, and helping. *Journal of Personality and Social Psychology, 53,* 94–103.

20. Buber, M. (1923). *I and thou* (2nd ed.). New York: Charles Scribner's Sons.

21. Gendlin, E. T. (1974). Client-centered and experiential therapy. In D. A. Wexler & L. N. Rice (Eds.), *Innovations in client-centered therapy* (pp. 211–246). New York: Wiley.

22. Bowlby, J. (1969). *Attachment.* New York: Basic; Hymer, S. (1988). *Confessions in psychotherapy.* New York: Gardner.

23. Szalita, A. B. (1976). Some thoughts on empathy. *Psychiatry, 39,* p. 151.

24. Rilke, R. M. (1934). *Letters to a young poet* (M. D. Herter Norton, Trans., pp. 72–73). New York: Norton.

25. Fraiberg, S., Adelson, E., & Shapiro, V. (1975). Ghosts in the nursery: A psychoanalytic approach to the problems of impaired infant-mother relationships. *American Academy of Child Psychiatry, 14,* 387–421.

26. Fraiberg, S., Adelson, E., & Shapiro, V. (1975). Ghosts in the nursery: A psychoanalytic approach to the problems of impaired infant-mother relationships. *American Academy of Child Psychiatry, 14,* p. 391.

27. Fraiberg, S., Adelson, E., & Shapiro, V. (1975). Ghosts in the nursery: A psychoanalytic approach to the problems of impaired infant-mother relationships. *American Academy of Child Psychiatry, 14,* pp. 396–397.

28. Greenberg, L. S., & Safran, J. D. (1987). *Emotion in psychotherapy* (p. 203). New York: Guilford.

29. See note 6.

30. Strupp, H. H., Fox, R. E., & Lessler, K. (1969). *Patients view their psychotherapy.* Baltimore: Johns Hopkins University Press.

31. Hammond, D. C., Hepworth, D. H., & Smith, V. G. (1977). *Improving therapeutic communication: A guide for developing effective techniques.* San Francisco: Jossey-Bass.

32. Rogers, C. R. (1958). The characteristics of a helping relationship. *Personnel and Guidance Journal, 37,* 6–16.

33. Brammer, L. M. (1973). *The helping relationship: Process and skills.* Englewood Cliffs, NJ: Prentice Hall.

34. Kennedy, E., & Charles, S. C. (1990). *On becoming a counselor: A basic guide for nonprofessional counselors.* New York: Continuum.

35. Hyman, R. B., & Woog, P. (1989). Flexibility, the dominant characteristic of effective helpers: A factor analytic study. *Measurement and Evaluation in Counseling and Development, 22,* p. 155.

36. Hyman, R. B., & Woog, P. (1989). Flexibility, the dominant characteristic of effective helpers: A factor analytic study. *Measurement and Evaluation in Counseling and Development, 22,* p. 152.

37. See note 33.

38. Susan Johnson, Family Support Coordinator for North Hospice, North Memorial Medical Center at Robbinsdale, Minnesota, kindly contributed this description.

39. Szasz, T. S., & Hollender, M. H. (1975). A contribution to the philosophy of medicine: The basic models of the doctor-patient relationship. In T. Millon (Ed.), *Medical behavioral science* (pp. 433–435). Philadelphia: W. B. Saunders.

40. Sobel, H. J., & Worden, J. W. (1982). *Practitioner's manual: Helping cancer patients cope* (p. 6). New York: Guilford.

41. Rogers, C. R. (1974). In retrospect: 46 years. *American Psychologist, 29,* p. 115.

42. Gendlin, E. T. (1981). *Focusing* (2nd ed.). New York: Bantam.

43. Gendlin, E. T. (1981). *Focusing* (2nd ed., p. 39). New York: Bantam.

44. Quoted in Bartlett, J. (1980). *Familiar quotations* (p. 396). Boston: Little, Brown.

45. Kahn, R. L., & Cannell, C. F. (1957). *The dynamics of interviewing.* New York: Wiley.

46. Suzuki, S. (1973). *Zen mind, beginner's mind* (p. 32). New York: Weatherhill.

47. Cousins, N. (1979). *Anatomy of an illness.* New York: Norton.

48. For a more complete discussion of this issue, see Temoshok, L., & Dreher, H. (1992). *The Type C connection: The behavioral links to cancer and your health.* New York: Random House.

49. Sobel, W. K. (1981). Behavioral treatment of depression in the dying patient. In H. J. Sobel (Ed.), *Behavior therapy in terminal care: A humanistic approach* (pp. 66–94). Cambridge, MA: Ballinger.

50. Brickman, P., Rabinowitz, V. C., Karuza, J., Coates, D., Cohn, E., & Kidder, L. (1982). Models of helping and coping. *American Psychologist, 37,* 368–384.

51. Brickman, P., Rabinowitz, V. C., Karuza, J., Coates, D., Cohn, E., & Kidder, L. (1982). Models of helping and coping. *American Psychologist, 37,* p. 368.

52. Frank, J. D. (1974). Psychotherapy: The restoration of morale. *American Journal of Psychiatry, 131,* 271–274.

53. DiMatteo, M. R., & DiNicola, D. D. (1981). *Achieving patient compliance: The psychology of the medical practitioner's role.* New York: Pergamon.

54. Tait, R., & Silver, R. C. (1989). Coming to terms with major negative life events. In J. S. Uleman & J. A. Bargh (Eds.), *Unintended thought* (p. 372). New York: Guilford.

55. Rae-Grant, Q. (1972). The art of being a failure as a consultant. In J. Zusman & D. L. Davidson (Eds.), *Practical aspects of mental health consultation* (pp. 71–82). Springfield, IL: Charles C Thomas.

Chapter 6. Healing Words: Communication Skills for Helping

1. Rogers, C. R. (1980). *A way of being* (p. 8). Boston: Houghton Mifflin.

2. Perlman, H. H. (1979). *Relationship: The heart of helping people* (p. 57). University of Chicago Press.

3. Martin, D. G. (1983). *Counseling and therapy skills* (p. 70). Pacific Grove, CA: Brooks/Cole.

4. Saposnek, D. T. (1980). Aikido: A model for brief strategic therapy. *Family Process, 19,* 227–238.

5. Brandon, D. (1976). *Zen in the art of helping* (p. 49). New York: Merloyd Lawrence.

6. Goodman, G., & Esterly, G. (1988). *The talk book: The intimate science of communicating in close relationships.* New York: Ballantine.

7. For descriptions of these programs, see Larson, D. (Ed.). (1984). *Teaching psychological skills: Models for giving psychology away.* Pacific Grove, CA: Brooks/Cole.

8. Larson, D. (Ed.). (1984). *Teaching psychological skills: Models for giving psychology away.* Pacific Grove, CA: Brooks/Cole.

9. Aspy, D. N. (1975). Empathy: Let's get the hell on with it. *The Counseling Psychologist, 5,* 10–14.

10. Egan, G., & Cowan, M. A. (1979). *People in systems: A model for development in the human-service professions and education* (p. 62). Pacific Grove, CA: Brooks/Cole.

11. Adapted from Moawad, R. (1978). *Increasing human effectiveness program guide.* Tacoma, WA: Edge Learning Institute. Moawad's model is in turn adapted from an ancient Arab proverb: "He who knows not and knows not that he knows not, is a fool. Shun him. He who knows not and knows that he knows not is simple. Teach him. He who knows, and knows not that he knows, is asleep. Wake him. He who knows, and knows that he knows, is wise. Follow him."

12. Gerald Goodman, personal communication, March 26, 1992.

13. Mehrabian, A. (1972). *Nonverbal communication.* Chicago: Aldine.

14. Lynch, J. J. *The language of the heart: The body's response to human dialogue.* New York: Basic.

15. Egan, G. (1982). *The skilled helper: Model, skills, and methods for effective helping* (2nd ed.). Pacific Grove, CA: Brooks/Cole.

16. For a more complete discussion of these and other microskills, see Ivey, A. E. (1988). *Intentional interviewing and counseling: Facilitating client development* (2nd ed.). Pacific Grove, CA: Brooks/Cole.

17. See note 6.

18. Ivey, A. E., & Gluckstern, N. B. (1982). *Basic attending skills* (2nd ed.). North Amherst, MA: Microtraining Associates.

19. See note 18.

20. Ivey, A. E. (1988). *Intentional interviewing and counseling* (2nd ed.). Pacific Grove, CA: Brooks/Cole.

21. All interview segments in this chapter have been transcribed from Larson, D. G. (Author and Presenter), & Mulpeters, P. M. (Executive Producer). (1991). *The caring helper: Skills for caregiving in grief and loss* [Film Series]. Menlo Park, CA: Catholic Television Network. Available from Pace Productions, P. O. Box 1344, San Carlos CA, 94070–7344.

22. Hammond, D. C., Hepworth, D. H., & Smith, V. G. (1977). *Improving therapeutic communication.* San Francisco: Jossey-Bass.

23. For a more complete description of this process, see Gendlin, E. T. (1981). *Focusing* (2nd ed.). New York: Bantam.

24. Robinson, F. P. (1950). *Principles and procedures of student counseling.* New York: Harper & Brothers.

25. Schwartzberg, S. S., & Janoff-Bulman, R. (1991). Grief and the search for meaning: Exploring the assumptive worlds of bereaved college students. *Journal of Social and Clinical Psychology, 10,* 270–288; Snyder, C. R., & Ford, C. E. (Eds.). (1987). *Coping with negative life events.* New York: Plenum.

26. Worden, W. J. (1982). *Grief counseling and grief therapy.* New York: Springer.

27. Rilke, R. M. (1984). *Letters to a young poet* (S. Mitchell, Trans., pp. 34–35). New York: Random House.

28. See note 20.

29. Ferrell, B. R., Cohen, M. Z., Rhiner, M., & Rozek, A. (1991). Pain as a metaphor for illness: Part 2. Family caregivers' management of pain. *Oncology Nursing Forum, 18,* 1315–1321; Janoff-Bulman, R., & Timko, C. (1987). Coping with traumatic life events: The role of denial in light

of people's assumptive worlds. In C. R. Snyder & C. E. Ford (Eds.), *Coping with negative life events: Clinical and social psychological perspectives* (pp. 135–159). New York: Plenum; Schwartzberg, S. S., & Janoff-Bulman, R. (1991). Grief and the search for meaning: Exploring the assumptive worlds of bereaved college students. *Journal of Social and Clinical Psychology, 10,* 270–288.

30. Ornston, P. S., Cuchetti, D. V., Levine, J., & Fierman, L. B. (1968). Some parameters of verbal behavior that reliably differentiate novice from experienced psychotherapists. *Journal of Abnormal Psychology, 73,* 240–244.

31. Boreing, M. L., & Adler, L. M. (1982). *Basic counseling skills for health professionals: An instructional guide* (Educational Monograph No. 1). San Francisco: Pacific Medical Center, Department of Psychological and Social Medicine.

32. See note 6.

33. Goodman, G., & Esterly, G. (1988). *The talk book: The intimate science of communicating in close relationships* (p. 216). New York: Ballantine.

34. Mencken, H. L. (1949). *A Mencken chrestomathy* (p. 443). New York: Knopf.

35. Kennedy, E., & Charles, S. C. (1990). *On becoming a counselor: A basic guide for nonprofessional counselors* (p. 67). New York: Continuum.

36. Korchin, S. J. (1976). *Modern clinical psychology.* New York: Basic.

37. Carkhuff, R. R. (1977). *The art of helping, III.* Amherst, MA: Human Resource Development Press; Carkhuff, R. R., & Anthony, W. A. (1976). *The skills of helping: An introduction to counseling skills.* Amherst, MA: Human Resource Development Press.

38. See note 22.

39. See note 31.

40. Wexler, M., & Adler, L. M. (1970). *Help the patient tell his story.* Oradell, NJ: Medical Economics.

41. Nouwen, H. J. M. (1974). Hospitality. *Monastic Studies, 10,* pp. 20–21.

42. See note 35.

43. Gazda, G., Childers, W., & Walters, R. (1982). *Interpersonal communication: A handbook for health professionals.* Rockville, MD: Aspen.

44. Lazarus, R. S. (1984). The trivialization of distress. In B. L. Hammonds & C. J. Scheirer (Eds.), *Psychology and health: The master lecture series* (Vol. 3, pp. 125–144). Washington, DC: American Psychological Association.

45. Beavers, R. W., & Kaslow, F. W. (1981). The anatomy of hope. *Journal of Marital and Family Therapy, 7,* 119–126.

46. Wortman, C., & Silver, R. (1989). The myths of coping with loss. *Journal of Consulting and Clinical Psychology, 57,* 349–357.

Chapter 7. The Caring Team

1. Quoted in Mount, B. M., & Voyer, J. (1980). Staff stress in palliative/ hospice care. In I. Ajemian & B. M. Mount (Eds.), *The R. V. H. manual on palliative/hospice care* (p. 466). New York: Arno Press.

2. Senge, P. M. (1990). *The fifth discipline: The art and practice of the learning organization* (p. 257). New York: Doubleday.

3. Rubin, I. M., Plovnick, M. S., & Fry, R. E. (1975). *Improving the coordination of care: A program for health team development.* Cambridge, MA: Ballinger.

4. Engel, G. L. (1977). The need for a new medical model: A challenge for biomedicine. *Science, 196,* 129–136.

5. Bailey, D. B. (1984). A triaxial model of the interdisciplinary team and group process. *Exceptional Children, 51,* 17–25.

6. Baldwin, D., Boufford, J. I., Eichorn, S. (1981, February). Making it work for everyone: Interdisciplinary health team development. In C. A. Garfield & D. G. Larson (Chairs), *The human dimension in health care: A national conference.* Unpublished proceedings of a conference conducted by the University of California, Santa Cruz Extension, Palo Alto.

7. See note 5.

8. Janis, I. (1982). *Groupthink.* Boston: Houghton Mifflin.

9. Dyer, W. G. (1977). *Team building: Issues and alternatives.* Reading, MA: Addison-Wesley.

10. Steele, F. T. (1975). *The open organization: The impact of secrecy and disclosure on people and organizations* (p. 6). Reading, MA: Addison-Wesley.

11. Senge, P. M. (1990). *The fifth discipline: The art and practice of the learning organization* (p. 237). New York: Doubleday.

12. Senge, P. M. (1990). *The fifth discipline: The art and practice of the learning organization* (p. 255). New York: Doubleday.

13. Senge, P. M. (1990). *The fifth discipline: The art and practice of the learning organization* (p. 284). New York: Doubleday.

14. Kohn, A. (1986). *No contest: The case against competition* (p. 156). Boston: Houghton Mifflin.

15. Quoted in Kohn, A. (1986). *No contest: The case against competition* (p. 157). Boston: Houghton Mifflin.

16. Margolis, H., & Fiorelli, J. S. (1984). An applied approach to facilitating interdisciplinary teamwork. *Journal of Rehabilitation, 50,* p. 16.

17. See note 3.

18. See note 3.

19. Ivey, A. E. (1988). *Intentional interviewing and counseling: Facilitating client development* (2nd ed.). Pacific Grove, CA: Brooks/Cole.

20. See note 9.

21. See note 3.

22. Gazda, G., Childers, W., & Walters, R. (1982). *Interpersonal communication: A handbook for health professionals.* Rockville, MD: Aspen.

23. Pines, A. M., & Aronson, E. (1988). *Career burnout: Causes and cures.* New York: Free Press; Richman, J. M. (1990). Groupwork in a hospice setting. *The Hospice Journal, 6,* 171–184; Scully, R. (1981). Staff support groups: Helping nurses to help themselves. *The Journal of Nursing Administration, 3,* 48–51.

24. Quoted in B. Stevenson (Ed.). (1967). *The home book of quotations: Classical and modern* (10th ed., p. 1783). New York: Dodd, Mead.

25. Maslach, C. (1982). *Burnout: The cost of caring.* Englewood Cliffs, NJ: Prentice Hall.

26. Nichols, K., & Jenkinson, J. (1991). *Leading a support group.* London: Chapman and Hall.

27. Weiner, M. F., Caldwell, T., & Tyson, J. (1983). Stresses and coping in ICU nursing: Why support groups fail. *General Hospital Psychiatry, 5,* p. 183.

28. Boreing, M. L., & Adler, L. M. (1982). *Facilitating support groups: An instructional guide* (NIMH Training Grant No. 15718, Group Facilitation Skills for Health Professionals). San Francisco, CA: Pacific Medical Center, Department of Psychological and Social Medicine.

29. California Self-Help Center (1985). *Common concern* [Audiotape program]. Los Angeles, CA: University of California at Los Angeles. Available from California Self-Help Center, UCLA, 405 Hilgard Avenue, Los Angeles, CA 90024 and from New Harbinger Publications, 5674 Shattuck Avenue, Oakland CA 94609. I contributed a specializing tape for this series making it applicable to hospice and oncology staff support groups. Research demonstrating the effectiveness of this program includes Larson, D. G. (1986). Developing effective hospice staff support groups: Pilot test of an innovative training program. *The Hospice Journal, 2,* 41–55.

30. Larson, D. G. (Author and Presenter), & Mulpeters, P. M. (Executive Producer). (1991). *The caring helper: Skills for caregiving in grief and loss: Tape 5. Making support groups work* [Film]. Menlo Park, CA: Catholic Television Network. Available from Pace Productions, P. O. Box 1344, San Carlos, CA 94070–7344.

31. Kirschenbaum, H., & Glaser, B. (1978). *Developing support groups.* La Jolla, CA: University Associates.

32. Nichols, K., & Jenkinson, J. (1991). *Leading a support group.* London: Chapman and Hall.

33. Moynihan, R. T., & Outlaw, E. (1984). Nursing support groups in a cancer center. *Journal of Psychosocial Oncology, 2,* 33–48.

34. For a detailed discussion of patient support groups in oncology, see Vugia, H. D. (1991). Support groups in oncology: Building hope through the human bond. *Journal of Psychosocial Oncology, 9,* 89–107.

35. See note 28.

36. Trotzer, J. P. (1979). *The counselor and the group.* Pacific Grove, CA: Brooks/Cole.

37. Vugia, H. D. (1991). Support groups in oncology: Building hope through the human bond. *Journal of Psychosocial Oncology, 9,* 89–107.

38. Parry, J. K. (1989). Mutual support groups for hospice staff: Planned or ad hoc? *Journal of Palliative Care, 5,* 34–36; Richman, J. M., & Rosenfeld, L. B. (1987). Stress reduction for hospice workers: A support group model. *The Hospice Journal, 3,* 205–221.

39. See note 37.

40. See note 29.

41. Kirschenbaum, H., & Glaser, B. (1978). *Developing support groups* (p. 38). La Jolla, CA: University Associates.

42. See note 1.

43. Pearson, P. H. (1983). The interdisciplinary team process, or the professionals' Tower of Babel. *Developmental Medicine and Child Neurology, 25,* 390–395.

44. Rubin, I. M., Plovnick, M. S., & Fry, R. E. (1975). *Improving the coordination of care: A program for health team development* (p. 235). Cambridge, MA: Ballinger.

45. Items adapted from Rubin, I. M., Plovnick, M. S., & Fry, R. E. (1975). *Improving the coordination of care: A program for health team development* (p. 3). Cambridge, MA: Ballinger.

46. See note 3.

47. See the following books: Dyer, W. G. (1977). *Team building: Issues and alternatives.* Reading, MA: Addison-Wesley; Rubin, I. M., Plovnick, M. S., & Fry, R. E. (1975). *Improving the coordination of care: A program for health team development.* Cambridge, MA: Ballinger; Varney, G. H. (1991). *Building productive teams: An action guide and resource book.* San Francisco: Jossey-Bass.

48. T. J. Ucko, personal communication, April 15, 1985. Idea for scale presented in Ucko, T. J., & Kazemek, E. A. (1986). Creating effective work teams. *Healthcare Financial Management, 41,* 80–81.

49. Larson, D. G. (1986, June). *Self-appraisal and self-renewal in the hospice team.* Paper presented at the National Hospice Organization Conference on Interdisciplinary Team Development, St. Paul, MN.

50. Kagan, N. (1984). Interpersonal Process Recall: Basic methods and recent research. In D. G. Larson (Ed.), *Teaching psychological skills: Models for giving psychology away* (pp. 229–244). Pacific Grove, CA: Brooks/Cole. For more information, contact Interpersonal Process Institute, University of Houston, 425 Farish Hall, Houston, TX 77204–5874.

Chapter 8. The Collective Caregiver: Toward a Caring Society

1. Einstein, A. (1934). *The world as I see it* (p. 237). New York: Covici Friede.

2. Seligman, M. E. (1990). *Learned optimism.* New York: Pocket Books.

3. Bellah, R. N., Madsen, R., Sullivan, W. M., Swidler, A., & Tipton, S. M. (1985). *The habits of the heart: Individualism and commitment in American life.* New York: Harper and Row.

4. See note 2.

5. Seligman, M. E. (1990). *Learned optimism* (p. 290). New York: Pocket Books.

6. Kanter, D. L., & Mirvis, P. H. (1989). *The cynical Americans.* San Franscisco: Jossey-Bass.

7. Hornstein, H. A. (1976). *Cruelty and kindness.* Englewood Cliffs, NJ: Prentice Hall.

8. Kohn, A. (1986). *No contest: The case against competition.* Boston: Houghton Mifflin.

9. Gerbner, G., & Gross, L. (1976). Living with television: The violence profile. *Journal of Communication, 26,* 173–199.

10. Rushton, J. P. (1980). *Altruism, socialization, and society.* New York: Prentice Hall.

11. Gordon, S. (1988, July 10). The crisis in caring. *Boston Globe Magazine,* pp. 22–23, 57–60, 68–73.

12. Kohn, A. (1990). *The brighter side of human nature: Altruism and empathy in everyday life* (pp. 267–268). New York: Basic.

13. Friedrich, L. K., & Stein, A. H. (1973). Aggressive and prosocial television programs and the natural behavior of preschool children. *Monographs of the Society for Research in Child Development, 38* (4, Serial No. 151).

14. Eisenberg, N. (1992). *The caring child.* Cambridge, MA: Harvard University Press.

15. Pilisuk, M., & Parks, S. H. (1988). Caregiving: Where families need help. *Social Work, 33,* 436–440.

16. Watkins, J. D. (1988). Responding to the HIV epidemic: A national strategy. *American Psychologist, 43,* 849–851.

17. For a more complete discussion of healthy systems, see the following: Anderson, R. E., & Carter, I. (1990). *Human behavior in the social environment: A social systems approach* (4th ed.). New York: Aldine De Gruyter; Ray, E. B., & Donohew, L. (Eds.). (1990). *Communication and health: Systems and applications.* Hillsdale, NJ: Erlbaum; Schwartz, G. E. (1984). Psychobiology of health: A new synthesis. In B. L. Hammonds & C. J. Scheirer (Eds.), *Psychology and health: The master lecture series* (Vol. 3, pp. 149–193). Washington, DC: American Psychological Association; Seeman, J. (1989). Toward a model of positive health. *American Psychologist, 44,* 1099–1109; Weinberger, D. A. (1990). The construct validity of the repressive-defensive coping style. In J. L. Singer (Ed.), *Repression and dissociation: Defense mechanisms and personality styles* (pp. 337–386). University of Chicago Press.

18. Brandt, A. M. (1986). AIDS: From social history to social policy. *Law, Medicine, and Health Care, 14,* 231–242.

19. Crawford, I., Humfleet, G., Ribordy, S. C., Ho, F. C., & Vickers, V. L. (1991). Stigmatization of AIDS patients by mental health professionals. *Professional Psychology: Research and Practice, 22,* 357–361; Herek, G. M., & Glunt, E. K. (1988). An epidemic of stigma: Public reactions to AIDS. *American Psychologist, 43,* 886–891.

20. Grossman, S. A., Sheidler, V. R., Swedeen, K., Mucenski, J., & Piantadosi, S. (1991). Correlation of patient and caregiver ratings of cancer pain. *Journal of Pain and Symptom Management, 6,* 53–57.

21. Murphy, P., & Perry, K. (1988). Hidden grievers. *Death Studies, 12,* 451–462.

22. Church, R. M. (1959). Emotional reaction of rats to the pain of others. *Journal of Comparative and Physiological Psychology, 52,* 132–134.

23. Clark, K. B. (1980). Empathy: A neglected topic in psychological research. *American Psychologist, 35,* p. 190.

24. Lynn, M., & Oldenquist, A. (1986). Egoistic and nonegoistic motives in social dilemmas. *American Psychologist, 41,* 529–534.

25. Schindler, C., & Lapid, G. (1989). *The great turning.* Santa Fe, NM: Bear and Company; Walsh, R. (1984). *Staying alive: The psychology of human survival.* Boulder, CO: New Science Library.

26. Quoted in Wynne-Tyson, J. (Compiler). *The extended circle: A dictionary of humane thought* (p. 316). Frontwell, Sussex: Centaur Press.

27. Quoted in Walsh, R. (1984). *Staying alive* (p. 71). Boulder, CO: New Science Library.

28. Saving the children. (1984, November 5). *Newsweek,* p. 46.

29. Rittner, C., & Myers, S. (Eds.). (1986). *The courage to care: Rescuers of the Jews during the Holocaust* (pp. 40–42). New York University Press.

NOTE 5: From *Basic Processes in Helping Relationships* (p. 2) edited by
T. A. Wills, 1982, New York: Academic Press. Copyright 1982 by Academic
Press. Reprinted by permission.

NOTE 9: From "Continuous Emotional Support During Labor in a US
Hospital" by J. Kennell, M. Klaus, S. McGrath, S. Robertson, and C. Hinkley,
1991, *Journal of the American Medical Association, 265,* p. 2201. Copyright
1991, American Medical Association. Reprinted by permission.

NOTE 13: From "Empathic: An Unappreciated Way of Being" by C. R.
Rogers, 1975, *The Counseling Psychologist, 5,* p. 4. Copyright © 1975 by
Sage Publications, Inc. Reprinted by permission of Sage Publications, Inc.

NOTE 27: From "Ghosts in the Nursery: A Psychoanalytic Approach to
the Problems of Impaired Infant-Mother Relationships" by S. Fraiberg,
E. Adelson, and V. Shapiro, 1975, *American Academy of Child Psychiatry,
14,* pp. 396–397. Copyright 1975 by Yale University Press. Reprinted by
permission.

NOTE 38: From Susan Johnson, Family Support Coordinator for North
Hospice, North Memorial Medical Center at Robbinsdale, Minnesota.
Reprinted by permission.

Chapter 6

NOTE 2: From *Relationship: The Heart of Helping People* (p. 57) by H. H.
Perlman, 1979, University of Chicago Press. Copyright © 1979 by the
University of Chicago. Reprinted by permission.

Chapter 7

NOTE 2: From *The Fifth Discipline: The Art and Practice of the Learning
Organization* (p. 257) by P. M. Senge, 1990, New York: Doubleday. Copyright
1990 by Doubleday, a division of Bantam, Doubleday, Dell Publishing
Group, Inc. Reprinted by permission.

Index

About the Author

Dale G. Larson (B.A., psychology, University of Chicago; Ph.D., clinical psychology, University of California, Berkeley) is professor of counseling psychology at Santa Clara University. A clinician and researcher, Dr. Larson was a summer scholar at the Stanford Center for Advanced Studies in the Behavioral Sciences and has lectured and conducted research in Europe as a Fulbright Scholar. He co-directed the pioneering Berkeley Hospice Training Project and created the widely used videotape training series, *The Caring Helper: Skills for Caregiving in Grief and Loss*. He has published widely on psychosocial issues in oncology and end-of-life care and was senior editor and a contributing author for "Finding Our Way: Living with Dying in America," a fifteen-article newspaper series funded by the Robert Woods Johnson Foundation. He lives with his wife, Deborah Kennedy, and environmental artist, and their son, Evan Larson, in San Jose, California.